Sunset

BEST HOME PLANS

Homes for Entertaining

Classic Italianate design fronts an open, contemporary floor plan perfect for entertaining. See plan E-3200 on page 209.

Sunset Publishing Corporation ■ **Menlo Park, California**

SUNSET BOOKS
President and Publisher:
 Susan J. Maruyama
Director, Sales & Marketing:
 Richard A. Smeby
Editorial Director:
 Bob Doyle
Production Director:
 Lory Day
Art Director:
 Vasken Guiragossian
Retail Sales Development Manager:
 Becky Ellis
Assistant Editor:
 Jody Mitori
Contributing Editor:
 Don Vandervort

**SUNSET PUBLISHING
CORPORATION**
Chairman:
 Jim Nelson
**President/Chief Executive
 Officer:** Stephen J. Seabolt
Chief Financial Officer:
 James E. Mitchell
**Director, Finance & Business
 Affairs:** Lawrence J. Diamond
Publisher:
 Anthony P. Glaves
Vice President, Manufacturing:
 Lorinda Reichert
Circulation Director:
 Robert I. Gursha
Editor, Sunset Magazine:
 Rosalie Muller Wright

Photographers: Mark Englund/
HomeStyles: 4, 5; Philip Harvey:
10 top, back cover; Stephen Marley:
11 top left and right; Russ Widstrand:
10 bottom; Tom Wyatt: 11 bottom.

Cover: Pictured is plan E-2604
on page 161. Cover design by Susan
Bryant and Naganuma Design &
Direction. Photography by Mark
Englund/ HomeStyles.

A Dream Come True

Planning and building a house is one of life's most creative and rewarding challenges. Whether you're seriously considering building a new home or you're just dreaming about it, this book offers a wealth of inspiration and information to help you get started.

On the following pages, you'll learn how to plan and manage a home-building project—and how to ensure its success. Then you'll discover more than 200 proven home plans, designed for families just like yours by architects and professional designers. Peruse the pages and study the floor plans; you're sure to find a home that's just right for you. When you're ready to order blueprints, you can simply call or mail in your order, and you'll receive the plans within days.

Enjoy the adventure!

For more information on Sunset's *Best Home
Plans Homes for Entertaining* or any other
Sunset book, call (800) 634-3095. For special
sales, bulk orders, and premium sales infor-
mation, call Sunset Custom Publishing
Services at (415) 324-5577.

Country-style home with a generous front porch welcomes guests into a spacious foyer that opens to the dining room, living room, family room, and island kitchen. Upstairs is a comfortable master suite and two more bedrooms. See plan GL-2161 on page 63.

Contents

A Warm Welcome

If entertaining family and friends is one of your great pleasures in life and you're considering building a new home, the wonderful home plans presented here will offer you plenty of inspiration. With inviting facades and foyers, large kitchens, formal dining rooms, and beckoning outdoor spaces, these home designs offer perfect solutions for people who love to entertain.

You'll find classic traditional homes, striking contemporary houses, country charmers, and even affordable starters that have the amenities and types of spaces you want. All are proven designs created by some of America's foremost residential architects and designers.

The two keys to success in building a home are capable project management and good design. The next few pages will walk you through some of the most important aspects of project management: you'll find an overview of the building process, directions for selecting the right plan and getting the most from it, and methods for working with a builder and other professionals.

The balance of the book presents professionally designed stock plans for homes in a wide range of styles and configurations. Once you find a plan that will work for you—perhaps with a few modifications made later to personalize it for your family—you can order construction blueprints for a fraction of the cost of a custom design, a savings of many thousands of dollars (see pages 12–15 for information on how to order).

Traditional two-story home offers ornate architectural detailing outside and generous spaces for entertaining inside. The large, bay-shaped kitchen easily accommodates more than one cook. Both the foyer and the spacious family room boast 18-foot ceilings. Three bedrooms and a huge master suite are upstairs. See plan FB-5347-HAST on page 216.

Striking portico lends elegance to this executive home. The living room features a sunken wet bar that extends into the pool area. The island kitchen services both the formal dining room with its tiered pedestal ceiling and a large breakfast room/family room. See plan HDS-99-154 on page 219.

Angular rooms and multiple levels add drama to this home's interior spaces. Vaulted ceilings open up the living room, dining room, and foyer. The master suite, three bedrooms, and a bath are located upstairs. See plan P-7664-4A & -4D on page 204.

Traditional and formal exterior masks a contemporary floor plan inside featuring angled spaces and 12-foot ceilings in the kitchen, living room, and dining area. A columned porch off the living room adds entertaining space. See plan E-2004 on page 55.

5

The Art of Building

As you embark on your home-building project, think of it as a trip—clearly not a vacation but rather an interesting, adventurous, at times difficult expedition. Meticulous planning will make your journey not only far more enjoyable but also much more successful. By careful planning, you can avoid—or at least minimize—some of the pitfalls along the way.

Start with realistic expectations of the road ahead. To do this, you'll want to gain an understanding of the basic house-building process, settle on a design that will work for you and your family, and make sure your project is actually doable. By taking those initial steps, you can gain a clear idea of how much time, money, and energy you'll need to invest to make your dream come true.

The Building Process

Your role in planning and managing a house-building project can be divided into two parts: prebuilding preparation and construction management.

■ **Prebuilding preparation.** This is where you should focus most of your attention. In the hands of a qualified contractor whose expertise you can rely on, the actual building process should go fairly smoothly. But during most of the prebuilding stage, you're generally on your own. Your job will be to launch the project and develop a talented team that can help you bring your new home to fruition.

When you work with stock plans, the prebuilding process usually goes as follows:

First, you research the general area where you want to live, selecting one or more possible home sites (unless you already own a suitable lot). Then you choose a basic house design, with the idea that it may require some modification. Finally, you analyze the site, the design, and your budget to determine if the project is actually attainable.

If you decide that it is, you purchase the land and order blueprints. If you want to modify them, you consult an architect, designer, or contractor. Once the plans are finalized, you request bids from contractors and arrange any necessary construction financing.

After selecting a builder and signing a contract, you (or your contractor) then file the plans with the building department. When the plans are approved, often several weeks—or even months—later, you're ready to begin construction.

■ **Construction management.** Unless you intend to act as your own contractor, your role during the building process is mostly one of quality control and time management. Even so, it's important to know the sequence of events and something about construction methods so you can discuss progress with your builder and prepare for any important decisions you may need to make along the way.

Decision-making is critical. Once construction begins, the builder must usually plunge ahead, keeping his carpenters and subcontractors progressing steadily. If you haven't made a key decision—which model bathtub or sink to install, for example—it can bring construction to a frustrating and expensive halt.

Usually, you'll make such decisions before the onset of building, but, inevitably, some issue or another will arise during construction. Being knowledgeable about the building process will help you anticipate and circumvent potential logjams.

Selecting a House Plan

Searching for the right plan can be a fun, interactive family experience—one of the most exciting parts of a house-building project. Gather the family around as you peruse the home plans in this book. Study the size, location, and configuration of each room; traffic patterns both inside the house and to the outdoors; exterior style; and how you'll use the available space. Discuss the pros and cons of the various plans.

Browse through pictures of homes in magazines to stimulate ideas. Clip the photos you like so you can think about your favorite options. When you visit the homes of friends, note special features that appeal to you. Also, look carefully at the homes in your neighborhood, noting their style and how they fit the site.

Mark those plans that most closely suit your ideals. Then, to narrow down your choices, critique each plan, using the following information as a guide.

■ **Overall size and budget.** How large a house do you want? Will the house you're considering fit your family's requirements? Look at the overall square footage and room sizes. If you have a hard time visualizing room sizes, measure some of the rooms in your present home and compare.

It's often better for the house to be a little too big than a little too small, but remember that every extra square foot will cost more money to build and maintain.

■ **Number and type of rooms.** Beyond thinking about the number of bedrooms and baths you want, consider your family's life-style and how you use space. Do you want both a family room and a living room? Do you need a formal dining space? Will you require some extra rooms, or "swing spaces," that can serve multiple purposes, such as a home office–guest room combination?

■ **Room placement and traffic patterns.** What are your preferences for locations of formal living areas, master bedroom, and children's rooms? Do you prefer a kitchen that's open to family areas or one that's private and out of the way? How much do you use exterior spaces and how should they relate to the interior?

Once you make those determinations, look carefully at the floor plan of the house you're considering to see if it meets your needs and if the traffic flow will be convenient for your family.

■ **Architectural style.** Have you always wanted to live in a Victorian farmhouse? Now is your chance to create a house that matches your idea of "home" (taking into account, of course, styles in your neighborhood). But don't let your preference for one particular architectural style dictate your home's floor plan. If the floor plan doesn't work for your family, keep looking.

■ **Site considerations.** Most people choose a site before selecting a plan—or at least they've zeroed in on the basic type of land where they'll situate their house. It sounds elementary, but choose a house that will fit the site.

When figuring the "footprint" of a house, you must know about any restrictions that will affect your home's height or proximity to the property lines. Call the local building department (look under city or county listings in the phone book) and get a very clear description of any restrictions, such as setbacks, height limits, and lot coverage, that will affect what you can build on the site (see "Working with City Hall," at right).

When you visit potential sites, note trees, rock outcroppings, slopes, views, winds, sun, neighboring homes, and other factors. All will impact on how your house works on a particular site.

Once you've narrowed down the choice of sites, consult an architect or building designer (see page 8) to help you evaluate how some potential houses will work on the sites you have in mind.

Is Your Project Doable?

Before you purchase land, make sure your project is doable. Although it's too early at this stage to pinpoint costs, making a few phone calls will help you determine whether your project is realistic. You'll be able to learn if you can afford to build the house, how long it will take, and what obstacles may stand in your way.

To get a ballpark estimate of cost, multiply a house's total square footage (of livable space) by the local average cost per square foot for new construction. (To obtain local averages, call a contractor, an architect, a realtor, or the local chapter of the National Association of Home Builders.) Some contractors may even be willing to give you a preliminary bid. Once you know approximate costs, speak to your lender to explore financing.

It's a good idea to discuss your project with several contractors (see page 8). They may be aware of problems in your area that could limit your options—bedrock that makes digging basements difficult, for example. These conversations are actually the first step in developing a list of contractors from which you'll choose the one who will build your home.

Working with City Hall

For any building project, even a minor one, it's essential to be familiar with building codes and other restrictions that can affect your project.

■ **Building codes,** generally implemented by the city or county building department, set the standards for safe, lasting construction. Codes specify minimum construction techniques and materials for foundations, framing, electrical wiring, plumbing, insulation, and all other aspects of a building. Although codes are adopted and enforced locally, most regional codes conform to the standards set by the national Uniform Building Code, Standard Building Code, or Basic Building Code. In some cases, local codes set more restrictive standards than national ones.

■ **Building permits** are required for home-building projects nearly everywhere. If you work with a contractor, the builder's firm should handle all necessary permits.

More than one permit may be needed; for example, one will cover the foundation, another the electrical wiring, and still another the heating equipment installation. Each will probably involve a fee and require inspections by building officials before work can proceed. (Inspections benefit *you*, as they ensure that the job is being done satisfactorily.) Permit fees are generally a percentage (1 to 1.5 percent) of the project's estimated value, often calculated on square footage.

It's important to file for the necessary permits. Failure to do so can result in fines or legal action against you. You can even be forced to undo the work performed. At the very least, your negligence may come back to haunt you later when you're ready to sell your house.

■ **Zoning ordinances,** particular to your community, restrict setbacks (how near to property lines you may build), your house's allowable height, lot coverage factors (how much of your property you can cover with structures), and other factors that impact design and building. If your plans don't conform to zoning ordinances, you can try to obtain a variance, an exception to the rules. But this legal work can be expensive and time-consuming. Even if you prove that your project won't negatively affect your neighbors, the building department can still refuse to grant the variance.

■ **Deeds and covenants** attach to the lot. Deeds set out property lines and easements; covenants may establish architectural standards in a neighborhood. Since both can seriously impact your project, make sure you have complete information on any deeds or covenants before you turn over a spadeful of soil.

Recruiting Your Home Team

A home-building project will inter-ject you and your family into the building business, an area that may be unfamiliar territory. Among the people you'll be working with are architects, designers, landscapers, contractors, and subcontractors.

Design Help

A qualified architect or designer can help you modify and personal-ize your home plan, taking into account your family's needs and budget and the house's style. In fact, you may want to consider consulting such a person while you're selecting a plan to help you articulate your needs.

Design professionals are capable of handling any or all aspects of the design process. For example, they can review your house plans, suggest options, and then provide rough sketches of the options on tracing paper. Many architects will even secure needed permits and negotiate with contractors or sub-contractors, as well as oversee the quality of the work.

Of course, you don't necessarily need an architect or designer to implement minor changes in a plan; although most contractors aren't trained in design, some can help you with modifications.

An open-ended, hourly-fee arrangement that you work out with your architect or designer allows for flexibility, but it often turns out to be more costly than working on a flat-fee basis. On a flat fee, you agree to pay a specific amount of money for a certain amount of work.

To find architects and designers, contact such trade associations as the American Institute of Architects (AIA), American Institute of Build-ing Designers (AIBD), American Society of Landscape Architects (ASLA), and American Society of Interior Designers (ASID). Although many professionals choose not to belong to trade associations, those who do have met the standards of their respective associations. For phone numbers of local branches, check the Yellow Pages.

■ **Architects** are licensed by the state and have degrees. They're trained in all facets of building design and construction. Although some can handle interior design and structural engineering, others hire specialists for those tasks.

■ **Building designers** are generally unlicensed but may be accredited by the American Institute of Building Designers. Their back-grounds are varied: some may be unlicensed architects in apprentice-ship; others are interior designers or contractors with design skills.

■ **Draftspersons** offer an economi-cal route to making simple changes on your drawings. Like building designers, these people may be unlicensed architect apprentices, engineers, or members of related trades. Most are accomplished at drawing up plans.

■ **Interior designers,** as their job title suggests, design interiors. They work with you to choose room fin-ishes, furnishings, appliances, and decorative elements. Part of their expertise is in arranging furnishings to create a workable space plan. Some interior designers are em-ployed by architectural firms; others work independently. Financial arrangements vary, depending on the designer's preference.

Related professionals are kitchen and bathroom designers, who con-centrate on fixtures, cabinetry, appliances, materials, and space planning for the kitchen and bath.

■ **Landscape architects, design-ers, and contractors** design out-door areas. Landscape architects are state-licensed to practice landscape design. A landscape designer usual-ly has a landscape architect's educa-tion and training but does not have a state license. Licensed landscape contractors specialize in garden construction, though some also have design skills and experience.

■ **Soils specialists and structural engineers** may be needed for proj-ects where unstable soils or uncom-mon wind loads or seismic forces must be taken into account. Any

structural changes to a house re-quire the expertise of a structural engineer to verify that the house won't fall down.

Services of these specialists can be expensive, but they're impera-tive in certain conditions to ensure a safe, sturdy structure. Your build-ing department will probably let you know if their services are re-quired.

General Contractors

To build your house, hire a licensed general contractor. Most states re-quire a contractor to be licensed and insured for worker's compensa-tion in order to contract a building project and hire other subcontrac-tors. State licensing ensures that contractors have met minimum training standards and have a spec-ified level of experience. Licensing does not guarantee, however, that they're good at what they do.

When contractors hire subcon-tractors, they're responsible for overseeing the quality of work and materials of the subcontractors and for paying them.

■ **Finding a contractor.** How do you find a good contractor? Start by getting referrals from people you know who have built or remodeled their home. Nothing beats a personal recommendation. The best contractors are usually busily moving from one satisfied client to another prospect, adver-tised only by word of mouth.

You can also ask local real estate brokers and lenders or even your building inspector for names of qualified builders. Experienced lumber dealers are another good source of names.

In the Yellow Pages, look under "Contractors–Building, General"; or call the local chapter of the National Association of Home Builders.

■ **Choosing a contractor.** Once you have a list of names of pro-spective builders, call several of them. On the telephone, ask first whether they handle your type of job and can work within your schedule. If they can, arrange a meeting with each one and ask them to be prepared with references of former clients and photos of previous jobs. Better still, meet them at one of their current work sites so you can get a glimpse of the quality of their work and how organized and thorough they are.

Take your plan to the meeting and discuss it enough to request a rough estimate (some builders will comply, while others will be reluctant to offer a ballpark estimate, preferring to give you a hard bid based on complete drawings). Don't hesitate to probe for advice or suggestions that might make building your house less expensive.

Be especially aware of each contractor's personality and how well you communicate. Good chemistry between you and your builder is a key ingredient for success.

Narrow down the candidates to three or four. Ask each for a firm bid, based on the exact same set of plans and specifications. For the bids to be accurate, your plans need to be complete and the specifications as precise as possible, calling out particular appliances, fixtures, floorings, roofing material, and so forth. (Some of these are specified in a stock-plan set; others are not.)

Call the contractors' references and ask about the quality of their work, their relationship with their clients, their promptness, and their readiness to follow up on problems. Visit former clients to check the contractor's work firsthand.

Be sure your final candidates are licensed, bonded, and insured for worker's compensation, public liability, and property damage. Also, try to determine how financially solvent they are (you can call their bank and credit references). Avoid contractors who are operating hand-to-mouth.

Don't automatically hire the contractor with the lowest bid if you don't think you'll get along well or if you have any doubts about the quality of the person's work. Instead, look for both the most reasonable bid and the contractor with the best credentials, references, terms, and compatibility with your family.

A word about bonds: You can request a performance bond that guarantees that your job will be finished by your contractor. If the job isn't completed, the bonding company will cover the cost of hiring another contractor to finish it. Bonds cost from 2 to 6 percent of the value of the project.

Your Building Contract

A building contract (see below) binds and protects both you and your contractor. It isn't just a legal document. It's also a list of the expectations of both parties. The best way to minimize the possibility of misunderstandings and costly changes later on is to write down every possible detail. Whether the contract is a standard form or one composed by you, have an attorney look it over before both you and the contractor sign it.

The contract should clearly specify all the work that needs to be done, including particular materials and work descriptions, the time schedule, and method of payment. It should be keyed to the working drawings.

A Sample Building Contract

Project and participants. Give a general description of the project, its address, and the names and addresses of both you and the builder.

Construction materials. Identify all construction materials by brand name, quality markings (species, grades, etc.), and model numbers where applicable. Avoid the clause "or equal," which allows the builder to substitute other materials for your choices. For materials you can't specify now, set down a budget figure.

Time schedule. Include both start and completion dates and specify that work will be "continuous." Although a contractor cannot be responsible for delays caused by strikes and material shortages, your builder should assume responsibility for completing the project within a reasonable period of time.

Work to be performed. State all work you expect the contractor to perform, from initial grading to finished painting.

Method and schedule of payment. Specify how and when payments are to be made. Typical agreements specify installment payments as particular phases of work are completed. Final payment is withheld until the job receives its final inspection and is cleared of all liens.

Waiver of liens. Protect yourself with a waiver of liens signed by the general contractor, the subcontractors, and all major suppliers. That way, subcontractors who are not paid for materials or services cannot place a lien on your property.

Personalizing Stock Plans

The beauty of buying stock plans for your new home is that they offer tested, well-conceived design at an affordable price. And stock plans dramatically reduce the time it takes to design a house, since the plans are ready when you are.

Because they were not created specifically for your family, stock plans may not reflect your personal taste. But it's not difficult to make revisions in stock plans that will turn your home into an expression of your family's personality. You'll surely want to add personal touches and choose your own finishes.

Ideally, the modifications you implement will be fairly minor. The more extensive the changes, the more expensive the plans. Major changes take valuable design time, and those that affect a house's structure may require a structural engineer's approval.

If you anticipate wholesale changes, such as moving a number of bearing walls or changing the roofline significantly, you may be better off selecting another plan. On the other hand, reconfiguring or changing the sizes of some rooms can probably be handled fairly easily.

Some structural changes may even be necessary to comply with local codes. Your area may have specific requirements for snow loads, energy codes, seismic or wind resistance, and so forth. Those types of modifications are likely to require the services of an architect or structural engineer.

Plan Modifications

Before you pencil in any changes, live with your plans for a while. Study them carefully—at your building site, if possible. Try to picture the finished house: how rooms will interrelate, where the sun will enter and at what angle, what the view will be from each window. Think about traffic patterns, access to rooms, room sizes, window and door locations, natural light, and kitchen and bathroom layouts.

Typical changes might involve adding windows or skylights to

bring in natural light or capture a view. Or you may want to widen a hallway or doorway for roomier access, extend a room, eliminate doors, or change window and door sizes. Perhaps you'd like to shorten a room, stealing the gained space for a large closet. Look closely at the kitchen; it's not difficult to reconfigure the layout if it makes the space more convenient for you.

Above all, take your time—this is your home and it should reflect your taste and needs. Make your changes now, during the planning stage. Once construction begins, it will take crowbars, hammers, saws, new materials, and, most significantly, time to alter the plans. Because changes are not part of your building contract, you can count on them being expensive extras once construction begins.

Specifying Finishes

One way to personalize a house without changing its structure is to substitute your favorite finishes for those specified on the plan.

Would you prefer a stuccoed exterior rather than the wood siding shown on the plan? In most cases, this is a relatively easy change. Do you like the look of a wood shingle roof rather than the composition shingles shown on the plan? This, too, is easy. Perhaps you would like to change the windows from sliders to casements, or upgrade to high-efficiency glazing. No problem. Many of those kinds of changes can be worked out with your contractor.

Inside, you may want hardwood where vinyl flooring is shown. In fact, you can—and should—choose types, colors, and styles of floorings, wall coverings, tile, plumbing fixtures, door hardware, cabinetry, appliances, lighting fixtures, and other interior details, for it's these materials that will personalize your home. For help in making selections, consult an architect or interior designer (see page 8).

Each material you select should be spelled out clearly and precisely in your building contract.

Finishing touches can transform a house built from stock plans into an expression of your family's taste and style. Clockwise, from far left: Colorful tilework and custom cabinetry enliven a bathroom (Design: Osburn Design); highly organized closet system maximizes storage space (Architect: David Jeremiah Hurley); low-level deck expands living space to outdoor areas (Landscape architects: The Runa Group, Inc.); built-ins convert the corner of a guest room into a home office (Design: Lynn Williams of The French Connection); French country cabinetry lends style and old-world charm to a kitchen (Design: Garry Bishop/Showcase Kitchens).

What the Plans Include

Complete construction blueprints are available for every house shown in this book. Clear and concise, these detailed blueprints are designed by licensed architects or members of the American Institute of Building Designers (AIBD). Each plan is designed to meet standards set down by nationally recognized building codes (the Uniform Building Code, Standard Building Code, or Basic Building Code) at the time and for the area where they were drawn.

Remember, however, that every state, county, and municipality has its own codes, zoning requirements, ordinances, and building regulations. Modifications may be necessary to comply with such local requirements as snow loads, energy codes, seismic zones, and flood areas.

Although blueprint sets vary depending on the size and complexity of the house and on the individual designer's style, each set may include the elements described below and shown at right.

■ **Exterior elevations** show the front, rear, and sides of the house, including exterior materials, details, and measurements.

■ **Foundation plans** include drawings for a full, partial, or daylight basement, crawlspace, pole, pier, or slab foundation. All necessary notations and dimensions are included. (Foundation options will vary for each plan. If the plan you choose doesn't have the type of foundation you desire, a generic conversion diagram is available.)

■ **Detailed floor plans** show the placement of interior walls and the dimensions of rooms, doors, windows, stairways, and similar elements for each level of the house.

■ **Cross sections** show details of the house as though it were cut in slices from the roof to the foundation. The cross sections give the home's construction, insulation, flooring, and roofing details.

■ **Interior elevations** show the specific details of cabinets (kitchen, bathroom, and utility room), fireplaces, built-in units, and other special interior features.

■ **Roof details** give the layout of rafters, dormers, gables, and other roof elements, including clerestory windows and skylights. These details may be shown on the elevation sheet or on a separate diagram.

■ **Schematic electrical layouts** show the suggested locations for switches, fixtures, and outlets. These details may be shown on the floor plan or on a separate diagram.

■ **General specifications** provide instructions and information regarding excavation and grading, masonry and concrete work, carpentry and woodwork, thermal and moisture protection, drywall, tile, flooring, glazing, and caulking and sealants.

Other Helpful Building Aids

In addition to the construction information on every set of plans, you can buy the following guides.

■ **Reproducible blueprints** are helpful if you'll be making changes to the stock plan you've chosen. These blueprints are line drawings produced on erasable, reproducible paper for the purpose of modification. When alterations are complete, working copies can be made.

■ **Itemized materials list** details the quantity, type, and size of materials needed to build your home. (This list is extremely helpful in obtaining an accurate construction bid. It's not intended for use to order materials.)

■ **Mirror-reverse plans** are useful if you want to build your home in the reverse of the plan that's shown. Because the lettering and dimensions read backwards, be sure to buy at least one regular-reading set of blueprints.

■ **Description of materials** gives the type and quality of materials suggested for the home. This form may be required for obtaining FHA or VA financing.

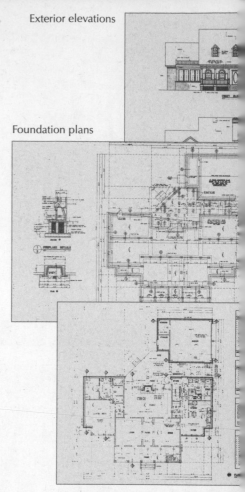

Exterior elevations

Foundation plans

Detailed floor plans

■ **How-to diagrams** for plumbing, wiring, solar heating, framing and foundation conversions show how to plumb, wire, install a solar heating system, convert plans with 2 by 4 exterior walls to 2 by 6 construction (or vice versa), and adapt a plan for a basement, crawlspace, or slab foundation. These diagrams are not specific to any one plan.

NOTE: Due to regional variations, local availability of materials, local codes, methods of installation, and individual preferences, detailed heating, plumbing, and electrical specifications are not included on plans. The duct work, venting, and other details will vary, depending on the heating and cooling system you use and the type of energy that operates it. These details and specifications are easily obtained from your builder or local supplier.

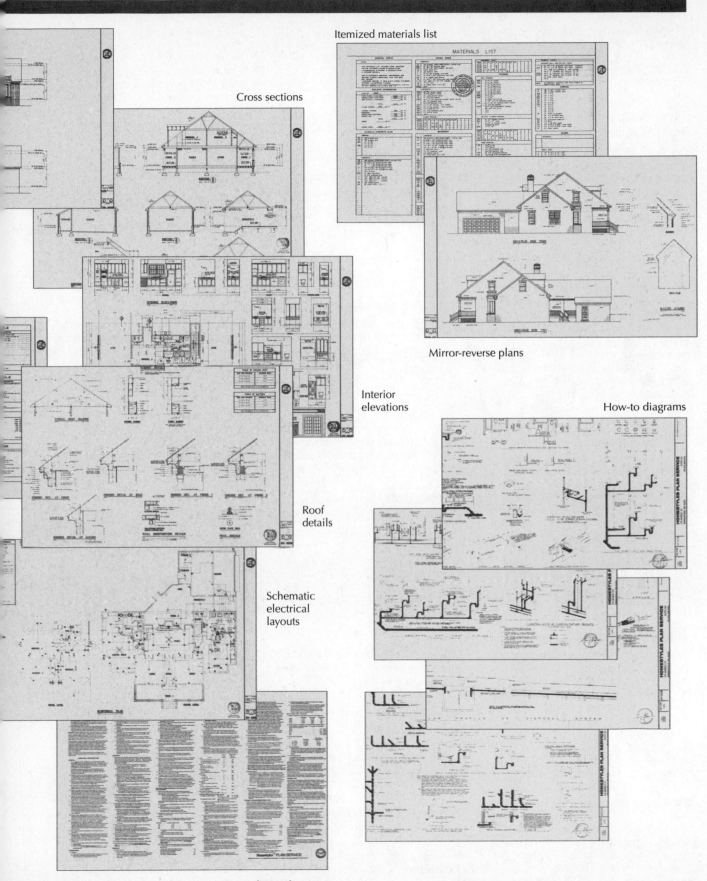

Itemized materials list

Cross sections

Mirror-reverse plans

Interior elevations

How-to diagrams

Roof details

Schematic electrical layouts

General specifications

Before You Order

Once you've chosen the one or two house plans that work best for you, you're ready to order blueprints. Before filling in the form on the facing page, note the information that follows.

How Many Blueprints Will You Need?

A single set of blueprints will allow you to study a home design in detail. You'll need more for obtaining bids and permits, as well as some to use as reference at the building site. If you'll be modifying your home plan, order a reproducible set (see page 12).

Figure you'll need at least one set each for yourself, your builder, the building department, and your lender. In addition, some subcontractors—foundation, plumber, electrician, and HVAC—may also need at least partial sets. If they do, ask them to return the sets when they're finished. The chart below can help you calculate how many sets you're likely to need.

Blueprint Checklist

___ Owner's set(s)

___ **Builder usually requires at least three sets:** one for legal documentation, one for inspections, and a minimum of one set for subcontractors.

___ **Building department requires at least one set.** Check with your local department before ordering.

___ **Lending institution usually needs one set for a conventional mortgage, three sets for FHA or VA loans.**

___ TOTAL SETS NEEDED

Blueprint Prices

The cost of having an architect design a new custom home typically runs from 5 to 15 percent of the building cost, or from $5,000 to $15,000 for a $100,000 home. A single set of blueprints for the plans in this book ranges from $295 to $505, depending on the house's size. Working with these drawings, you can save enough on design fees to add a deck, a swimming pool, or a luxurious kitchen.

Pricing is based on "total finished living space." Garages, porches, decks, and unfinished basements are not included.

Building Costs

Building costs vary widely, depending on a number of factors, includ-

Price Code (Size)	1 Set	4 Sets	7 Sets	Reproducible Set
AAA (under 500 sq. ft.)	$245	$295	$330	$430
AA (500-999 sq. ft.)	$285	$335	$370	$470
A (1,000-1,499 sq. ft.)	$325	$375	$410	$510
B (1,500-1,999 sq. ft.)	$365	$415	$450	$550
C (2,000-2,499 sq. ft.)	$405	$455	$490	$590
D (2,500-2,999 sq. ft.)	$445	$495	$530	$630
E (3,000-3,499 sq. ft.)	$485	$535	$570	$670
F (3,500-3,999 sq. ft.)	$525	$575	$610	$710
G (4,000-4,499 sq. ft.)	$565	$615	$650	$750
H (4,500-4,999 sq. ft.)	$605	$655	$690	$790
I (5,000 sq. ft. & above)	$645	$695	$730	$830

ing local material and labor costs and the finishing materials you select. For help estimating costs, see "Is Your Project Doable?" on page 7.

Foundation Options & Exterior Construction

Depending on your site and climate, your home will be built with a slab, pier, pole, crawlspace, or basement foundation. Exterior walls will be framed with either 2 by 4s or 2 by 6s, determined by structural and insulation standards in your area. Most contractors can easily adapt a home to meet the foundation and/or wall requirements for your area. Or ask for a conversion how-to diagram (see page 12).

Service & Blueprint Delivery

Service representatives are available to answer questions and assist you in placing your order. Every effort is made to process and ship orders within 48 hours.

Returns & Exchanges

Each set of blueprints is specially printed and shipped to you in response to your specific order; consequently, requests for refunds cannot be honored. However, if the prints you order cannot be used, you may exchange them for another plan from any Sunset home plan book. For an exchange, you must return all sets of plans within 30 days. A nonrefundable service charge will be assessed for all exchanges; for more information, call the toll-free number on the facing page. Note: Reproducible sets cannot be exchanged.

Compliance with Local Codes & Regulations

Because of climatic, geographic, and political variations, building codes and regulations vary from one area to another. These plans are authorized for your use expressly conditioned on your obligation and agreement to comply strictly with all local building codes, ordinances, regulations, and requirements, including permits and in-spections at time of construction.

Architectural & Engineering Seals

With increased concern about energy costs and safety, many cities and states now require that an architect or engineer review and "seal" a blueprint prior to construction. To find out whether this is a requirement in your area, contact your local building department.

License Agreement, Copy Restrictions & Copyright

When you purchase your blueprints, you are granted the right to use those documents to construct a single unit. All the plans in this publication are protected under the Federal Copyright Act, Title XVII of the United States Code and Chap-ter 37 of the Code of Federal Regu-lations. Each designer retains title and ownership of the original documents. The blueprints licensed to you cannot be used by or resold to any other person, copied, or reproduced by any means. The copying restrictions do not apply to reproducible blueprints. When you buy a reproducible set, you may modify and reproduce it for your own use.

Blueprint Order Form

Complete this order form in just three easy steps. Then mail in your order or, for faster service, call toll-free.

1. Blueprints & Accessories

BLUEPRINT CHART

Price Code	1 Set	4 Sets	7 Sets	Reproducible Set*
AAA	$245	$295	$330	$430
AA	$285	$335	$370	$470
A	$325	$375	$410	$510
B	$365	$415	$450	$550
C	$405	$455	$490	$590
D	$445	$495	$530	$630
E	$485	$535	$570	$670
F	$525	$575	$610	$710
G	$565	$615	$650	$750
H	$605	$655	$690	$790
I	$645	$695	$730	$830

*A reproducible set is produced on erasable paper for the purpose of modification. It is only available for plans with prefixes A, AG, AGH, AH, AHP, APS, AX, B, C, CC, CPS, DCL, DD, DW, E, EOF, FB, GL, GML, GSA, H, HDS, HFL, J, K, KD, KLF, L, LRD, LS, M, NW, OH, PH, PI, RD, S, SDG, THD, U, UDG, V.

_____

Prices subject to change

Mirror-Reverse Sets: $50 surcharge. From the total number of sets you ordered above, choose the number you want to be reversed. *Note: All writing on mirror-reverse plans is backwards. Order at least one regular-reading set.*

Itemized Materials List: One set $50; each additional set $15. Details the quantity, type, and size of materials needed to build your home.

Description of Materials: Sold in a set of two for $50 (for use in obtaining FHA or VA financing).

Typical How-To Diagrams: One set $20; two sets $30; three sets $40; four sets $45. General guides on plumbing, wiring, and solar heating, plus information on how to convert from one foundation or exterior framing to another. *Note: These diagrams are not specific to any one plan.*

2. Sales Tax & Shipping

Determine your subtotal and add appropriate local state sales tax, plus shipping and handling (see chart below).

SHIPPING & HANDLING

	1–3 Sets	4–6 Sets	7 or More Sets	Reproducible Set
U.S. Regular (5–6 business days)	$17.50	$20.00	$22.50	$17.50
U.S. Express (2–3 business days)	$29.50	$32.50	$35.00	$29.50
Canada Regular (2–3 weeks)	$20.00	$22.50	$25.00	$20.00
Canada Express (5–6 business days)	$35.00	$40.00	$45.00	$35.00
Overseas/Airmail (7–10 business days)	$57.50	$67.50	$77.50	$57.50

3. Customer Information

Choose the method of payment you prefer. Include check, money order, or credit card information, complete name and address portion, and mail, fax, or call using the information at the right.

SS19

COMPLETE THIS FORM

Plan Number _____ **Price Code** _____

Foundation _____
(Review your plan carefully for foundation options—basement, pole, pier, crawlspace, or slab. Many plans offer several options; others offer only one.)

Number of Sets: $_____
(See chart at left)
☐ One Set
☐ Four Sets
☐ Seven Sets
☐ One Reproducible Set

Additional Sets _____ $_____
($40 each)

Mirror-Reverse Sets _____ $_____
($50 surcharge)

Itemized Materials List $_____
Only available for plans with prefixes AH, AHP, APS*, AX*, B*, C, CAR, CC, CDG*, CPS, DD*, DW, E, GSA, H, HFL, I*, J, K, LMB*, LRD, NW*, P, PH, R, S, THD, U, UDG, VL. *Not available on all plans. Please call before ordering.

Description of Materials $_____
Only available for plans with prefixes AHP, C, DW, H, J, K, P, PH, VL.

Typical How-To Diagrams $_____
☐ Plumbing ☐ Wiring ☐ Solar Heating ☐ Foundation & Framing Conversion

SUBTOTAL $_____

SALES TAX $_____

SHIPPING & HANDLING $_____

GRAND TOTAL $_____

☐ Check/money order enclosed (in U.S. funds)
☐ VISA ☐ MasterCard ☐ AmEx ☐ Discover

Credit Card # _____ **Exp. Date** _____

Signature _____

Name _____

Address _____

City _____ **State** ____ **Country** _____

Zip _____ **Daytime Phone** (____)_____
☐ Please check if you are a contractor.

Mail form to: Sunset/HomeStyles Plan Service
P.O. Box 50670
Minneapolis, MN 55405

Or fax to: (612) 338-1626

FOR FASTER SERVICE CALL 1-800-820-1283

SS19

Classic Country-Style

- At the center of this rustic country-style home is an enormous living room with a flat beamed ceiling and a massive stone fireplace. A sunny patio and a covered rear porch are just steps away.
- The adjoining eating area and kitchen provide plenty of room for casual dining and meal preparation. The eating area is visually enhanced by a 14-ft. sloped ceiling with false beams. The kitchen includes a snack bar, a pantry closet and a built-in spice cabinet.
- The formal dining room gets plenty of pizzazz from a stone-faced wall and an arched planter facing the living room.
- The secluded master suite has it all, including a private bath, a separate dressing area and a large walk-in closet with built-in shelves.
- The two remaining bedrooms have big closets and easy access to a full bath.

Plan E-1808	
Bedrooms: 3	**Baths:** 2
Living Area:	
Main floor	1,800 sq. ft.
Total Living Area:	**1,800 sq. ft.**
Garage	605 sq. ft.
Exterior Wall Framing:	2x4
Foundation Options:	
Crawlspace	
Slab	

(All plans can be built with your choice of foundation and framing. A generic conversion diagram is available. See order form.)

BLUEPRINT PRICE CODE: B

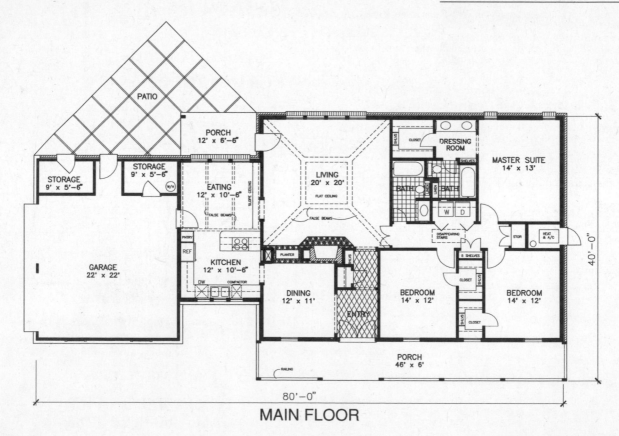

MAIN FLOOR

TO ORDER THIS BLUEPRINT,
CALL TOLL-FREE 1-800-820-1283

Plan E-1808

PRICES AND DETAILS
ON PAGES 12-15

Cozy Covered Porches

- Twin dormers give this raised one-story design the appearance of a two-story. Two covered porches and a deck supplement the main living areas with plenty of outdoor entertaining space.
- The large central living room features a dramatic fireplace, a 12-ft. ceiling with a skylight and access to both porch areas.
- Double doors open to a bayed eating area, which overlooks the adjoining deck and includes a sloped ceiling that rises to 12 ft. in the kitchen. An angled snack bar and a pantry are also featured.
- The elegant master suite is tucked to one side of the home and also overlooks the backyard and deck. Laundry facilities and garage access are nearby.
- Across the home, two additional bedrooms share another full bath.

Plan E-1826

Bedrooms: 3	Baths: 2
Living Area:	
Main floor	1,800 sq. ft.
Total Living Area:	**1,800 sq. ft.**
Garage	550 sq. ft.
Storage	84 sq. ft.
Exterior Wall Framing:	2x6

Foundation Options:

Crawlspace
Slab
(All plans can be built with your choice of foundation and framing. A generic conversion diagram is available. See order form.)

BLUEPRINT PRICE CODE: B

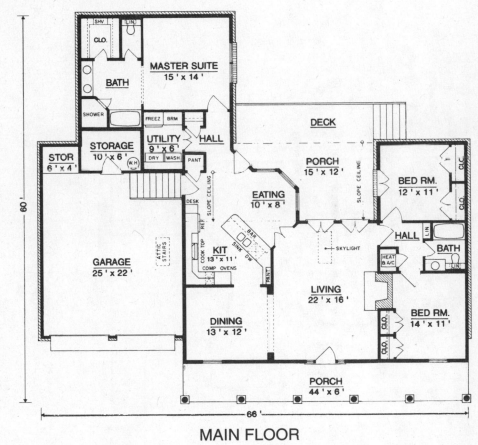

MAIN FLOOR

Simple Roofline Characterizes Country Home

Characterized by a simple roof line, the country-style home is among the most popular categories in today's real estate market. The brick masonry facade accented by shutters and an expansive bow window at the living room add to the comfortable country character of this three-bedroom design.

Inside, an informal family gathering area is carefully separated from the formal living/dining portion by a double door off the entry and a versatile pocket door to the dining room. The kitchen island counter is large enough to accommodate a family of six. A French door opens off the nook to a covered patio. The octagonal projection of the nook adds interest to the rear exterior wall as well as visually enhancing the interior.

Double doors open to an expansive master bedroom area characteristic of much larger homes. The third bedroom is conveniently located for the independent resident or guest, or may effectively serve as a secluded den/study for those not requiring a third bedroom.

Whether rural or urban, this home will blend well and look comfortable in a variety of settings.

55'-0"

54'-0"

Nook
11/0x10/6

Family
13/6x17/6

Master
12/0x16/0

Dining
10/0x10/0

Kit.

walk in wardrobe

Living
17/0x13/6

Entry

linen

Bdrm. 2
11/0x11/0

built in

Bdrm. 3
11/0x10/6

Garage
19/0x22/0

PLAN R-1030
WITHOUT BASEMENT
(CRAWLSPACE FOUNDATION)

Total living area:
(Not counting garage)   1,801 sq. ft.

Blueprint Price Code B

Plan R-1030

TO ORDER THIS BLUEPRINT,
CALL TOLL-FREE 1-800-820-1283

PRICES AND DETAILS
ON PAGES 12-15

Outstanding One-Story

- This sharp one-story home has an outstanding floor plan, attractively enhanced by a stately brick facade.
- A vestibule introduces the foyer, which flows between the formal living spaces at the front of the home.
- The large living room features a 14-ft., 8-in. sloped ceiling and dramatic, high windows. The spacious dining room has easy access to the kitchen.

- The expansive family room is the focal point of the home, with a 16-ft. beamed cathedral ceiling, a slate-hearth fireplace and sliding glass doors to a backyard terrace.
- The adjoining kitchen has a snack bar and a sunny dinette framed by a curved window wall that overlooks the terrace.
- Included in the sleeping wing is a luxurious master suite with a private bath. A skylighted dressing room and a big walk-in closet are also featured.
- The two secondary bedrooms share a hall bath that has a dual-sink vanity. A half-bath is near the mud/laundry room.

Plan K-278-M

Bedrooms: 3	Baths: 2½
Living Area:	
Main floor	1,803 sq. ft.
Total Living Area:	**1,803 sq. ft.**
Standard basement	1,778 sq. ft.
Garage and storage	586 sq. ft.
Exterior Wall Framing:	2x4 or 2x6

Foundation Options:

Standard basement
Slab
(All plans can be built with your choice of foundation and framing. A generic conversion diagram is available. See order form.)

BLUEPRINT PRICE CODE:	B

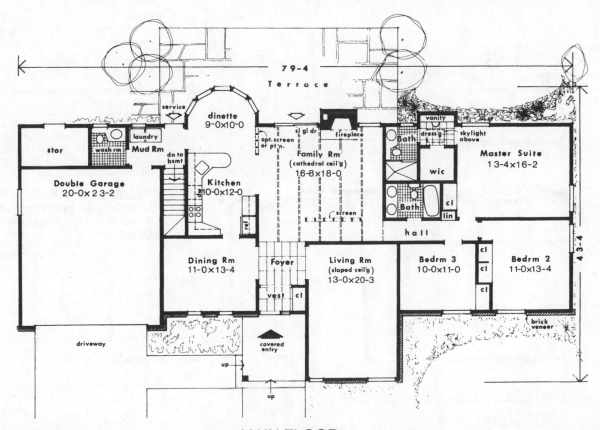

MAIN FLOOR

A Present From the Past

- A covered front porch with Victorian trim and an exterior with half-round windows and classic, high-pitched gables give today's homebuyers a present from the past.
- Arriving guests enjoy an open view into the Great Room with fireplace and the formal dining room with window wall.
- The kitchen incorporates a breakfast bay with rear access and adjacent laundry room.
- Up the double-stairs, lit by a round-top window, are three bedrooms and two full baths.
- All of the main-floor rooms are enhanced by 10-ft. ceilings. The upper floor has standard 8-ft. ceilings.

Plan V-1803

Bedrooms: 3	Baths: 2½
Living Area:	
Upper floor	875 sq. ft.
Main floor	928 sq. ft.
Total Living Area:	**1,803 sq. ft.**
Exterior Wall Framing:	2x6

Foundation Options:
Crawlspace
(Typical foundation & framing conversion diagram available—see order form.)

BLUEPRINT PRICE CODE:	B

MAIN FLOOR

UPPER FLOOR

TO ORDER THIS BLUEPRINT, CALL TOLL-FREE 1-800-820-1283   Plan V-1803   *PRICES AND DETAILS ON PAGES 12-15*

Warm Glow

- With a nod toward contemporary style, this home displays a warm, glowing country countenance.
- On lazy summer nights, you'll remind passersby of a wistful Rockwell painting as you adjust your Adirondack chair on the covered front porch and kick back with a tall, chilly cola at your elbow.
- Inside, the radiant, 20-ft., 8-in. entry spills directly into the living room, which boasts an impressive 17-ft. vaulted ceiling.
- All common areas are convenient to the kitchen, which includes a snack bar to feed those hungry kids after school. From the neighboring breakfast nook, sliding glass doors open to a large backyard patio—an excellent space for fun mini-picnics.
- Cozy gatherings are assured in the family room, where a handsome fireplace provides warmth and peace.
- Past an airy loft, the master suite beckons from behind double doors. Here, a tray ceiling rises gracefully to 8 feet. In the master bath, a shower refreshes you quickly, while a whirlpool tub soothes those aching muscles.
- Your children share another bath and sleep well in two roomy bedrooms.

Plan AG-1802	
Bedrooms: 3	**Baths:** 2½
Living Area:	
Upper floor	840 sq. ft.
Main floor	990 sq. ft.
Total Living Area:	**1,830 sq. ft.**
Standard basement	950 sq. ft.
Garage	400 sq. ft.
Exterior Wall Framing:	2x4
Foundation Options:	

Standard basement

(All plans can be built with your choice of foundation and framing. A generic conversion diagram is available. See order form.)

BLUEPRINT PRICE CODE:	**B**

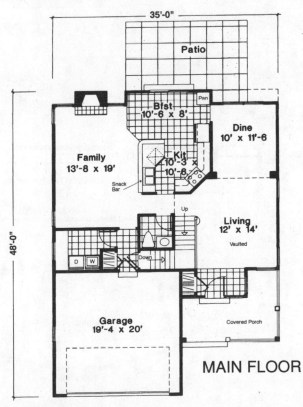

MAIN FLOOR

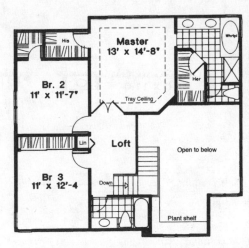

UPPER FLOOR

Indoor-Outdoor Living

- Attention-getting pentagonal-shaped home is ideal for full-time or vacation living.
- Huge, two-story high living/dining area takes up half of the main floor, ideal for family gatherings.
- Compact, but functional kitchen features breakfast bar and adjacent laundry room that can also serve as a pantry and/or mudroom.
- Open stairway leads to second-floor balcony hallway overlooking the main level living area.
- Upper level has room for two additional bedrooms and a second bath.

Plans H-855-2 & -2A

Bedrooms: 3	Baths: 2

Space:	
Upper floor:	660 sq. ft.
Main floor:	1,174 sq. ft.

Total living area:	1,834 sq. ft.
Basement:	approx. 1,174 sq. ft.
Garage:	277 sq. ft.

Exterior Wall Framing:	2x4

Foundation options:
Daylight basement (Plan H-855-2).
Crawlspace (Plan H-855-2A).
(Foundation & framing conversion diagram available — see order form.)

Blueprint Price Code:

Without basement	B
With basement	E

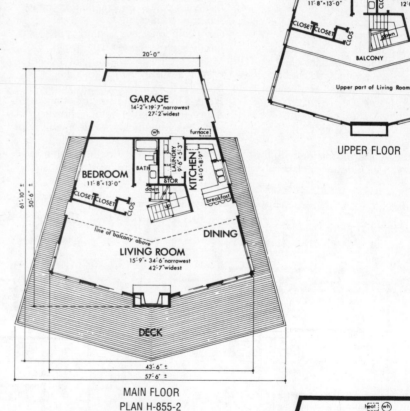

UPPER FLOOR

MAIN FLOOR
PLAN H-855-2
WITH BASEMENT

PLAN H-855-2A
WITHOUT BASEMENT

SCALE

BASEMENT

TO ORDER THIS BLUEPRINT, CALL TOLL-FREE 1-800-820-1283

Plans H-855-2 & -2A

PRICES AND DETAILS ON PAGES 12-15

Sunny Surprises

- A clean-lined roof with wide overhangs blends this home into the landscape, and a low-walled entrance court adds to the effect.
- Inside, you'll find many sunny surprises, including bow windows in the living and dining rooms, a beautiful kitchen and a bright semi-circular dinette area.
- The spacious family room or den features a 10½-ft. cathedral ceiling.

A large fireplace is centered on a bright wall of glass. Sliding glass doors provide access to a lovely backyard terrace. A decorative screen separates the family room from the main hall.
- The quiet master suite includes a private bath, a walk-in closet and a skylighted dressing area.
- A hall bath with a dual-sink vanity serves the two front-facing bedrooms.
- The double garage offers two storage areas, plus a choice of door locations.

Plan K-167-R

Bedrooms: 3	**Baths:** 2

Living Area:	
Main floor	1,834 sq. ft.
Total Living Area:	**1,834 sq. ft.**
Standard basement	1,768 sq. ft.
Garage and storage	619 sq. ft.
Exterior Wall Framing:	2x4 or 2x6

Foundation Options:
Standard basement
Slab
(All plans can be built with your choice of foundation and framing. A generic conversion diagram is available. See order form.)

BLUEPRINT PRICE CODE:	B

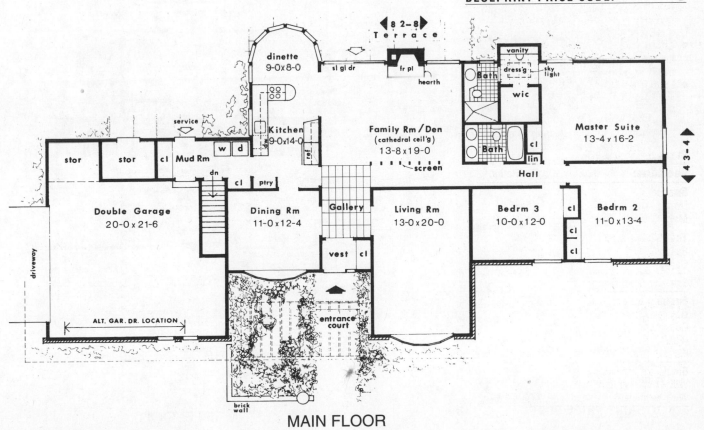

MAIN FLOOR

Unique Inside and Out

- This delightful design is as striking on the inside as it is on the outside.
- The focal point of the home is the huge Grand Room, which features a vaulted ceiling, plant shelves and lots of glass, including a clerestory window. French doors flanking the fireplace lead to the covered porch and the two adjoining sun decks.
- The centrally located kitchen offers easy access from any room in the house, and a full bath, a laundry area and the garage entrance are nearby.
- The two main-floor master suites are another unique design element of the home. Both of the suites showcase a volume ceiling, a sunny window seat, a walk-in closet, a private bath and French doors that open to a sun deck.
- Upstairs, two guest suites overlook the vaulted Grand Room below.

Plan EOF-13

Bedrooms: 4	Baths: 3
Living Area:	
Upper floor	443 sq. ft.
Main floor	1,411 sq. ft.
Total Living Area:	**1,854 sq. ft.**
Garage	264 sq. ft.
Storage	50 sq. ft.
Exterior Wall Framing:	2x6

Foundation Options:

Crawlspace

(Typical foundation & framing conversion diagram available—see order form.)

BLUEPRINT PRICE CODE:	B

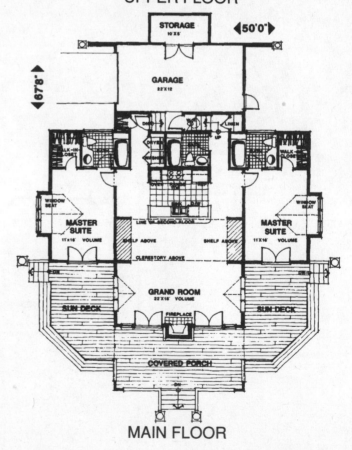

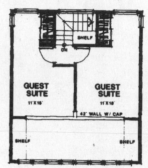

UPPER FLOOR

MAIN FLOOR

Plan EOF-13

PRICES AND DETAILS ON PAGES 12-15

Classic Ranch

- With decorative brick quoins, a columned porch and stylish dormers, the exterior of this classic one-story provides an interesting blend of Early American and European design.
- Flowing from the foyer, the bay-windowed dining room is enhanced by an 11½-ft.-high stepped ceiling.
- The spacious Great Room, separated from the dining room by a columned arch, features a stepped ceiling, a built-in media center and a striking fireplace. Lovely French doors lead to a big backyard patio.
- The breakfast room, which shares an eating bar with the kitchen, boasts a ceiling that slopes to 12 feet. French doors access a covered rear porch.
- The master bedroom has a 10-ft. tray ceiling, a sunny bay window and a roomy walk-in closet. The master bath features a whirlpool tub in a bayed nook and a separate shower.
- The front-facing bedroom is enhanced by a 10-ft.-high vaulted area over an arched transom window.

Plan AX-93304

Bedrooms: 3	Baths: 2
Living Area:	
Main floor	1,860 sq. ft.
Total Living Area:	**1,860 sq. ft.**
Standard basement	1,860 sq. ft.
Garage/utility/storage	434 sq. ft.
Exterior Wall Framing:	2x4

Foundation Options:

Standard basement
Crawlspace
Slab
(All plans can be built with your choice of foundation and framing. A generic conversion diagram is available. See order form.)

BLUEPRINT PRICE CODE:	**B**

VIEW INTO GREAT ROOM

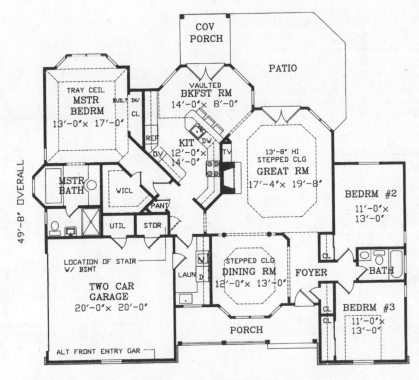

MAIN FLOOR

Attainable Luxury

- This traditional ranch home offers a large, central living room with a 12-ft. ceiling, a corner fireplace and an adjoining patio.
- The U-shaped kitchen easily services both the formal dining room and the bayed eating area.
- The luxurious master suite features a large bath with separate vanities and dressing areas.
- Two secondary bedrooms share a second full bath.
- A covered carport boasts a decorative brick wall and attic space above. Two additional storage areas provide plenty of room for gardening supplies and sports equipment.

Plan E-1812

Bedrooms: 3	Baths: 2
Living Area:	
Main floor	1,860 sq. ft.
Total Living Area:	**1,860 sq. ft.**
Carport	484 sq. ft.
Storage	132 sq. ft.
Exterior Wall Framing:	2x6

Foundation Options:

Crawlspace

Slab

(All plans can be built with your choice of foundation and framing. A generic conversion diagram is available. See order form.)

BLUEPRINT PRICE CODE: B

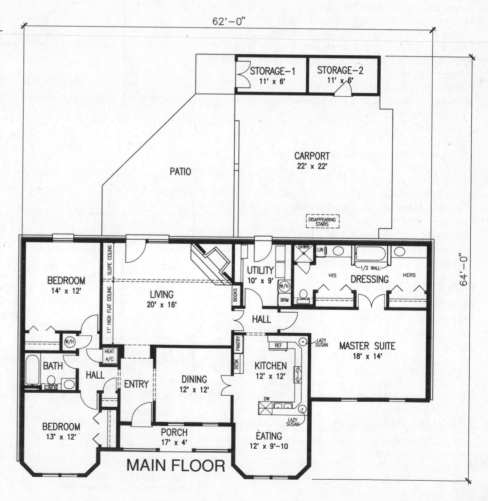

MAIN FLOOR

Plan E-1812

Up-to-Date Country Styling

- Nearly surrounded by a covered wood porch, this traditional 1,860-sq.-ft. farm-styled home is modernized for today's active, up-to-date family.
- Inside, the efficient floor plan promotes easy mobility with vast openness and a minimum of cross-traffic.
- The spacious living and dining area is warmed by a fireplace with a stone hearth; sliding glass doors off the dining room open to the porch.
- The U-shaped country kitchen is centrally located and overlooks a bright breakfast nook and a big family room with a woodstove and its own sliding glass doors to a patio.
- On the upper floor is a large master bedroom with corner windows, a dressing area and a private bath. Two secondary bedrooms share a second bath with a handy dual-sink vanity.

Plans P-7677-2A & -2D

Bedrooms: 3	Baths: 2½
Living Area:	
Upper floor	825 sq. ft.
Main floor	1,035 sq. ft.
Total Living Area:	**1,860 sq. ft.**
Daylight basement	1,014 sq. ft.
Garage	466 sq. ft.
Exterior Wall Framing:	2x6
Foundation Options:	**Plan #**
Daylight basement	P-7677-2D
Crawlspace	P-7677-2A

(All plans can be built with your choice of foundation and framing. A generic conversion diagram is available. See order form.)

BLUEPRINT PRICE CODE:	**B**

UPPER FLOOR

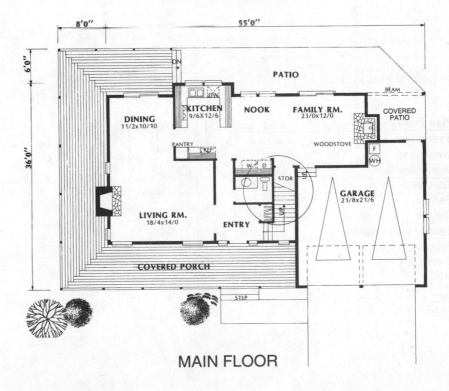

MAIN FLOOR

Impressive Master Suite

- This attractive one-story home features an impressive master suite located apart from the secondary bedrooms.
- A lovely front porch opens to the entry, which flows to the formal dining room, the rear-oriented living room and the secondary bedroom wing.
- The living room boasts a large corner fireplace, a ceiling that slopes to 11 ft. and access to a backyard patio.
- A U-shaped kitchen services the dining room and its own eating area. It also boasts a built-in desk, a handy pantry closet and access to the nearby laundry room and carport.
- The wide master bedroom hosts a lavish master bath with a spa tub, a separate shower and his-and-hers dressing areas.
- Across the home, the two secondary bedrooms share another full bath.

Plan E-1818

Bedrooms: 3	Baths: 2
Living Area:	
Main floor	1,868 sq. ft.
Total Living Area:	**1,868 sq. ft.**
Carport	484 sq. ft.
Storage	132 sq. ft.
Exterior Wall Framing:	2x6

Foundation Options:

Crawlspace

Slab

(All plans can be built with your choice of foundation and framing. A generic conversion diagram is available. See order form.)

BLUEPRINT PRICE CODE:	B

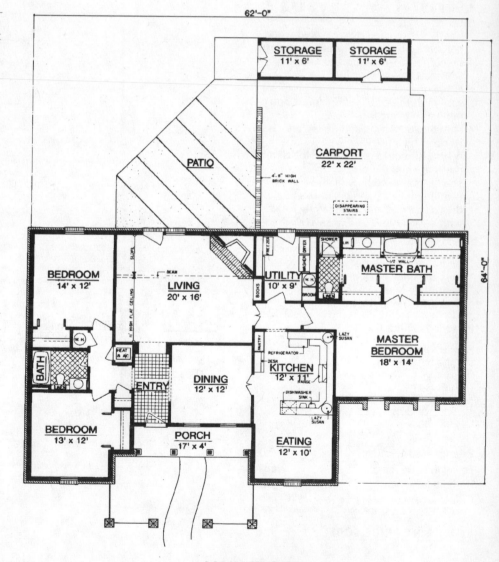

MAIN FLOOR

Plan E-1818

Showy One-Story

- Dramatic windows embellish the exterior of this showy one-story home.
- Inside, the entry provides a sweeping view of the living room, where sliding glass doors open to the backyard patio and flank a dramatic fireplace.
- Skylights accent the living room's 12-ft. sloped ceiling, while arched openings define the formal dining room.
- Double doors lead from the dining room to the kitchen and informal eating area. The kitchen features a built-in work desk and a pantry. An oversized utility room adjoins the kitchen and accesses the two-car garage.
- A 10-ft. tray ceiling adorns the master suite. The private bath is accented with a skylight above the fabulous fan-shaped marble tub. His-and-hers vanities, a separate shower and a huge walk-in closet are also featured.
- Two more bedrooms and a full bath are located at the other end of the home.
- The front-facing bedroom boasts a 12-ft. sloped ceiling.

Plan E-1830

Bedrooms: 3	Baths: 2
Living Area:	
Main floor	1,868 sq. ft.
Total Living Area:	**1,868 sq. ft.**
Garage and storage	616 sq. ft.
Exterior Wall Framing:	2x6

Foundation Options:

Crawlspace

Slab

(All plans can be built with your choice of foundation and framing. A generic conversion diagram is available. See order form.)

BLUEPRINT PRICE CODE:	**B**

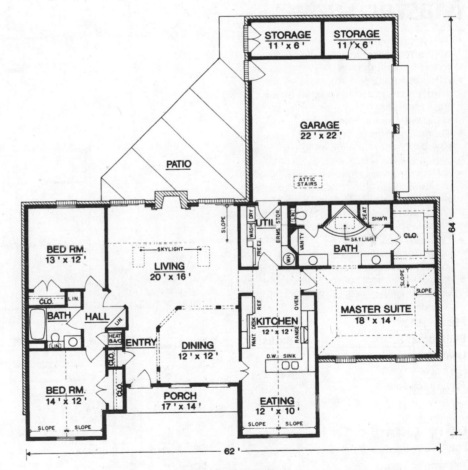

MAIN FLOOR

Attractive and Cozy Cottage

- This cozy country cottage is attractive, economical and easy to build.
- A striking front door with oval glass and sidelights opens directly into the huge living room, which is warmed by a nice fireplace. French doors provide access to the expansive covered front porch.
- The dining room is brightened by a boxed-out area with lots of glass.
- The efficient kitchen includes a snack bar, a windowed sink and a lazy Susan.
- The quiet main-floor master bedroom offers porch access through French doors. The master bath boasts a garden tub, a separate shower, two vanities and a walk-in closet.
- A powder room and a convenient laundry room round out the main floor.
- Upstairs, two bedrooms share another full bath. Hall closets provide additional storage space.
- A storage area for outdoor equipment is offered in the secluded carport.

Plan J-86131

Bedrooms: 3	Baths: 2½
Living Area:	
Upper floor	500 sq. ft.
Main floor	1,369 sq. ft.
Total Living Area:	**1,869 sq. ft.**
Standard basement	1,369 sq. ft.
Carport and storage	540 sq. ft.
Exterior Wall Framing:	2x4

Foundation Options:

Standard basement
Crawlspace
Slab
(All plans can be built with your choice of foundation and framing.
A generic conversion diagram is available. See order form.)

BLUEPRINT PRICE CODE: B

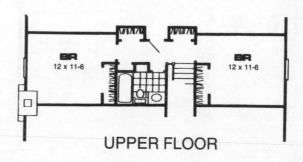

UPPER FLOOR

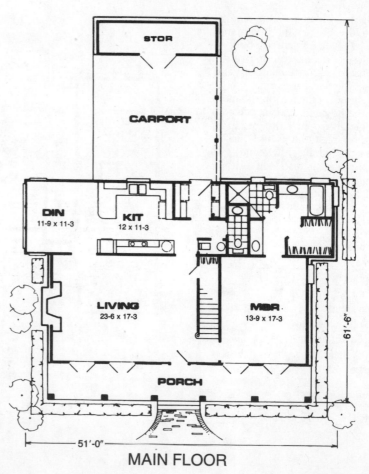

MAIN FLOOR

TO ORDER THIS BLUEPRINT,
CALL TOLL-FREE 1-800-820-1283

Plan J-86131

PRICES AND DETAILS
ON PAGES 12-15

Two-Story Great Room

- An expansive two-story-high Great Room, with an oversized hearth and high transom windows, is the highlight of this updated traditional design.
- The cozy front porch and bright, open foyer welcome visitors.
- A 16-ft. vaulted ceiling in the Great Room creates an open expanse as it merges with the nice-sized dining room. Sliding glass doors open to the backyard from the dining area, and the adjoining island kitchen boasts a pantry and windows above the sink.
- The main-floor master suite is in a separate wing for privacy and features a whirlpool tub and a separate shower.
- Upstairs, a balcony joins two bedrooms and a hall bath. The balcony overlooks the Great Room and the foyer.

Plan PI-92-510

Bedrooms: 3	Baths: 2½
Living Area:	
Upper floor	574 sq. ft.
Main floor	1,298 sq. ft.
Total Living Area:	**1,872 sq. ft.**
Daylight basement	1,298 sq. ft.
Garage	660 sq. ft.
Exterior Wall Framing:	2x6

Foundation Options:

Daylight basement

(All plans can be built with your choice of foundation and framing. A generic conversion diagram is available. See order form.)

BLUEPRINT PRICE CODE:	B

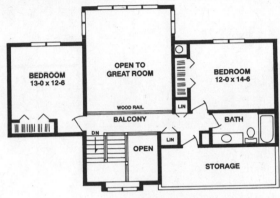

UPPER FLOOR

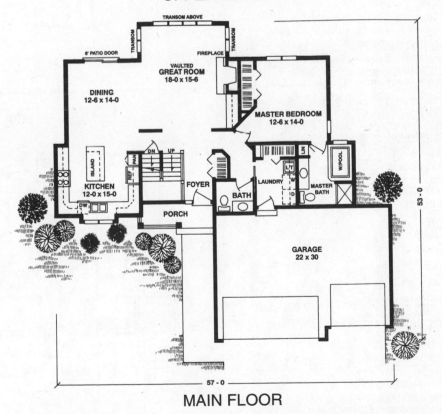

MAIN FLOOR

TO ORDER THIS BLUEPRINT, CALL TOLL-FREE 1-800-820-1283

Plan PI-92-510

PRICES AND DETAILS ON PAGES 12-15

31

Customize Your Floor Plan!

- An optional bonus room and a choice between a loft or a bedroom allow you to customize the floor plan of this striking two-story traditional.

- The 18-ft. vaulted foyer leads guests past a handy powder room and directly into the living areas. Straight ahead is an 18-ft. vaulted family room with a handsome centered fireplace. To the right of the foyer is the formal dining room. The spaces are pleasantly set off by a beautiful open-railed staircase.

- The sunny breakfast room is open to the island kitchen. A pantry closet, a lot of counter space and direct access to the laundry room and the garage add to the kitchen's efficiency.

- The main-floor master suite is a treasure, with its 11-ft. tray ceiling and vaulted, amenity-filled master bath.

- Upstairs, two bedrooms, a full bath and an optional loft and bonus room provide plenty of opportunity for expansion and customization.

Plan FB-1874

Bedrooms: 3+	**Baths:** 2½
Living Area:	
Upper floor	554 sq. ft.
Main floor	1,320 sq. ft.
Bonus room	155 sq. ft.
Total Living Area:	**2,029 sq. ft.**
Daylight basement	1,320 sq. ft.
Garage	240 sq. ft.
Storage	38 sq. ft.
Exterior Wall Framing:	2x4

Foundation Options:

Daylight basement

(All plans can be built with your choice of foundation and framing. A generic conversion diagram is available. See order form.)

BLUEPRINT PRICE CODE: C

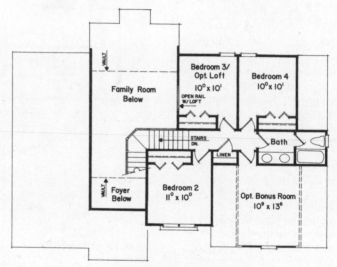

UPPER FLOOR

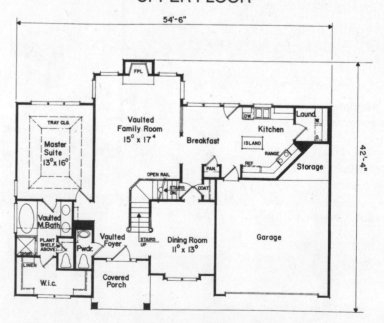

MAIN FLOOR

Plan FB-1874

PRICES AND DETAILS
ON PAGES 12-15

Upscale Charm

- Country charm and the very latest in conveniences mark this upscale home. To add extra appeal, all of the living areas are housed on one floor, yet may be expanded to the upper floor later.
- Set off from the foyer, the dining room is embraced by elegant columns. Arched windows in the dining room and in the bedroom across the hall echo the delicate detailing of the covered front porch.
- Straight ahead, the family room flaunts a wall of French doors overlooking a covered back porch and a large deck.
- A curved island snack bar smoothly connects the gourmet kitchen to the sunny breakfast area, which features a dramatic 13-ft. vaulted ceiling brightened by skylights. All other rooms have 9-ft. ceilings. A nearby computer room and a laundry/utility room with a recycling center are other amenities.
- The master bedroom's private bath includes a dual-sink vanity and a floor-to-ceiling storage unit with a built-in chest of drawers. Other extras include a step-up spa tub and a separate shower.

Plan J-92100

Bedrooms: 3+	Baths: 2
Living Area:	
Main floor	1,877 sq. ft.
Total Living Area:	**1,877 sq. ft.**
Upper floor (future areas)	1,500 sq. ft.
Standard basement	1,877 sq. ft.
Garage and storage	551 sq. ft.
Exterior Wall Framing:	2x4

Foundation Options:

Standard basement

Crawlspace

Slab

(All plans can be built with your choice of foundation and framing. A generic conversion diagram is available. See order form.)

BLUEPRINT PRICE CODE:	B

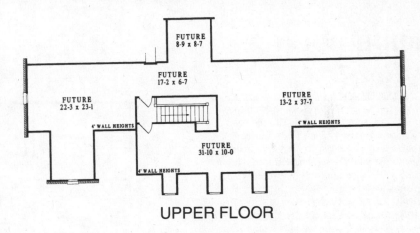

UPPER FLOOR

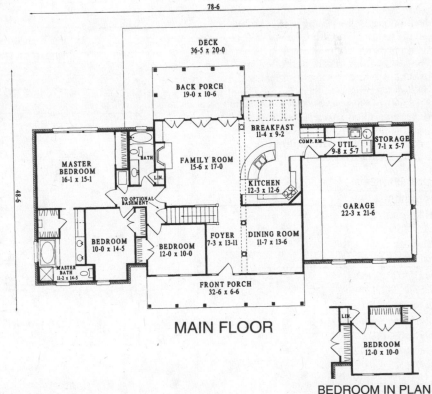

MAIN FLOOR

BEDROOM IN PLAN
WITHOUT BASEMENT

Remember When?

- Remember when porch swings creaked in the summer air, a glass of iced tea sweated beside you and the nights seemed to last forever? This country home recalls those days with a nostalgic covered porch and a peaceful interior.
- From the sidelighted foyer, the massive Great Room unfolds, offering a rustic stone fireplace that rises to the ceiling. French doors lead to a backyard patio.
- Wide-open spaces enhance the kitchen and the adjoining dining area. The big island snack bar will be a favorite spot when the kids come home from school.
- The upper-floor master bedroom provides plenty of room to relax, and includes a private bath.
- Business matters may be attended to in the home office space just down the hall, while two bedrooms with desks allow private space for children or overnight guests.

Plan J-9507

Bedrooms: 3	Baths: 2½
Living Area:	
Upper floor	947 sq. ft.
Main floor	931 sq. ft.
Total Living Area:	**1,878 sq. ft.**
Standard basement	931 sq. ft.
Carport	455 sq. ft.
Exterior Wall Framing:	**2x4**

Foundation Options:
Standard basement
Crawlspace
Slab
(All plans can be built with your choice of foundation and framing. A generic conversion diagram is available. See order form.)

BLUEPRINT PRICE CODE:	B

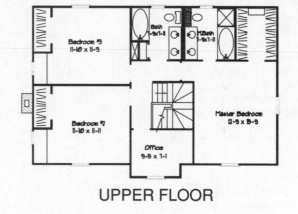

UPPER FLOOR

BASEMENT STAIRWAY LOCATION

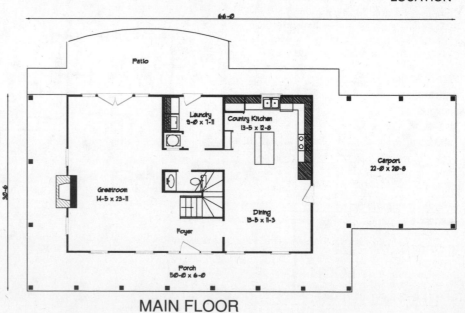

MAIN FLOOR

TO ORDER THIS BLUEPRINT, CALL TOLL-FREE 1-800-820-1283

Plan J-9507

PRICES AND DETAILS ON PAGES 12-15

Sunny, Spacious Two-Story

- Captivating exterior angles and numerous windows are just the beginning of what this exciting two-story design has to offer.
- The covered double-door entry leads into the impressive two-story-high foyer.
- Straight ahead, the living room features a 17-ft., 4-in. ceiling, a striking fireplace and built-in shelves. The open formal dining room is expanded by a 10½-ft.

vaulted ceiling. Both rooms access a secluded patio.
- A 10½-ft. vaulted ceiling soars above the gourmet kitchen, which offers a sunny breakfast nook and a convenient pass-through to the dining room.
- The main-floor master suite has it all, including a large walk-in closet and a luxurious bath with double vanities, a corner tub and a separate shower.
- A decorative plant shelf accents the stairway to the upper floor, where there are two bedrooms, a nice-sized loft and a large bath, as well as breathtaking views of the first floor.

Plan HDS-99-176

Bedrooms: 3+	Baths: 2½
Living Area:	
Upper floor	649 sq. ft.
Main floor	1,230 sq. ft.
Total Living Area:	**1,879 sq. ft.**
Garage	400 sq. ft.
Exterior Wall Framing:	2x4

Foundation Options:

Slab

(All plans can be built with your choice of foundation and framing. A generic conversion diagram is available. See order form.)

BLUEPRINT PRICE CODE: **B**

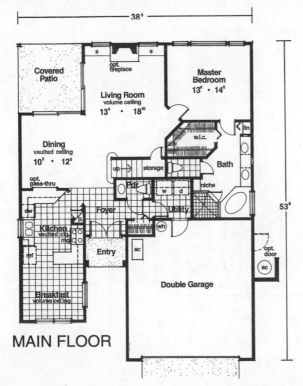

MAIN FLOOR

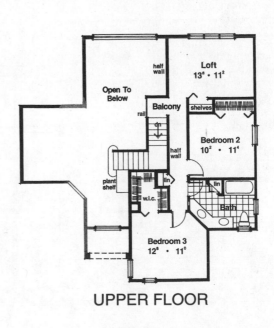

UPPER FLOOR

Exemplary Colonial

- Inside this traditionally designed home is an exciting floor plan for today's lifestyles.
- The classic center-hall arrangement of this Colonial allows easy access to each of the living areas.
- Plenty of views are possible from the formal rooms at the front of the home, as well as from the informal areas at the rear.
- The spacious kitchen offers lots of counter space, a handy work island, a laundry closet and a sunny bayed breakfast nook.
- The adjoining family room shows off a fireplace and elegant double doors to the rear. An optional set of double doors opens to the living room.
- The beautiful master suite on the upper level boasts a 10-ft., 10-in. vaulted ceiling, two closets, dual sinks, a garden tub and a separate shower.

Plan CH-100-A

Bedrooms: 4	**Baths:** 2½

Living Area:	
Upper floor	923 sq. ft.
Main floor	965 sq. ft.
Total Living Area:	**1,888 sq. ft.**
Basement	952 sq. ft.
Garage	462 sq. ft.
Exterior Wall Framing:	2x4

Foundation Options:

Daylight basement
Standard basement
Crawlspace

(All plans can be built with your choice of foundation and framing. A generic conversion diagram is available. See order form.)

BLUEPRINT PRICE CODE: B

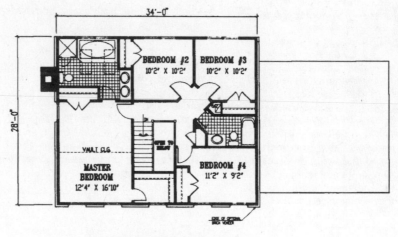

UPPER FLOOR

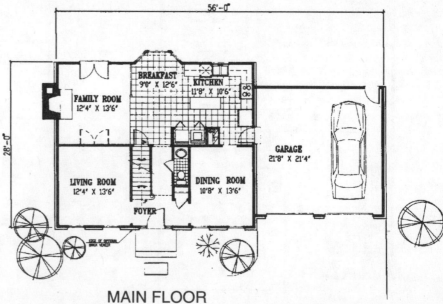

MAIN FLOOR

Plan CH-100-A

A Real Original

- This home's round window, elegant entry and transom windows create an eye-catching, original look.
- Inside, high ceilings and tremendous views let the eyes wander. The foyer provides an exciting look at an expansive deck and inviting spa through the living room's tall windows. The windows frame a handsome fireplace, while a 10-ft. ceiling adds volume and interest.
- To the right of the foyer is a cozy den or home office with its own fireplace, 10-ft. ceiling and dramatic windows.
- The spacious kitchen/breakfast area features an oversized snack bar island and opens to a large screen porch. Within easy reach are the laundry room and the entrance to the garage.
- The bright formal dining room overlooks the deck and boasts a ceiling that vaults up to 10 feet.
- The secluded master suite looks out to the deck as well, with access through a patio door. The private bath features a dynamite corner spa tub, a separate shower and a large walk-in closet.
- A second bedroom and bath complete the main floor.

Plan B-90065

Bedrooms: 2+	Baths: 2
Living Area:	
Main floor	1,889 sq. ft.
Total Living Area:	**1,889 sq. ft.**
Screen porch	136 sq. ft.
Standard basement	1,889 sq. ft.
Garage	406 sq. ft.
Exterior Wall Framing:	2x6

Foundation Options:

Standard basement

(All plans can be built with your choice of foundation and framing. A generic conversion diagram is available. See order form.)

BLUEPRINT PRICE CODE: B

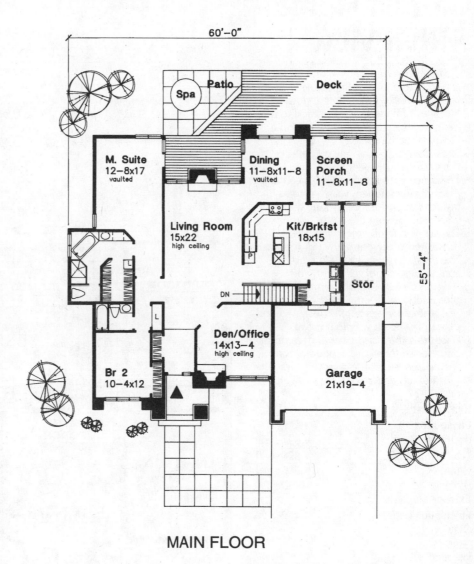

MAIN FLOOR

Garden Home with a View

- This clever design proves that privacy doesn't have to be compromised even in high-density urban neighborhoods. From within, views are oriented to a beautiful, lush entry courtyard and a covered rear porch.
- The exterior appearance is sheltered, but warm and welcoming.
- The innovative interior design centers on a unique kitchen, which directs traffic away from the working areas while still serving the entire home.
- The sunken family room features a 14-ft. vaulted ceiling and a warm fireplace.
- The master suite is highlighted by a sumptuous master bath with an oversized shower and a whirlpool tub, plus a large walk-in closet.
- The formal living room is designed and placed in such a way that it can become a third bedroom, a den, or an office or study room, depending on family needs and lifestyles.

Plan E-1824

Bedrooms: 2+	Baths: 2
Living Area:	
Main floor	1,891 sq. ft.
Total Living Area:	**1,891 sq. ft.**
Garage	506 sq. ft.
Storage	60 sq. ft.
Exterior Wall Framing:	2x4

Foundation Options:

Crawlspace
Slab
(All plans can be built with your choice of foundation and framing. A generic conversion diagram is available. See order form.)

BLUEPRINT PRICE CODE: B

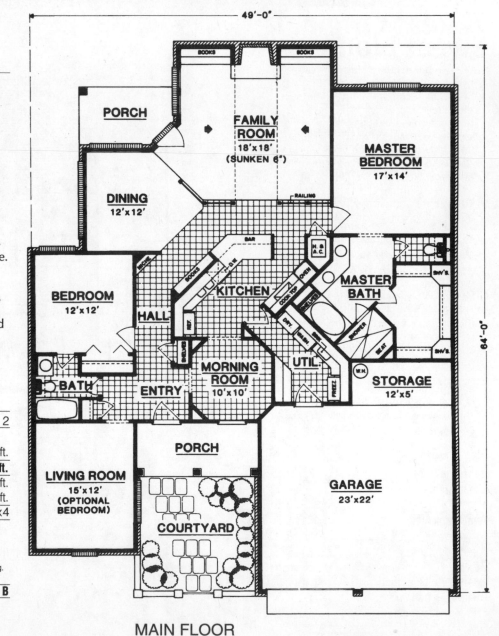

MAIN FLOOR

Plan E-1824

Sweet Home

- The sweet facade of this charming home looks as if it were plucked straight out of a European hamlet. The stone exterior, decorated dormers and cute porch combine to present a charming invitation to guests.
- Inside, the floor plan takes advantage of the compact square footage. A tiled foyer leads into a unique curved gallery that wraps around the central Great Room. On the left, a half-wall allows a view into the dining room.
- A wall of windows adds brightness and cheer to the Great Room, where a shuttered pass-through to the kitchen lets the chef visit with guests. French doors open to a railed deck that is the perfect site for drinks with friends.
- Between the kitchen and the breakfast nook, a serving counter provides a spot to set snacks. The kitchen's island cooktop makes meal preparation easier.
- The Great Room, the breakfast nook and the kitchen boast 12-ft. ceilings. All other rooms feature 9-ft. ceilings.
- The master suite's sunny bay serves as a cozy sitting area to retreat to each day.

Plan DW-1892

Bedrooms: 3	Baths: 2
Living Area:	
Main floor	1,892 sq. ft.
Total Living Area:	**1,892 sq. ft.**
Standard basement	1,892 sq. ft.
Exterior Wall Framing:	2x4

Foundation Options:

Standard basement

Crawlspace

Slab

(All plans can be built with your choice of foundation and framing. A generic conversion diagram is available. See order form.)

BLUEPRINT PRICE CODE:	B

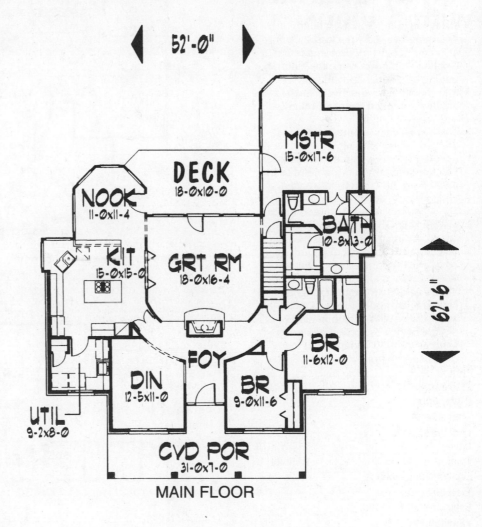

52'-0"

62'-6"

MAIN FLOOR

Family Charmer

- Designed with families in mind, this charming two-story packs plenty of excitement in its modest square footage.
- Dual bay windows grace the exterior, adding traditional appeal.
- A skylight bathes the 16½-ft.-high vaulted entry and the open-railed stairway with light.
- The living room features a 14½-ft. vaulted ceiling leading up to a cased-opening overlook in the third bedroom.
- The formal dining room is mere steps away from the kitchen, for serving convenience, and opens to a rear patio.
- The efficient kitchen features a corner garden sink. The bright breakfast nook boasts sliding glass doors to the patio.
- The inviting family room includes a cozy fireplace and a handy wet bar.
- The main floor also has a laundry room off the garage and a powder room.
- The three bedrooms upstairs include a master suite with a walk-in closet and a private bath. The second bedroom features a bayed window seat that overlooks the front yard.

Plans P-7681-3A & -3D

Bedrooms: 3	Baths: 2½
Living Area:	
Upper floor	875 sq. ft.
Main floor	1,020 sq. ft.
Total Living Area:	**1,895 sq. ft.**
Daylight basement	925 sq. ft.
Garage	419 sq. ft.
Exterior Wall Framing:	2x4
Foundation Options:	**Plan #**
Daylight basement	P-7681-3D
Crawlspace	P-7681-3A

(All plans can be built with your choice of foundation and framing. A generic conversion diagram is available. See order form.)

BLUEPRINT PRICE CODE:	**B**

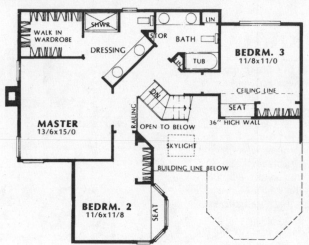

UPPER FLOOR

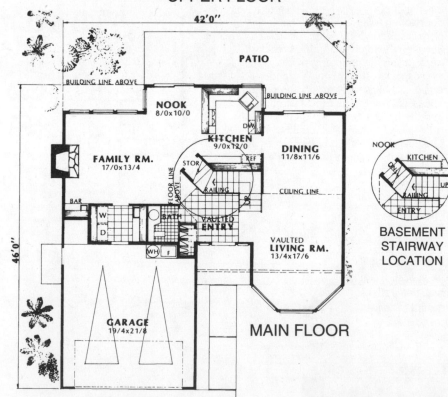

MAIN FLOOR

BASEMENT STAIRWAY LOCATION

Plans P-7681-3A & -3D

PRICES AND DETAILS ON PAGES 12-15

Playful Floor Plan

- High, hip roofs and a recessed entry give this home a smart-looking exterior. A dynamic floor plan—punctuated with angled walls, high ceilings and playful window treatments—gives the home an exciting interior.
- The sunken Great Room, the circular dining room and the angled island kitchen are the heartbeat of the home. The Great Room offers a 14-ft. vaulted ceiling, a fireplace, a built-in corner entertainment center and tall arched windows overlooking the backyard.

- An angled railing separates the Great Room from the open kitchen and dining room. An atrium door next to the glassed-in dining area leads to the backyard. The kitchen includes an island snack bar and a garden window.
- The master bedroom is nestled into one corner for quiet and privacy. This deluxe suite features two walk-in closets and a luxurious whirlpool bath.
- An extra-large laundry area, complete with a clothes-folding counter and a coat closet, is accessible from the three-car garage.
- The home is expanded by 9-ft. ceilings throughout, with the exception of the vaulted Great Room.

Plan PI-90-435	
Bedrooms: 3	**Baths:** 2
Living Area:	
Main floor	1,896 sq. ft.
Total Living Area:	**1,896 sq. ft.**
Daylight basement	1,889 sq. ft.
Garage	667 sq. ft.
Exterior Wall Framing:	2x6
Foundation Options:	

Daylight basement
(All plans can be built with your choice of foundation and framing. A generic conversion diagram is available. See order form.)

BLUEPRINT PRICE CODE:	**B**

MAIN FLOOR

Master Bedroom 13' x 17'

Sunken Great Room 16'-6" x 18'

Vaulted Ceiling

Dining Room 14' x 11'

Kitchen 13' x 14'

Snack Bar

Foyer

Bedroom 11' x 11'

Bedroom 10'-6" x 15'

3 Car Garage 29' x 23'

F.P.

Whirlpool

68'-0"

44'-0"

Town-and-Country Classic

- A railed front porch, a charming cupola and stylish shutters add town and country flair to this classic one-story.
- The welcoming entry flows into the vaulted family room, which boasts a 14-ft. vaulted ceiling with exposed beams, a handsome fireplace and a French door to a backyard patio.

- The living room and the formal dining room are separated by a half-wall with decorative wooden spindles. The adjoining kitchen features wraparound counter space. The eating nook has a laundry closet and garage access.
- The master bedroom enjoys a private bath with a separate dressing and a roomy walk-in closet.
- Two additional bedrooms are serviced by a compartmentalized hallway bath.
- The two-car garage includes a separate storage area at the back.

Plan E-1815

Bedrooms: 3	Baths: 2
Living Area:	
Main floor	1,898 sq. ft.
Total Living Area:	**1,898 sq. ft.**
Garage and storage	513 sq. ft.
Exterior Wall Framing:	2x4

Foundation Options:

Crawlspace
Slab
(All plans can be built with your choice of foundation and framing. A generic conversion diagram is available. See order form.)

BLUEPRINT PRICE CODE:	B

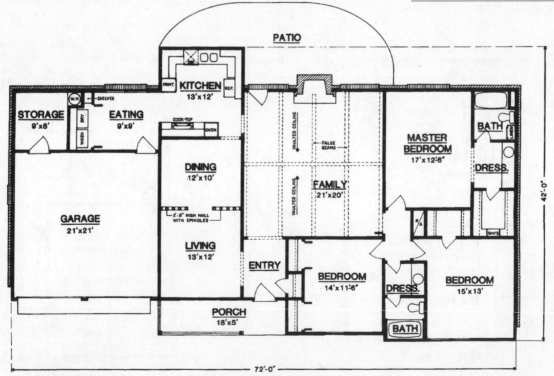

MAIN FLOOR

Plan E-1815

PRICES AND DETAILS ON PAGES 12-15

Octagonal Dining Bay

- Classic traditional styling is recreated with a covered front porch and triple dormers with half-round windows.
- Off the entry porch, double doors reveal the reception area, with a walk-in closet and a half-bath.

- The living room features a striking fireplace and leads to the dining room, with its octagonal bay.
- The island kitchen overlooks the dinette and the family room, which features a second fireplace and sliding glass doors to a rear deck.
- Upstairs, the master suite boasts a walk-in closet and a whirlpool bath. A skylighted hallway connects three more bedrooms and another full bath.

Plan K-680-R	
Bedrooms: 4	**Baths: 2½**
Living Area:	
Upper floor	853 sq. ft.
Main floor	1,047 sq. ft.
Total Living Area:	**1,900 sq. ft.**
Standard basement	1,015 sq. ft.
Garage and storage	472 sq. ft.
Exterior Wall Framing:	2x4 or 2x6

Foundation Options:

Standard basement

Slab

(All plans can be built with your choice of foundation and framing. A generic conversion diagram is available. See order form.)

BLUEPRINT PRICE CODE:	B

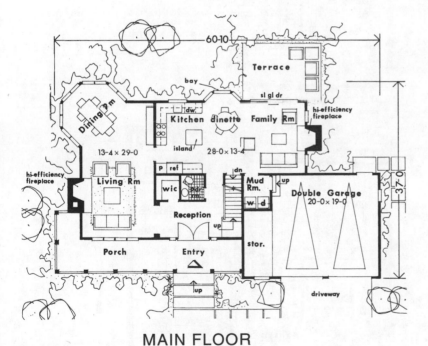

MAIN FLOOR

UPPER FLOOR

VIEW INTO LIVING ROOM AND DINING ROOM

CH-210-A

CH-210-B

Outstanding Options

- A functional floor plan and the option of two exteriors make this traditional home an outstanding choice.
- Guests will be impressed by the large, light-filled living room, with its classic columns and optional fireplace. The adjoining dining room offers an optional bay window.
- The adjacent kitchen offers an island work area and a sunny breakfast nook tucked into a large bay window.
- An open railing separates the nook from the skylighted family room, which boasts a 10½-ft. vaulted ceiling, a cozy fireplace and outdoor access through triple French doors.
- A utility room and a half-bath are located near the garage entrance.
- Upstairs, the master bedroom flaunts a 10-ft. vaulted ceiling, a huge walk-in closet and a private luxury bath with a whirlpool tub. Two additional bedrooms share another full bath.

Plans CH-210-A & -B

Bedrooms: 3	Baths: 2½
Living Area:	
Upper floor	823 sq. ft.
Main floor	1,079 sq. ft.
Total Living Area:	**1,902 sq. ft.**
Basement	978 sq. ft.
Garage	400 sq. ft.
Exterior Wall Framing:	2x4

Foundation Options:

Daylight basement
Standard basement
Crawlspace

(All plans can be built with your choice of foundation and framing. A generic conversion diagram is available. See order form.)

BLUEPRINT PRICE CODE:	B

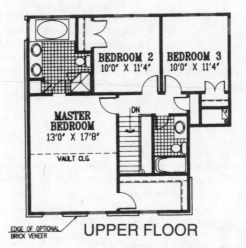

UPPER FLOOR

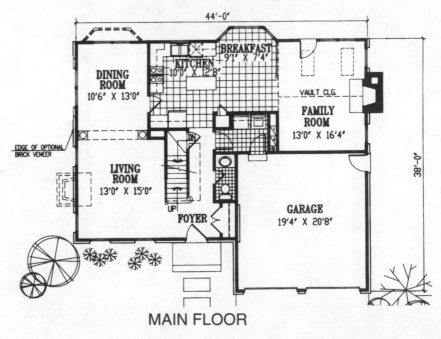

MAIN FLOOR

TO ORDER THIS BLUEPRINT, CALL TOLL-FREE 1-800-820-1283

Plans CH-210-A & -B

PRICES AND DETAILS ON PAGES 12-15

Spacious and Open

- A brilliant wall of windows invites guests into the two-story-high foyer of this striking traditional home.
- At the center of this open floor plan, the sunken family room boasts a 21-ft. vaulted ceiling and a striking fireplace with flanking windows.
- The cozy dinette merges with the family room and the island kitchen, creating a spacious, open atmosphere. A pantry closet, a laundry room, a half-bath and garage access are all nearby.
- The formal living and dining rooms are found at the front of the home. The living room boasts a 10½-ft. cathedral ceiling and a lovely window arrangement.
- The main-floor master bedroom has a 10-ft., 10-in. tray ceiling, a walk-in closet and a lush bath designed for two.
- Upstairs, two bedrooms share another full bath and a balcony landing that overlooks the family room and foyer.

Plan A-2207-DS

Bedrooms: 3	Baths: 2½
Living Area:	
Upper floor	518 sq. ft.
Main floor	1,389 sq. ft.
Total Living Area:	**1,907 sq. ft.**
Standard basement	1,389 sq. ft.
Garage	484 sq. ft.
Exterior Wall Framing:	2x6

Foundation Options:

Standard basement

(All plans can be built with your choice of foundation and framing. A generic conversion diagram is available. See order form.)

BLUEPRINT PRICE CODE:	B

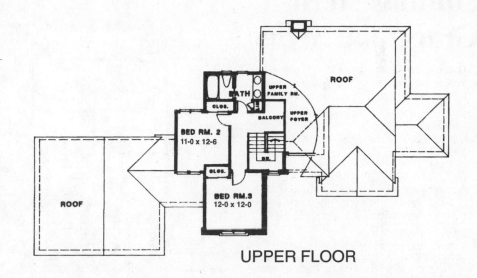

UPPER FLOOR

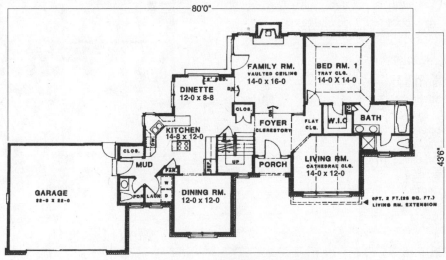

MAIN FLOOR

Southwestern Grace and Style

- This exciting home, perfect for narrow lots, is highlighted by a clay tile roof, a stucco exterior and a built-in planter.
- The tiled foyer leads into the 17½-ft. vaulted living room, which opens into the dining room to create an air of spaciousness.
- The L-shaped kitchen features a garden sink and plenty of work space.
- A breathtaking 11½-ft. cathedral ceiling accents the expansive family room, which offers a fireplace and sliding glass doors to a covered patio.
- The stunning master suite has its own doors to the covered patio, plus a huge walk-in closet and a private bath with a whirlpool tub.
- The study or guest room has convenient access to a hall bath.
- Two upper-floor bedrooms share a full bath and a balcony overlooking the living room.

Plan Q-1915-1A

Bedrooms: 3+	Baths: 3
Living Area:	
Upper floor	515 sq. ft.
Main floor	1,400 sq. ft.
Total Living Area:	**1,915 sq. ft.**
Garage	390 sq. ft.
Exterior Wall Framing:	2x4

Foundation Options:

Slab

(All plans can be built with your choice of foundation and framing. A generic conversion diagram is available. See order form.)

BLUEPRINT PRICE CODE:	B

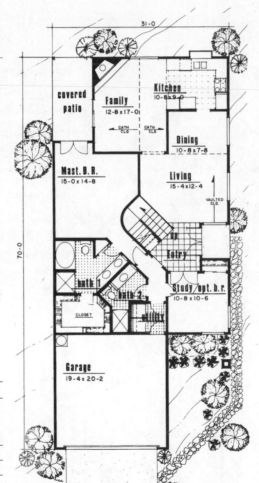

MAIN FLOOR

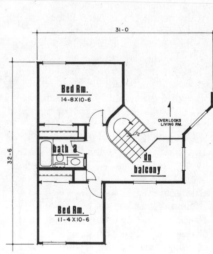

UPPER FLOOR

TO ORDER THIS BLUEPRINT,
CALL TOLL-FREE 1-800-820-1283

Plan Q-1915-1A

PRICES AND DETAILS
ON PAGES 12-15

Soaring Design

- Dramatic windows soar to the peak of this prowed chalet, offering unlimited views of outdoor scenery.
- The spacious living room flaunts a fabulous fireplace, a soaring 26-ft. vaulted ceiling, a striking window wall and sliding glass doors to a wonderful wraparound deck.
- An oversized window brightens a dining area on the left side of the living room. The sunny, L-shaped kitchen is spacious and easily accessible.
- The secluded main-floor bedroom has convenient access to a full bath, a linen closet, a good-sized laundry room and the rear entrance.
- A central, open-railed staircase leads to the upper floor, which contains two more bedrooms and a full bath.
- A skylighted balcony is the high point of this design, offering a railed overlook into the living room below and sweeping outdoor vistas through the wall of windows.
- The optional daylight basement provides another fireplace in a versatile recreation room. The extra-long, tuck-under garage includes plenty of room for hobbies, while the service room offers additional storage space.

Plans H-930-1 & -1A	
Bedrooms: 3	**Baths:** 2
Living Area:	
Upper floor	710 sq. ft.
Main floor	1,210 sq. ft.
Daylight basement	605 sq. ft.
Total Living Area:	**1,920/2,525 sq. ft.**
Tuck-under garage/shop	605 sq. ft.
Exterior Wall Framing:	2x6
Foundation Options:	**Plan #**
Daylight basement	H-930-1
Crawlspace	H-930-1A
(All plans can be built with your choice of foundation and framing. A generic conversion diagram is available. See order form.)	
BLUEPRINT PRICE CODE:	**B/D**

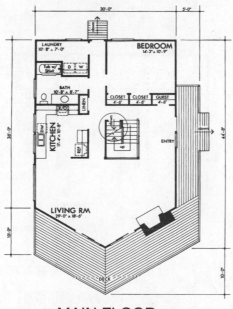

DAYLIGHT BASEMENT

STAIRWAY AREA IN CRAWLSPACE VERSION

MAIN FLOOR

UPPER FLOOR

Farmhouse for Today

- An inviting covered porch and decorative dormer windows lend traditional warmth and charm to this attractive design.
- The up-to-date interior includes ample space for entertaining as well as for daily family activities.
- The elegant foyer is flanked on one side by the formal, sunken living room and on the other by a sunken family room with a fireplace and an entertainment center. Each room features an 8½-ft. tray ceiling and views of the porch.
- The dining room flows from the living room to increase the entertaining space.
- The kitchen/nook/laundry area forms a large expanse for casual family living and domestic chores.
- Upstairs, the grand master suite includes a large closet and a private bath with a garden tub, a designer shower and a private deck.
- A second full bath serves the two secondary bedrooms.

Plan U-87-203

Bedrooms: 3	Baths: 2½
Living Area:	
Upper floor	857 sq. ft.
Main floor	1,064 sq. ft.
Total Living Area:	**1,921 sq. ft.**
Standard basement	1,064 sq. ft.
Garage	552 sq. ft.
Exterior Wall Framing:	2x4 or 2x6

Foundation Options:

Standard basement
Crawlspace
Slab
(All plans can be built with your choice of foundation and framing. A generic conversion diagram is available. See order form.)

BLUEPRINT PRICE CODE: **B**

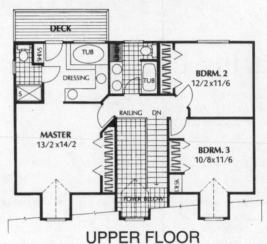

UPPER FLOOR

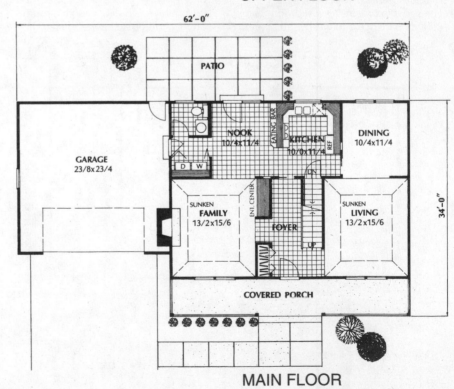

MAIN FLOOR

Plan U-87-203

PRICES AND DETAILS
ON PAGES 12-15

Irresistible Master Suite

- This traditional three-bedroom home features a main-floor master suite that is hard to resist, with an inviting window seat and a delightful bath.
- The home is introduced by a covered front entry, topped by a dormer with a half-round window.
- Just off the front entry, the formal dining room is distinguished by a tray ceiling and a large picture window overlooking the front porch.
- Straight back, the Great Room features a 16-ft.-high vaulted ceiling with a window wall facing the backyard. The fireplace can be enjoyed from the adjoining kitchen and breakfast area.
- The gourmet kitchen includes a corner sink, an island cooktop and a walk-in pantry. A 12-ft. vaulted ceiling expands the breakfast nook, which features a built-in desk and backyard deck access.
- The spacious master suite offers a 14-ft. vaulted ceiling and a luxurious private bath with a walk-in closet, a garden tub, a separate shower and a dual-sink vanity with a sit-down makeup area.
- An open-railed stairway leads up to another full bath that serves two additional bedrooms.

Plan B-89061

Bedrooms: 3	Baths: 2½
Living Area:	
Upper floor	436 sq. ft.
Main floor	1,490 sq. ft.
Total Living Area:	**1,926 sq. ft.**
Standard basement	1,490 sq. ft.
Garage	400 sq. ft.
Exterior Wall Framing:	2x4

Foundation Options:

Standard basement

(All plans can be built with your choice of foundation and framing. A generic conversion diagram is available. See order form.)

BLUEPRINT PRICE CODE: **B**

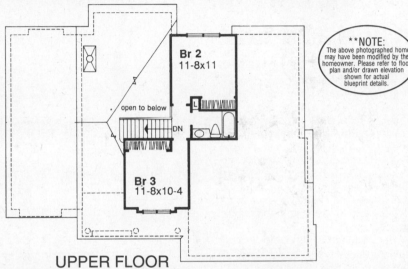

UPPER FLOOR

NOTE:
The above photographed home may have been modified by the homeowner. Please refer to floor plan and/or drawn elevation shown for actual blueprint details.

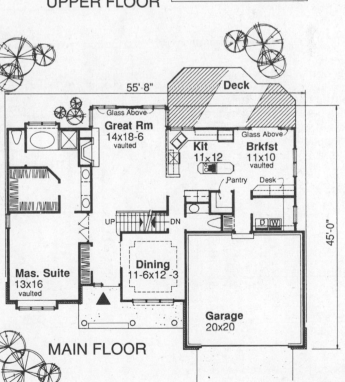

MAIN FLOOR

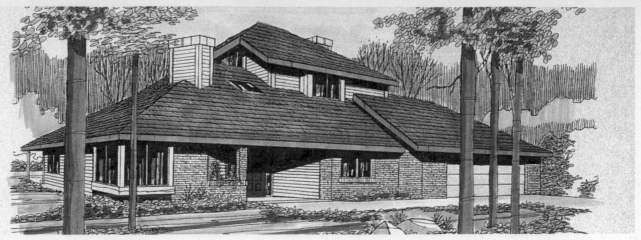

Spacious Styling Inside and Out

- Wood siding, brick accents, clean rooflines and contemporary styling highlight the exterior of this home.
- A built-in planter accents the covered entry, which opens to a skylighted foyer. Angling gracefully to the left is the 12½-ft.-high vaulted living room with a corner boxed-out window and a handsome fireplace.
- The adjoining dining room, also with a 12½-ft. vaulted ceiling, gives way to a 13-ft. vaulted, skylighted nook with an attached deck.
- A 19-ft. vaulted ceiling presides over the gourmet kitchen, which offers an angled eating bar and a pass-through to the family room.
- The family room has its own fireplace, along with sliding glass doors that open to a second backyard deck.
- The upper-floor master suite boasts a boxed-out window, a walk-in wardrobe and a private bath with twin sinks.
- The second upper-floor bedroom also has a boxed-out window and its own bath. The main-floor den could be converted into an extra bedroom or a guest room.

Plans P-7689-3A & -3D

Bedrooms: 2+	Baths: 3
Living Area:	
Upper floor	576 sq. ft.
Main floor	1,358 sq. ft.
Total Living Area:	**1,934 sq. ft.**
Daylight basement	1,358 sq. ft.
Garage	537 sq. ft.
Exterior Wall Framing:	2x4
Foundation Options:	**Plan #**
Daylight basement	P-7689-3D
Crawlspace	P-7689-3A

(All plans can be built with your choice of foundation and framing. A generic conversion diagram is available. See order form.)

BLUEPRINT PRICE CODE:	B

UPPER FLOOR

BASEMENT STAIRWAY LOCATION

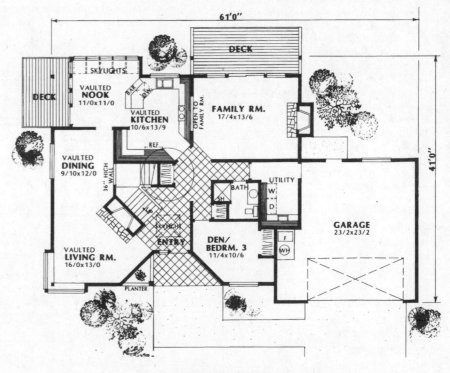

MAIN FLOOR

Plans P-7689-3A & -3D

PRICES AND DETAILS ON PAGES 12-15

Elegance
Inside and Out

- The raised front porch of this home is finely detailed with wood columns, railings, moldings, and French doors with half-round transoms.
- The living room, dining room and entry have 12-ft.-high ceilings. Skylights illuminate the living room, which offers a fireplace and access to a roomy deck.
- The efficient kitchen permits easy service to both the dining room and the casual eating area.
- The master suite features a raised tray ceiling and an enormous skylighted bath with a walk-in closet, dual vanities and a large quarter-circle spa tub surrounded by a mirror wall.
- On the left, two secondary bedrooms are insulated from the more active areas of the home by an efficient hallway, and also share another full bath.

Plan E-1909

Bedrooms: 3	Baths: 2
Living Area:	
Main floor	1,936 sq. ft.
Total Living Area:	**1,936 sq. ft.**
Garage	484 sq. ft.
Storage	132 sq. ft.
Exterior Wall Framing:	2x6

Foundation Options:

Crawlspace

Slab

(All plans can be built with your choice of foundation and framing. A generic conversion diagram is available. See order form.)

BLUEPRINT PRICE CODE: B

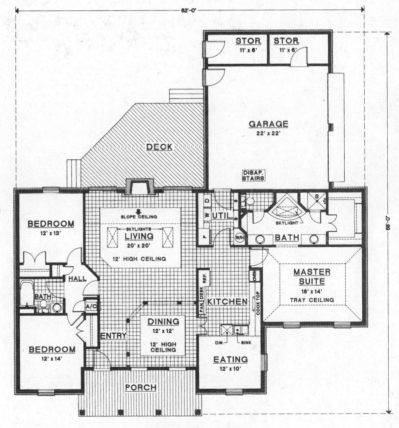

MAIN FLOOR

Family Home, Formal Accents

- Captivating roof angles and European detailing highlight the exterior of this graceful home.
- The generous foyer is flanked by the spacious living and dining rooms, both with tall, ornate windows.
- Beyond the foyer lies an expansive family room, highlighted by a dramatic

fireplace and sliding glass doors that open to a sunny patio.
- The kitchen makes use of an L-shaped counter and a central island to maximaze efficiency. The adjacent breakfast room offers casual dining. A nearby utility room features a washer and dryer and a door to the backyard.
- The large master suite boasts two closets and a private bath with a dual-sink vanity and a step-up tub.
- Across the hall, two additional bedrooms share a second full bath.

Plan C-8103

Bedrooms: 3	**Baths:** 2

Living Area:	
Main floor	1,940 sq. ft.
Total Living Area:	**1,940 sq. ft.**
Daylight basement	1,870 sq. ft.
Garage	400 sq. ft.
Exterior Wall Framing:	2x4

Foundation Options:

Daylight basement
Crawlspace
Slab
(All plans can be built with your choice of foundation and framing. A generic conversion diagram is available. See order form.)

BLUEPRINT PRICE CODE:	B

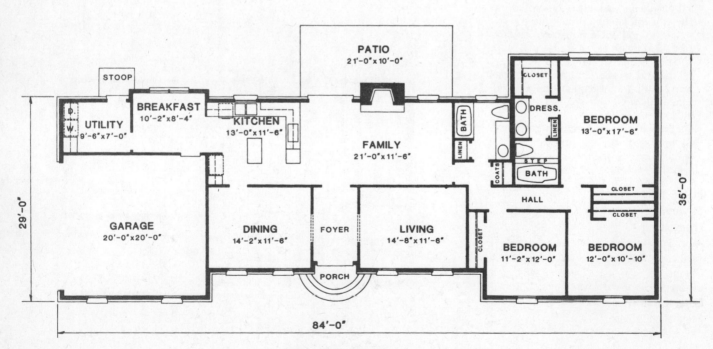

MAIN FLOOR

Plan C-8103

PRICES AND DETAILS ON PAGES 12-15

Excellent Family Design

- Long, sloping rooflines and bold design features make this home attractive in any neighborhood.
- The vaulted entry ushers visitors into the impressive Great Room with its 12½-ft. vaulted ceiling, clerestory windows and warm woodstove. A rear window wall overlooks an expansive deck.
- The magnificent kitchen opens to the informal dining area and includes a functional work island and a wet bar.
- A skylighted laundry room, a skylighted bath and two bedrooms complete the main floor. The rear-facing bedroom opens to the deck, and the front bedroom boasts a lovely window seat.
- The upstairs consists of a master bedroom retreat with a 10½-ft. vaulted ceiling. Highlights include a walk-in closet and a luxurious private bath with a spa tub.
- The optional daylight basement adds lots of space for recreation and entertaining, plus a fourth bedroom and a large shop/storage area.

Plans P-528-2A & -2D

Bedrooms: 3+	Baths: 2-3
Living Area:	
Upper floor	498 sq. ft.
Main floor	1,456 sq. ft.
Daylight basement	1,410 sq. ft.
Total Living Area:	**1,954/3,364 sq. ft.**
Garage	502 sq. ft.
Exterior Wall Framing:	2x6
Foundation Options:	**Plan #**
Daylight basement	P-528-2D
Crawlspace	P-528-2A
(All plans can be built with your choice of foundation and framing. A generic conversion diagram is available. See order form.)	
BLUEPRINT PRICE CODE:	**B/E**

UPPER FLOOR

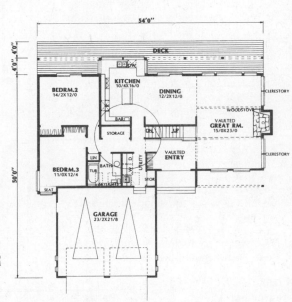

MAIN FLOOR

STAIRWAY AREA IN CRAWLSPACE VERSION

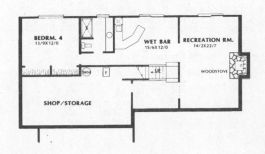

DAYLIGHT BASEMENT

Vaulted Ceilings Expand Interior

- A dignified exterior and a gracious, spacious interior combine to make this an outstanding plan for today's families.
- A step down from the vaulted entry, the living room offers a 12-ft.-high vaulted ceiling brightened by an arch-top boxed window and a nice fireplace.
- The vaulted dining room ceiling rises to more than 15 ft., and sliding glass doors open to a unique central atrium.
- The island kitchen shares a snack bar with the bayed nook and provides easy service to the dining room.
- The spacious family room boasts a sloped ceiling that peaks at 18 ft. and a woodstove that warms the entire area.
- The master suite is first-class all the way, with a spacious sleeping room and an opulent bath, which features a walk-in closet, a sunken garden tub, a separate shower and a skylighted dressing area with a dual-sink vanity.
- Two secondary bedrooms have window seats and share another full bath.

Plans P-7697-4A & -4D

Bedrooms: 3	Baths: 2
Living Area:	
Main floor (crawlspace version)	2,003 sq. ft.
Main floor (basement version)	2,030 sq. ft.
Total Living Area:	**2,003/2,030 sq. ft.**
Daylight basement	2,015 sq. ft.
Garage	647 sq. ft.
Exterior Wall Framing:	**2x6**
Foundation Options:	**Plan #**
Daylight basement	P-7697-4D
Crawlspace	P-7697-4A

(All plans can be built with your choice of foundation and framing. A generic conversion diagram is available. See order form.)

BLUEPRINT PRICE CODE:	**C**

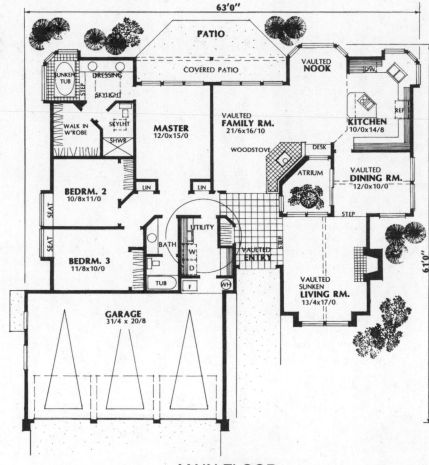

MAIN FLOOR

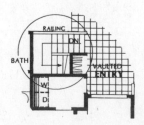

BASEMENT STAIRWAY LOCATION

TO ORDER THIS BLUEPRINT, CALL TOLL-FREE 1-800-820-1283

Plans P-7697-4A & -4D

PRICES AND DETAILS ON PAGES 12-15

Photo by Mark Englund/HomeStyles

French Garden Design

- A creative, angular design gives this traditional French garden home an exciting, open and airy floor plan.
- Guests enter through a covered, columned porch that opens into the large, angled living and dining rooms.
- High 12-ft. ceilings highlight the living and dining area, which also features corner windows, a wet bar, a cozy fireplace and access to a huge covered backyard porch.
- The angled walk-through kitchen, also with a 12-ft.-high ceiling, offers plenty of work space and an adjoining informal eating nook that faces a delightful private courtyard. The nearby utility area has extra freezer space, a walk-in pantry and garage access.
- The home's bedrooms are housed in two separate wings. One wing boasts a luxurious master suite, which features a large walk-in closet, an angled tub and a separate shower.
- Two large bedrooms in the other wing share a hall bath. Each bedroom has a walk-in closet.

Plan E-2004

Bedrooms: 3	Baths: 2

Living Area:	
Main floor	2,023 sq. ft.
Total Living Area:	**2,023 sq. ft.**
Garage	484 sq. ft.
Storage	87 sq. ft.
Exterior Wall Framing:	**2x6**

Foundation Options:

Crawlspace
Slab

(All plans can be built with your choice of foundation and framing. A generic conversion diagram is available. See order form.)

BLUEPRINT PRICE CODE: C

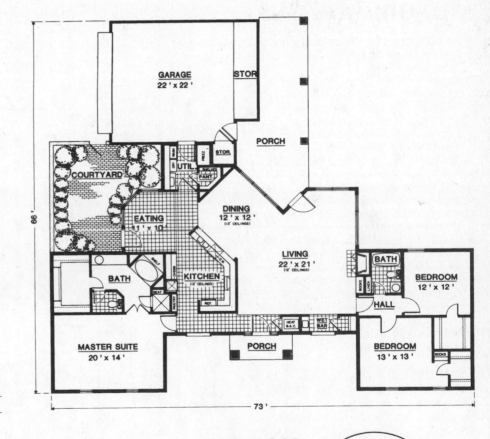

MAIN FLOOR

**NOTE:
The above photographed home may have been modified by the homeowner. Please refer to floor plan and/or drawn elevation shown for actual blueprint details.

Personality Plus

- An artful blend of contemporary and traditional elements gives this design its own personality.
- The innovative interior begins with a 16½-ft.-high vaulted entry. A coat closet is creatively tucked into one corner, while a beautiful stairway has a windowed landing that floods the hall with light.
- The living room is simply stunning, with its 16½-ft. vaulted ceiling, inviting woodstove and wall of glass facing the backyard. Traffic flows smoothly into the adjoining dining room, which offers access to a partially covered patio.
- The bright, open kitchen combines with the nook. A 14-ft. vaulted ceiling, a nice-sized eating bar and double doors to a patio further expand the area.
- Upstairs, the master suite is graced with five windows, a large dressing area and a compartmentalized bath. The two front bedrooms boast eye-catching round-top windows.

Plans P-6597-2A & -2D

Bedrooms: 3	Baths: 2½
Living Area:	
Upper floor	1,085 sq. ft.
Main floor	950 sq. ft.
Total Living Area:	**2,035 sq. ft.**
Daylight basement	950 sq. ft.
Garage	597 sq. ft.
Exterior Wall Framing:	2x4
Foundation Options:	**Plan #**
Daylight basement	P-6597-2D
Crawlspace	P-6597-2A

(All plans can be built with your choice of foundation and framing. A generic conversion diagram is available. See order form.)

BLUEPRINT PRICE CODE:	C

UPPER FLOOR

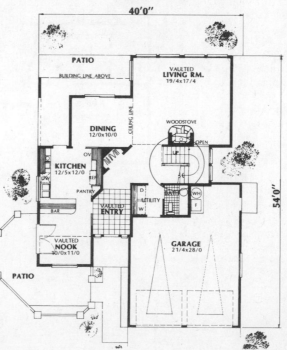

MAIN FLOOR

BASEMENT STAIRWAY LOCATION

Elaborate Entry

- This home's important-looking covered entry greets guests with heavy, banded support columns, sunburst transom windows and dual sidelights.
- Once inside the home, the 15-ft.-high foyer is flanked by the formal living and dining rooms, which have 10½-ft. vaulted ceilings. Straight ahead and beyond five decorative columns lies the spacious family room.
- Surrounded by 8-ft.-high walls, the family room features a 13-ft. vaulted ceiling, a fireplace and sliding doors to a covered patio. A neat plant shelf above the fireplace adds style.
- The bright and airy kitchen has a 13-ft. ceiling and serves the family room and the breakfast area, which is enhanced by a corner window and a French door.
- The master suite enjoys a 13-ft. vaulted ceiling and features French-door patio access, a large walk-in closet and a private bath with a corner platform tub and a separate shower.
- Across the home, three secondary bedrooms share a hall bath, which boasts private access to the patio.

Plan HDS-90-806

Bedrooms: 4	Baths: 2

Living Area:

Main floor	2,041 sq. ft.
Total Living Area:	**2,041 sq. ft.**
Garage	452 sq. ft.

Exterior Wall Framing:
2x4 or 8-in. concrete block

Foundation Options:
Slab
(All plans can be built with your choice of foundation and framing. A generic conversion diagram is available. See order form.)

BLUEPRINT PRICE CODE:	C

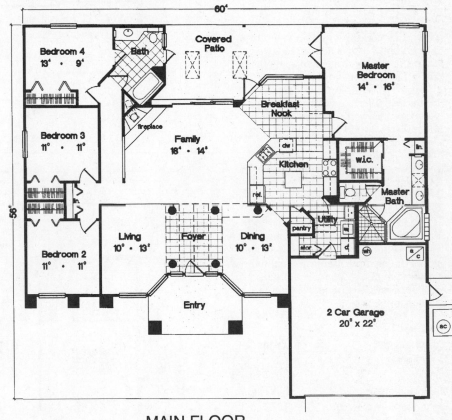

MAIN FLOOR

NOTE:
The above photographed home may have been modified by the homeowner. Please refer to floor plan and/or drawn elevation shown for actual blueprint details.

Picture-Perfect!

- With graceful arches, columns and railings, the wonderful front porch makes this home the picture of country charm. Decorative chimneys, shutters and quaint dormers add more style.
- Inside, the foyer shows off sidelights and a fantail transom. The foyer is flanked by the dining room and a bedroom, both of which boast porch views and arched transoms. All three areas are expanded by 10-ft. ceilings.
- The living room also flaunts a 10-ft. ceiling, plus a fireplace and French doors that open to a skylighted porch. The remaining rooms offer 9-ft. ceilings.
- The L-shaped kitchen has an island cooktop and a sunny breakfast nook.
- A Palladian window arrangement brightens the sitting alcove in the master suite. Other highlights include porch access and a fantastic bath with a garden tub and a separate shower.
- The upper floor is perfect for future expansion space.

Plan J-9401

Bedrooms: 3+	Baths: 2½
Living Area:	
Main floor	2,089 sq. ft.
Total Living Area:	**2,089 sq. ft.**
Upper floor (unfinished)	878 sq. ft.
Standard basement	2,089 sq. ft.
Garage and storage	530 sq. ft.
Exterior Wall Framing:	2x4

Foundation Options:
Standard basement
Crawlspace
Slab
(All plans can be built with your choice of foundation and framing. A generic conversion diagram is available. See order form.)

BLUEPRINT PRICE CODE: C

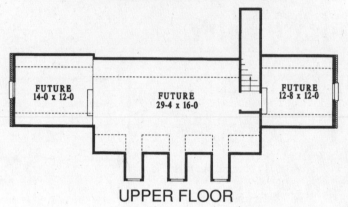

UPPER FLOOR

MAIN FLOOR

TO ORDER THIS BLUEPRINT,
CALL TOLL-FREE 1-800-820-1283

Plan J-9401

PRICES AND DETAILS
ON PAGES 12-15

State-of-the-Art Floor Plan

- This design's state-of-the-art floor plan begins with a two-story-high foyer that introduces a stunning open staircase and a bright Great Room.
- The Great Room is expanded by a 17-ft. vaulted ceiling and a window wall with French doors that open to a rear deck.
- Short sections of half-walls separate the Great Room from the open kitchen and dining room. Natural light streams in through a greenhouse window above the sink and lots of glass facing the deck.
- The main-floor master suite has a 9-ft. coved ceiling and private access to an inviting hot tub on the deck. Walk-in closets frame the entrance to the luxurious bath, highlighted by a 10-ft. vaulted ceiling and an arched window above a raised spa tub.
- Upstairs, a balcony hall leads to two bedrooms and a continental bath, plus a den and a storage room.

Plan S-2100

Bedrooms: 3+	Baths: 2½
Living Area:	
Upper floor	660 sq. ft.
Main floor	1,440 sq. ft.
Total Living Area:	**2,100 sq. ft.**
Standard basement	1,440 sq. ft.
Garage	552 sq. ft.
Exterior Wall Framing:	2x6

Foundation Options:
Standard basement
Crawlspace
Slab
(All plans can be built with your choice of foundation and framing. A generic conversion diagram is available. See order form.)

BLUEPRINT PRICE CODE: C

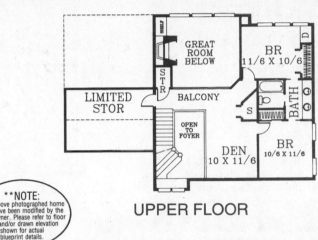

**NOTE:
The above photographed home may have been modified by the homeowner. Please refer to floor plan and/or drawn elevation shown for actual blueprint details.

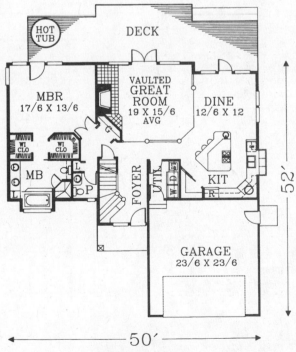

UPPER FLOOR

MAIN FLOOR

Classic Victorian

- This classic exterior is built around an interior that offers all the amenities desired by today's families.
- In from the covered front porch, the entry features a curved stairway and a glass-block wall to the dining room.
- A step down from the entry, the Great Room boasts a dramatic 24½-ft. cathedral ceiling and provides ample space for large family gatherings.
- The formal dining room is available for special occasions, while the 13-ft.-high breakfast nook serves everyday needs.
- The adjoining island kitchen offers plenty of counter space and opens to a handy utility room and a powder room.
- The deluxe main-floor master suite features a 14½-ft. cathedral ceiling and an opulent private bath with a garden spa tub and a separate shower.
- Upstairs, two secondary bedrooms share a full bath and a balcony overlooking the Great Room below.
- Plans for a two-car garage are available upon request.

Plan DW-2112

Bedrooms: 3	Baths: 2½
Living Area:	
Upper floor	514 sq. ft.
Main floor	1,598 sq. ft.
Total Living Area:	**2,112 sq. ft.**
Standard basement	1,598 sq. ft.
Exterior Wall Framing:	2x4

Foundation Options:

Standard basement
Crawlspace
Slab

(All plans can be built with your choice of foundation and framing. A generic conversion diagram is available. See order form.)

BLUEPRINT PRICE CODE: C

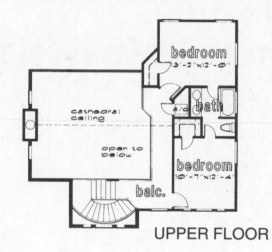

UPPER FLOOR

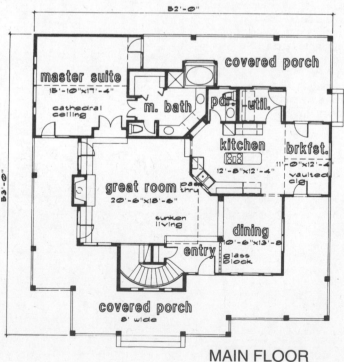

MAIN FLOOR

Today's Tradition

- This two-story country home combines traditional standards with the exciting new designs of today.
- Visitors are welcomed by the wrap-around porch and the symmetrical bay windows of the living and dining rooms.
- The front half of the main floor lends itself to entertaining as the angled entry creates a flow between the formal areas.
- French doors lead from the living room to the spacious family room, which boasts a beamed ceiling, a warm fireplace and porch access.
- The super kitchen features an island cooktop with a snack bar. A nice-sized laundry room is nearby.
- The spacious upper level hosts a master suite with two walk-in closets and a large bath with a dual-sink vanity, a tub and a separate shower. Three more bedrooms share another full bath.

Plan AGH-2143

Bedrooms: 4	Baths: 2½
Living Area:	
Upper floor	1,047 sq. ft.
Main floor	1,096 sq. ft.
Total Living Area:	**2,143 sq. ft.**
Daylight basement	1,096 sq. ft.
Garage	852 sq. ft.
Exterior Wall Framing:	2x6

Foundation Options:

Daylight basement

(All plans can be built with your choice of foundation and framing. A generic conversion diagram is available. See order form.)

BLUEPRINT PRICE CODE: C

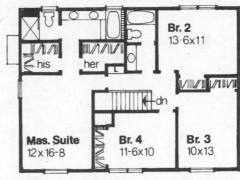

UPPER FLOOR

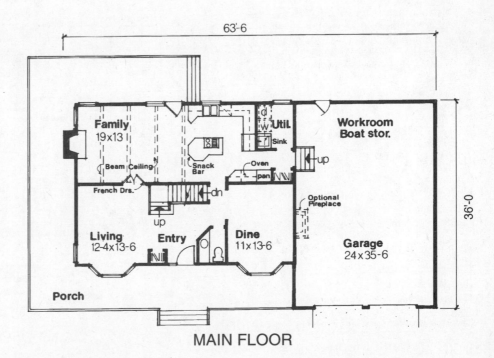

MAIN FLOOR

Open, Flowing Floor Plan

- Open, flowing rooms punctuated with wonderful windows enhance this spacious four-bedroom home.
- The two-story-high foyer is brightened by an arched window above. To the left lies the living room, which flows into the family room. An inviting fireplace and windows overlooking a rear terrace highlight the family room.
- The centrally located kitchen serves both the formal dining room and the dinette, with a view of the family room beyond. Sliding glass doors in the dinette open to a lovely terrace.
- Upstairs, the master suite features an arched window and a walk-in closet with a dressing area. The private master bath includes a dual-sink vanity, a skylighted whirlpool tub and a separate shower.
- The three remaining bedrooms share another skylighted bath.

Plan AHP-9020

Bedrooms: 4	Baths: 2½
Living Area:	
Upper floor	1,021 sq. ft.
Main floor	1,125 sq. ft.
Total Living Area:	**2,146 sq. ft.**
Standard basement	1,032 sq. ft.
Garage	480 sq. ft.
Exterior Wall Framing:	2x6

Foundation Options:

Standard basement

Crawlspace

Slab

(All plans can be built with your choice of foundation and framing. A generic conversion diagram is available. See order form.)

BLUEPRINT PRICE CODE: **C**

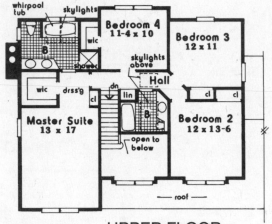

UPPER FLOOR

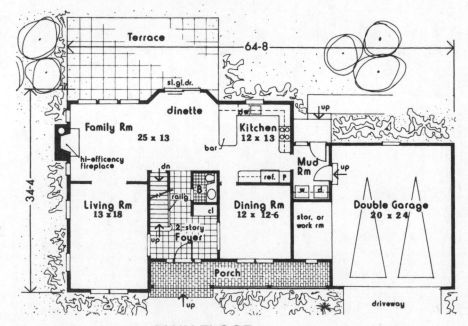

MAIN FLOOR

TO ORDER THIS BLUEPRINT, CALL TOLL-FREE 1-800-820-1283

Plan AHP-9020

PRICES AND DETAILS ON PAGES 12-15

Front Porch Invites Visitors

- This neat and well-proportioned design exudes warmth and charm.
- The roomy foyer connects the formal dining room and living room for special occasions, and the living and family rooms join together to create abundant space for large gatherings.
- The large kitchen, dinette and family room flow from one to the other for great casual family living.
- Upstairs, the roomy master suite is complemented by a master bath available in two configurations. The unique library is brightened by a beautiful arched window.

Plan GL-2161

Bedrooms: 3	Baths: 2½
Living Area:	
Upper floor	991 sq. ft.
Main floor	1,170 sq. ft.
Total Living Area	**2,161 sq. ft.**
Standard basement	1,170 sq. ft.
Garage	462 sq. ft.
Exterior Wall Framing	**2x6**

Foundation Options:

Standard basement

(All plans can be built with your choice of foundation and framing. A generic conversion diagram is available. See order form.)

BLUEPRINT PRICE CODE	**C**

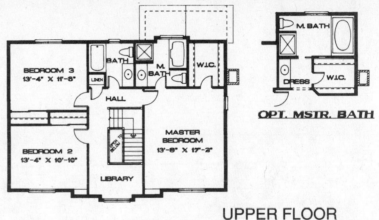

UPPER FLOOR

OPT. MSTR. BATH

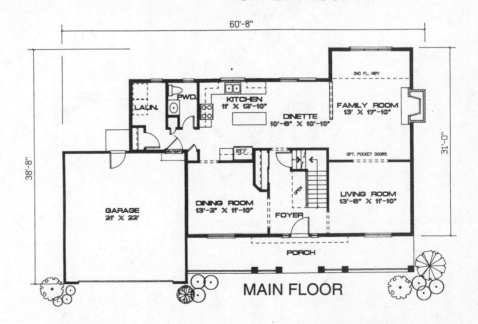

MAIN FLOOR

Striking Vertical Design

- Unique roof deck and massive wrap-around main level deck harbor an equally exciting interior.
- Large sunken living room is brightened by a three-window skylight and also features a log-sized fireplace.
- U-shaped kitchen is just off the entry, adjacent to handy laundry area.
- Second-story balcony overlooks the large living room and entryway below.

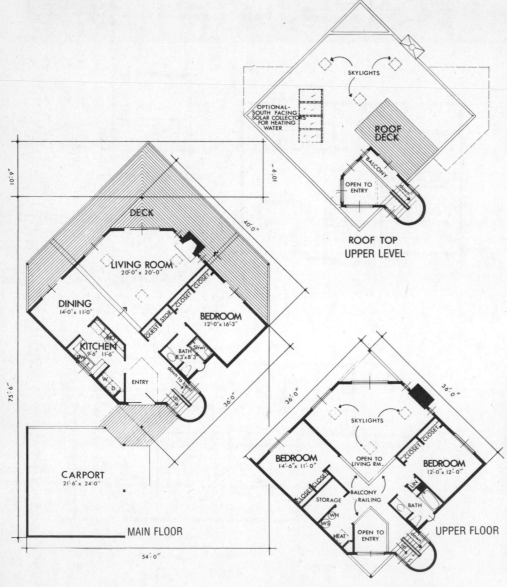

ROOF TOP
UPPER LEVEL

MAIN FLOOR

UPPER FLOOR

Plans H-935-1 & -1A

Bedrooms: 3	Baths: 2

Space:	
Upper floor:	844 sq. ft.
Main floor:	1,323 sq. ft.

Total living area:	**2,167 sq. ft.**
Basement:	approx. 1,323 sq. ft.
Carport:	516 sq. ft.

Exterior Wall Framing:	2x6

Foundation options:
Standard basement (Plan H-935-1).
Crawlspace (Plan H-935-1A).
(Foundation & framing conversion diagram available — see order form.)

Blueprint Price Code:	C

Morning Glory

- This melodious country-style home opens itself to the sights and sounds of nature with front and rear porches, and dazzling window treatments.
- From the sidelighted entry, a long hall leads to the right, introducing three secondary bedrooms. Along the way, you'll find plenty of closet space for coats and board games.
- There's plenty of gathering room in the family room, where a solid fireplace warms the spirit. The bird-watcher in your family can set up camp at the large boxed-out window to the rear.

- The cheery breakfast nook flaunts its own boxed-out window and a glassy door to the backyard porch.
- A raised bar joins the nook to the kitchen, which incorporates cabinets into its center island. Just a few steps brings you to the formal dining room for an exquisite meal.
- On the other side of the home, the master suite is enhanced by a charming window seat. The private bath is packed with essentials, including twin walk-in closets, a whirlpool tub beneath a radiant window, and a dual-sink vanity. The sit-down shower is sure to be a morning eye-opener!

Plan RD-1944	
Bedrooms: 4	**Baths:** 2
Living Area:	
Main floor	1,944 sq. ft.
Total Living Area:	**1,944 sq. ft.**
Standard basement	1,750 sq. ft.
Garage and storage	538 sq. ft.
Exterior Wall Framing:	2x4

Foundation Options:

Standard basement
Crawlspace
Slab
(All plans can be built with your choice of foundation and framing. A generic conversion diagram is available. See order form.)

BLUEPRINT PRICE CODE:	B

MAIN FLOOR

73'-0"
48'-1"

STORAGE
WIH
STOR.
UTIL.
NOOK
9'-0" CLG.
11'-6" x 8'-0"
PORCH
WINDOW SEAT
MASTER SUITE
10'-0" BOXED CEILING
12'-0" x 15'-6"
B.1
9'-0" CLG.
SHOWER
RAISED BAR
KITCH.
13'-0" x 13'-0"
ISLAND CABINET
9'-0" HIGH CEILING
FAMILY RM.
12'-0" HIGH CEILING
15'-0" x 19'-0"
SHLVS.
B.2
LIN.
BED RM.4
9'-0" HIGH CEILING
10'-0" x 10'-6"
GARAGE
20'-6" x 21'-6"
DINING RM.
10'-0" BOXED CEILING
11'-0" x 12'-0"
ENTRY
STOR.
LIN.
STOR.
PORCH
BED RM.2
9'-0" HIGH CEILING
11'-0" x 11'-6"
DESK
BED RM.3
9'-0" HIGH CEILING
10'-0" x 11'-0"
WINDOW SEAT

Country Living

- A covered porch, half-round transom windows and three dormers give this home its warm, nostalgic appeal. Shuttered windows and a louvered vent beautify the side-entry, two-car garage.

- Designed for the ultimate in country living, the floor plan starts off with a dynamic Great Room that flows to a bayed dining area. A nice fireplace adds warmth, while a French door provides access to a backyard covered porch. A powder room is just steps away.

- A 12-ft., 4-in. vaulted ceiling presides over the large country kitchen, which offers a bayed nook, an oversized breakfast bar and a convenient pass-through to the rear porch.

- The exquisite master suite boasts a tray ceiling, a bay window and an alcove for built-in shelves or extra closet space. Other amenities include a large walk-in closet and a compartmentalized bath.

- Upstairs, 9-ft. ceilings enhance two more bedrooms and a second full bath. Each bedroom boasts a cozy dormer window and two closets.

Plan AX-93311

Bedrooms: 3	Baths: 2½
Living Area:	
Upper floor	570 sq. ft.
Main floor	1,375 sq. ft.
Total Living Area:	**1,945 sq. ft.**
Standard basement	1,280 sq. ft.
Garage	450 sq. ft.
Exterior Wall Framing:	2x4

Foundation Options:

Standard basement

Crawlspace

Slab

(All plans can be built with your choice of foundation and framing. A generic conversion diagram is available. See order form.)

BLUEPRINT PRICE CODE: **B**

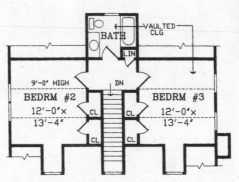

VIEW INTO GREAT ROOM

UPPER FLOOR

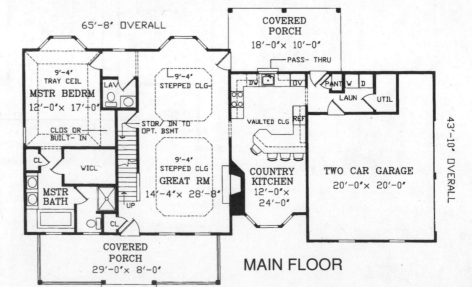

MAIN FLOOR

Plan AX-93311

PRICES AND DETAILS
ON PAGES 12-15

Cozy Bungalow

- This pleasing L-shaped design packs a lot of living space into its floor plan.
- The large family room at the center of the home extends to two outdoor living spaces: a screened porch and a big patio or deck. For colder days, the warm fireplace will come in handy.
- Formal occasions will be well received in the spacious living/dining room at the front of the home. Each area offers a nice view of the front porch.
- The airy kitchen includes a pantry, a windowed sink and lots of counter space. Attached is a cozy breakfast bay and, beyond that, a laundry room.
- Secluded to the rear of the sleeping wing, the master suite boasts a private symmetrical bath with a garden tub, a separate shower and his-and-hers vanities and walk-in closets.
- Two secondary bedrooms and another full bath complete the sleeping wing.

Plan C-8620

Bedrooms: 3	Baths: 2
Living Area:	
Main floor	1,950 sq. ft.
Total Living Area:	**1,950 sq. ft.**
Daylight basement	1,950 sq. ft.
Garage	420 sq. ft.
Exterior Wall Framing:	2x4

Foundation Options:

Daylight basement
Crawlspace
Slab
(All plans can be built with your choice of foundation and framing. A generic conversion diagram is available. See order form.)

BLUEPRINT PRICE CODE: B

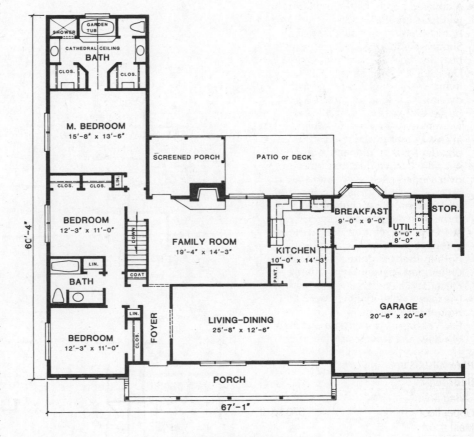

MAIN FLOOR

Two-Story Traditional

- A lovely front porch adorns the facade of this traditional beauty.
- Virtually barrier-free, this open design offers plenty of room to roam; the family room, kitchen and eating area form a continuous dining or entertaining expanse with fireplace, bay window and worktop island.
- Formal dining is done opposite the kitchen in the front-facing dining room.
- The living room can be closed off with pocket doors.
- The large master bedroom and two secondary bedrooms are found on the second floor, which also reveals an open balcony.

Plan GL-1950

Bedrooms: 3	Baths: 2½

Space:

Upper floor:	912 sq. ft.
Main floor:	1,038 sq. ft.
Total living area:	**1,950 sq. ft.**
Garage:	484 sq. ft.

Exterior Wall Framing:	2x6

Foundation options:
Standard basement.
(Foundation & framing conversion diagram available — see order form.)

Blueprint Price Code:	B

UPPER FLOOR

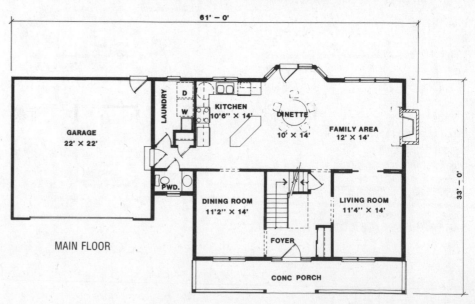

MAIN FLOOR

Plan GL-1950

PRICES AND DETAILS ON PAGES 12-15

Living on a Sloping Lot

- The interesting roofline, attractive front deck and dramatic windows of this stylish family home give it lasting contemporary appeal.
- The two-story entry opens up to the spacious living room, which boasts floor-to-ceiling windows and an 11½-ft. vaulted ceiling with exposed beams.

- The adjoining dining area provides access to a wraparound railed deck.
- The updated kitchen offers a walk-in pantry, an eating bar and a breakfast nook with sliding glass doors to a second railed deck.
- A fireplace and access to a rear patio highlight the attached family room.
- Upstairs, a washer and dryer in the hall bath are convenient to all three bedrooms, making laundry a breeze.
- The master bedroom has an 11½-ft. vaulted ceiling and a private bath.

Plan P-7737-4D

Bedrooms: 3	Baths: 2½
Living Area:	
Upper floor	802 sq. ft.
Main floor	1,158 sq. ft.
Total Living Area:	**1,960 sq. ft.**
Tuck-under garage	736 sq. ft.
Exterior Wall Framing:	2x6

Foundation Options:

Crawlspace
(All plans can be built with your choice of foundation and framing. A generic conversion diagram is available. See order form.)

BLUEPRINT PRICE CODE: B

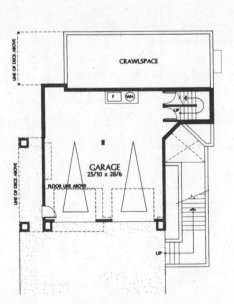

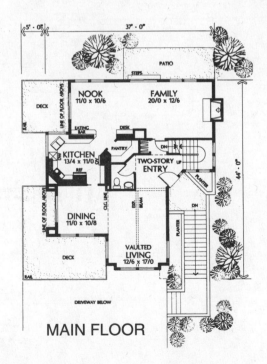

MAIN FLOOR

UPPER FLOOR

Morning Room with a View

- This modern-looking ranch is stylishly decorated with a pair of arched-window dormers, handsome brick trim and a covered front porch.
- Inside, the dining room is set off by columns, as it merges with the entry.
- The main living areas are oriented to the rear, where a huge central family room offers a patio view and a fireplace that may also be enjoyed from the bayed morning room and adjoining kitchen.
- The walk-through kitchen features a pantry, a snack bar to the family room and easy service to the formal dining room across the hall.
- The secluded master suite boasts a wide window seat and a private bath with a walk-in closet, a corner garden tub and a separate shower.
- Across the home, the three secondary bedrooms share another full bath. The fourth bedroom may double as a study.
- High 10-ft. ceilings are found throughout the home, except in the secondary bedrooms.

Plan DD-1962-1

Bedrooms: 3+	Baths: 2
Living Area:	
Main floor	1,962 sq. ft.
Total Living Area:	**1,962 sq. ft.**
Standard basement	1,962 sq. ft.
Garage	386 sq. ft.
Exterior Wall Framing:	2x4

Foundation Options:

Standard basement

Crawlspace

Slab

(All plans can be built with your choice of foundation and framing. A generic conversion diagram is available. See order form.)

BLUEPRINT PRICE CODE: B

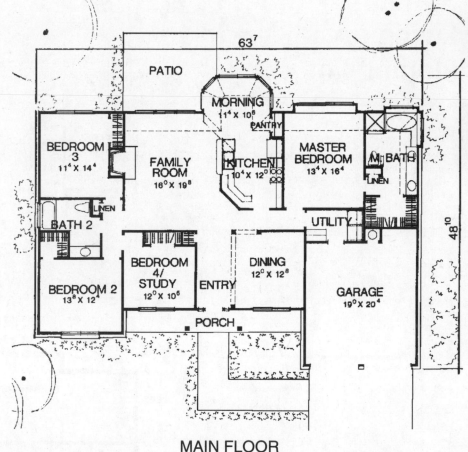

MAIN FLOOR

Plan DD-1962-1

PRICES AND DETAILS ON PAGES 12-15

Stunning Home

- A stunning picture window arrangement highlights this split-foyer home, which is perfect for a sloping lot.
- Inside, a half-staircase leads up to the sunken living room. A 14-ft. cathedral ceiling soars over the room, which offers a spectacular view through a floor-to-ceiling wall of windows.
- A charming two-way stone fireplace is shared with the dining room, which features a 12-ft. cathedral ceiling. Sliding glass doors open to a backyard deck that beckons you for a summer afternoon barbecue.
- Nearby, a cheery bayed breakfast nook extends to the galley-style kitchen.
- In the master bedroom, sliding glass doors offer private deck access. The master bath boasts a garden tub and a dual-sink vanity.
- Across the hall, two good-sized bedrooms with large closets are serviced by a centrally located bath.
- Downstairs, a fun recreation room with handy built-in shelves is a great spot for boisterous family get togethers.

Plan AX-8486-A

Bedrooms: 3	Baths: 2
Living Area:	
Main floor	1,630 sq. ft.
Daylight basement (finished)	334 sq. ft.
Total Living Area:	**1,964 sq. ft.**
Daylight basement (unfinished)	754 sq. ft.
Tuck-under garage and storage	510 sq. ft.
Exterior Wall Framing:	2x4

Foundation Options:

Daylight basement

(All plans can be built with your choice of foundation and framing. A generic conversion diagram is available. See order form.)

BLUEPRINT PRICE CODE:	B

MAIN FLOOR

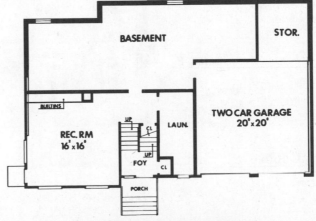

DAYLIGHT BASEMENT

Big, Vaulted Great Room

- Behind this home's unpretentious facade lies an exciting and highly livable floor plan.
- The 16-ft.-high vaulted entry leads visitors to the impressive Great Room, where a corner fireplace rises to meet the 16-ft. exposed-beam ceiling.
- The skylighted central kitchen has a 12-ft. vaulted ceiling and a nice pantry.
- The sunny nook includes a 12-ft. ceiling, a built-in work desk and access to a large patio.
- Elegant double doors open to the dazzling master suite, which includes a skylighted dressing area wth a 12-ft. ceiling. An enormous walk-in closet and a sumptuous bath with a sunken tub are also featured.
- Two secondary bedrooms share another full bath at the opposite end of the home, near the laundry room.

Plans P-6577-3A & -3D

Bedrooms: 3	Baths: 2
Living Area:	
Main floor (crawlspace version)	1,978 sq. ft.
Main floor (basement version)	2,047 sq. ft.
Total Living Area:	**1,978/2,047 sq. ft.**
Daylight basement	1,982 sq. ft.
Garage	438 sq. ft.
Exterior Wall Framing:	2x4
Foundation Options:	**Plan #**
Daylight basement	P-6577-3D
Crawlspace	P-6577-3A

(All plans can be built with your choice of foundation and framing. A generic conversion diagram is available. See order form.)

BLUEPRINT PRICE CODE:	**B/C**

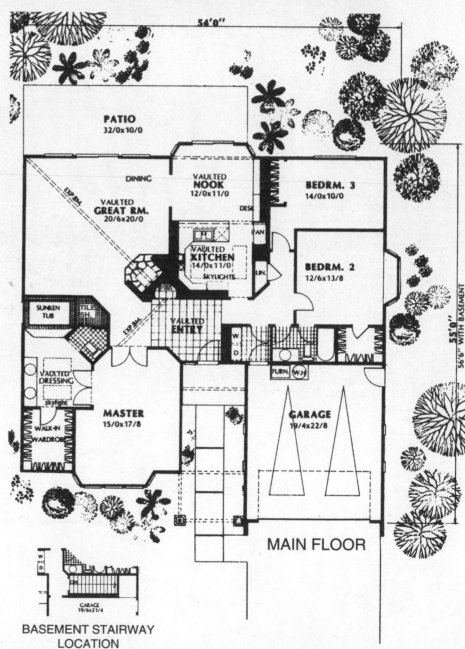

MAIN FLOOR

BASEMENT STAIRWAY LOCATION

Plans P-6577-3A & -3D

PRICES AND DETAILS ON PAGES 12-15

A Splash of Style

- Eye-catching keystones, arched window arrangements and a varied roofline give this home a refreshing splash of style.
- Inside, the 10-ft., 8-in.-high entry leads to the dining room and the Great Room. A 12-ft. sloped ceiling expands the Great Room, which features a brick fireplace that soars to the ceiling.
- A sunny bay brightens the cheery breakfast nook and the adjacent kitchen. A built-in desk, a pantry, an island workstation and a nearby powder room make the most of this busy area.
- A split staircase at the center of the plan leads to the upper-floor bedrooms.
- A 13-ft., 4-in. cathedral ceiling, a sunny bay and a plant ledge spice up the master bedroom. The private bath boasts a whirlpool tub under an 11-ft., 4-in. sloped ceiling. Two vanities and a separate shower are also included.
- The secondary bedrooms share a split hall bath. The front bedroom has a built-in bookcase and an 11-ft., 4-in. sloped ceiling; the left, rear bedroom has a 13-ft., 10-in. cathedral ceiling.

Plan CC-1990-M

Bedrooms: 4	Baths: 2½
Living Area:	
Upper floor	967 sq. ft.
Main floor	1,023 sq. ft.
Total Living Area:	**1,990 sq. ft.**
Standard basement	1,023 sq. ft.
Garage	685 sq. ft.
Exterior Wall Framing:	2x4

Foundation Options:

Standard basement

(All plans can be built with your choice of foundation and framing. A generic conversion diagram is available. See order form.)

BLUEPRINT PRICE CODE: B

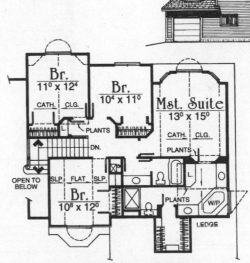

REAR VIEW

UPPER FLOOR

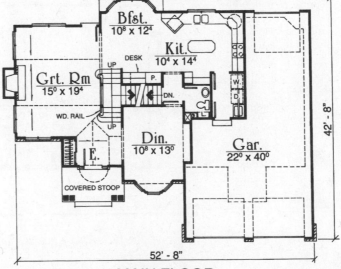

MAIN FLOOR

Relax on the Front Porch

- With its wraparound covered porch, this quaint two-story home makes summer evenings a breeze.
- Inside, a beautiful open stairway welcomes guests into the vaulted foyer, which connects the formal areas. The front-facing living and dining rooms have views of the covered front porch.
- French doors open from the living room to the family room, where a fireplace and corner windows warm and brighten this spacious activity area.
- The breakfast nook, set off by a half-wall, hosts a handy work desk and opens to the back porch.
- The country kitchen offers an oversized island, a pantry closet and illuminating windows flanking the corner sink.
- The upper-floor master suite boasts two walk-in closets and a private bath with a tub and a separate shower. Two more bedrooms, another full bath and a laundry room are also included.

Plan AGH-1997

Bedrooms: 3	Baths: 2½
Living Area:	
Upper floor	933 sq. ft.
Main floor	1,064 sq. ft.
Total Living Area:	**1,997 sq. ft.**
Standard basement	1,064 sq. ft.
Garage	662 sq. ft.
Exterior Wall Framing:	2x6

Foundation Options:

Standard basement

(All plans can be built with your choice of foundation and framing. A generic conversion diagram is available. See order form.)

BLUEPRINT PRICE CODE: B

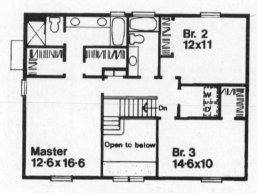

UPPER FLOOR

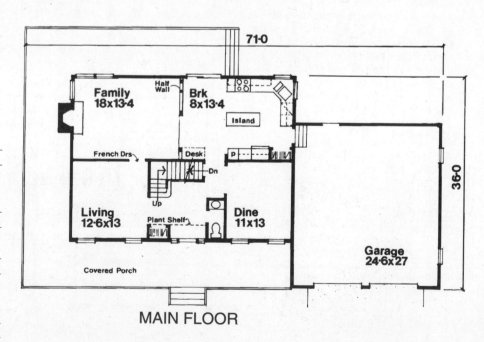

MAIN FLOOR

TO ORDER THIS BLUEPRINT, CALL TOLL-FREE 1-800-820-1283

Plan AGH-1997

PRICES AND DETAILS ON PAGES 12-15

Interior Angles Add Excitement

- Interior angles add a touch of excitement to this one-story home.
- A pleasantly charming exterior combines wood and stone to give the plan a solid, comfortable look for any neighborhood.
- Formal living and dining rooms flank the entry, which leads into the large family room, featuring a fireplace, a 19-ft. high vaulted ceiling and built-in bookshelves. A covered porch and a sunny patio are just steps away.
- The adjoining eating area with a built-in china cabinet angles off the roomy kitchen. Note the pantry and the convenient utility room.
- The master bedroom suite is both spacious and private, and includes a dressing room, a large walk-in closet and a secluded bath.
- The three secondary bedrooms are also zoned for privacy, and share a compartmentalized bath.

Plan E-1904

Bedrooms: 4	Baths: 2½
Living Area:	
Main floor	1,997 sq. ft.
Total Living Area:	**1,997 sq. ft.**
Garage	484 sq. ft.
Storage	104 sq. ft.
Exterior Wall Framing:	2x4

Foundation Options:

Crawlspace
Slab
(All plans can be built with your choice of foundation and framing. A generic conversion diagram is available. See order form.)

BLUEPRINT PRICE CODE: **B**

MAIN FLOOR

European Charm

- This distinguished European home offers today's most luxurious features.
- In the formal living and dining rooms, 15-ft. vaulted ceilings add elegance.
- The informal areas are oriented to the rear of the home, entered through French doors in the foyer. The family room features a 12-ft. tray ceiling, a fireplace with an adjoining media center and a view of a backyard deck.

- The open kitchen and breakfast area is bright and cheerful, with a window wall and French-door deck access.
- Double doors lead into the luxurious master suite, which showcases a 14-ft. vaulted ceiling and a see-through fireplace that is shared with the spa bath. The splashy bath includes a dual-sink vanity, a separate shower and a wardrobe closet and dressing area.
- Two more bedrooms, one with private deck access, and a full bath are located on the opposite side of the home.
- Unless otherwise mentioned, 9-ft. ceilings enhance every room.

Plan APS-2006	
Bedrooms: 3	Baths: 2
Living Area:	
Main floor	2,006 sq. ft.
Total Living Area:	2,006 sq. ft.
Daylight basement	2,006 sq. ft.
Garage	448 sq. ft.
Exterior Wall Framing:	2x4
Foundation Options:	

Daylight basement
Slab

(All plans can be built with your choice of foundation and framing. A generic conversion diagram is available. See order form.)

BLUEPRINT PRICE CODE:	C

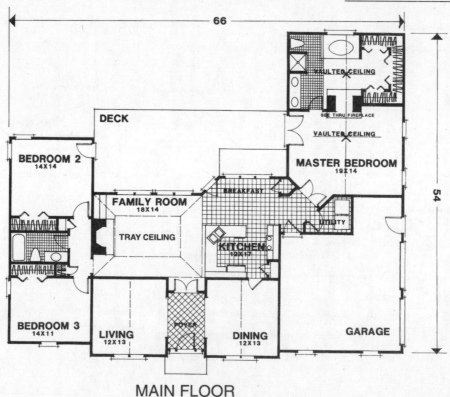

MAIN FLOOR

Plan APS-2006

Ever-Popular Floor Plan

- Open living spaces that are well integrated with outdoor areas give this plan its popularity.
- The covered porch ushers guests into a roomy entry that separates the formal entertaining areas.
- Double doors open to the huge family room, which boasts a 13-ft. vaulted ceiling accented by rustic beams, a raised-hearth fireplace and built-in book-shelves. Glass doors lead to a covered porch and an adjoining patio, creating a perfect poolside setting.
- A bayed eating area is open to the family room, separated only by a decorative half-wall, and features a large china hutch and great views. The adjacent kitchen has an angled sink for easy service to the family room and the eating area. The utility room and the garage are close by.
- The master suite is secluded to the rear of the home, with a private bath and access to the patio. The two remaining bedrooms share a dual-access bath.

Plan E-2000	
Bedrooms: 3	**Baths:** 2
Living Area:	
Main floor	2,009 sq. ft.
Total Living Area:	**2,009 sq. ft.**
Garage and storage	550 sq. ft.
Exterior Wall Framing:	2x4
Foundation Options:	
Crawlspace	
Slab	

(All plans can be built with your choice of foundation and framing. A generic conversion diagram is available. See order form.)

BLUEPRINT PRICE CODE: C

MAIN FLOOR

A Little Bit Country

- This up-to-date design is enhanced by a country-style front porch, striking columns and a high round-top window.
- The covered porch leads guests into the sidelighted entry foyer, which extends its 17-ft. ceiling into the Great Room. Dramatic quarter-round transoms beautifully set off the handsome fireplace centered on the rear wall.
- Double doors lead into the bayed breakfast nook, where sliding glass doors provide access to a sunny patio.

- The island kitchen has a planning desk and a pantry. A broom closet, a half-bath and a laundry room are nearby.
- The formal dining room is brightened by front-facing windows.
- The secluded main-floor master suite boasts a 12-ft.-high vaulted ceiling and his-and-hers walk-in closets. The private master bath features a garden whirlpool tub, a sit-down shower and a dual-sink vanity.
- Upstairs, a railed balcony overlooks the Great Room below. A full bath with two sinks is shared by three bedrooms.
- The front bedroom is brightened by a lovely arched window under a 9½-ft. vaulted area.

Plan AG-2004	
Bedrooms: 4	**Baths:** 2½
Living Area:	
Upper floor	615 sq. ft.
Main floor	1,415 sq. ft.
Total Living Area:	**2,030 sq. ft.**
Standard basement	1,390 sq. ft.
Garage	400 sq. ft.
Exterior Wall Framing:	2x4

Foundation Options:

Standard basement
(All plans can be built with your choice of foundation and framing. A generic conversion diagram is available. See order form.)

BLUEPRINT PRICE CODE: C

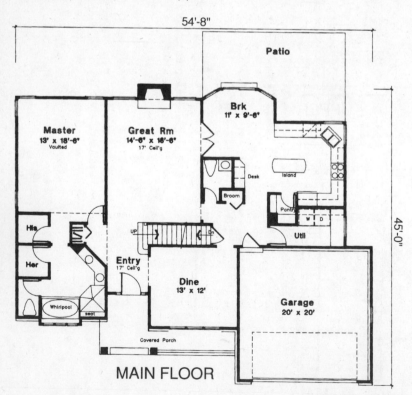

MAIN FLOOR

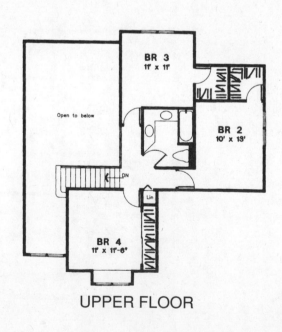

UPPER FLOOR

TO ORDER THIS BLUEPRINT, CALL TOLL-FREE 1-800-820-1283

Plan AG-2004

PRICES AND DETAILS ON PAGES 12-15

Country Appeal

- A spacious covered front porch adds to the country appeal of this classic farmhouse-style home.
- The inviting central foyer showcases a curved open-railed stairway. The adjacent living room boasts a handsome fireplace and a 9½-ft.-high vaulted sitting area brightened by a large Palladian-style window.
- Formal entertaining can be expanded to the dining room, which offers sliding glass doors to a backyard terrace.
- Updated and efficient, the good-sized kitchen includes an eating bar and a windowed sink. The adjoining dinette also expands to the terrace through sliding glass doors. Nearby is a laundry/mudroom with a service entry and garage access.
- Upstairs, an open-railed balcony overlooks the foyer. The deluxe master bedroom features a private bath and a separate dressing area.
- Three additional upper-floor bedrooms are serviced by a second full bath.

Plan HFL-1040-MB

Bedrooms: 4	Baths: 2½
Living Area:	
Upper floor	936 sq. ft.
Main floor	1,094 sq. ft.
Total Living Area:	**2,030 sq. ft.**
Standard basement	1,022 sq. ft.
Garage	420 sq. ft.
Exterior Wall Framing:	2x6

Foundation Options:

Standard basement

Slab

(All plans can be built with your choice of foundation and framing. A generic conversion diagram is available. See order form.)

BLUEPRINT PRICE CODE: C

VIEW INTO LIVING ROOM

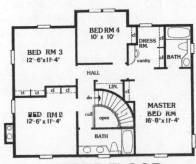

UPPER FLOOR

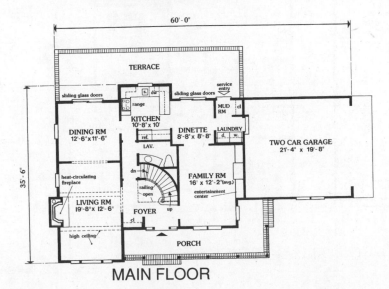

MAIN FLOOR

Charming One-Story

- The charming facade of this home conceals an exciting angled interior with many accesses to the outdoors.
- At the center of the floor plan is a spacious family activity area that combines the Great Room, the breakfast room and the kitchen.
- The sunny sunken Great Room features a 12½-ft. cathedral ceiling and an exciting two-sided fireplace. The adjacent breakfast room offers French doors to a covered backyard patio.

- The unique angled kitchen has a bright sink, a serving bar and plenty of counter space. Across the hall are the dining room, the laundry room and access to the three-car garage.
- The secluded master bedroom boasts a 12½-ft. cathedral ceiling, a roomy walk-in closet and French doors to a private covered patio. The lavish master bath has a bright garden tub, a separate shower and a dual-sink vanity.
- The secondary bedrooms both have walk-in closets. The rear-facing bedroom has patio access through its own full bath. The parlor off the entry could serve as a fourth bedroom, a guest room or a home office.

Plan Q-2033-1A	
Bedrooms: 3+	**Baths:** 3
Living Area:	
Main floor	2,033 sq. ft.
Total Living Area:	**2,033 sq. ft.**
Garage	592 sq. ft.
Exterior Wall Framing:	2x4

Foundation Options:

Slab

(All plans can be built with your choice of foundation and framing. A generic conversion diagram is available. See order form.)

BLUEPRINT PRICE CODE: C

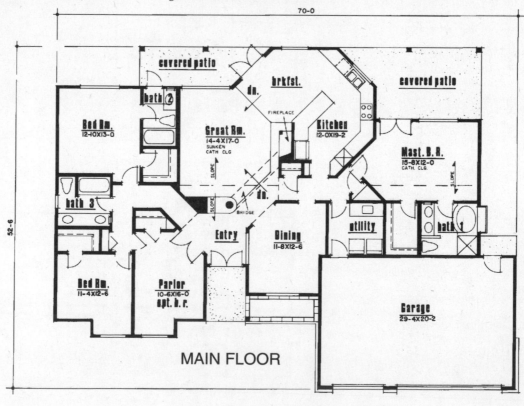

MAIN FLOOR

Plan Q-2033-1A

Spacious Contemporary

- Perfect for a sloping or scenic site, this home features a large deck, a patio, lots of windows and a walk-out basement.
- Guests are welcomed by a roomy front porch with a decorative planter.
- The 14-ft. vaulted entry leads to a spectacular Great Room with a 13-ft. vaulted ceiling, a fireplace and a rear window wall. The dining area's vaulted ceiling rises to 14 feet. French doors provide deck access.
- The kitchen boasts a unique angled serving counter and a bright sink.
- The main-floor master suite offers a window seat, a walk-in closet and a private bath with a skylighted dressing area that has his-and-hers sinks. A 14-ft. vaulted ceiling adds a dramatic effect.
- Two bedrooms and a full bath share the daylight basement with a roomy family room, which boasts a second fireplace and sliding glass doors to a sunny patio.

Plan P-6606-2D

Bedrooms: 3	Baths: 2½
Living Area:	
Main floor	1,140 sq. ft.
Daylight basement	935 sq. ft.
Total Living Area:	**2,075 sq. ft.**
Garage	451 sq. ft.
Exterior Wall Framing:	2x6

Foundation Options:

Daylight basement

(All plans can be built with your choice of foundation and framing. A generic conversion diagram is available. See order form.)

BLUEPRINT PRICE CODE: C

MAIN FLOOR

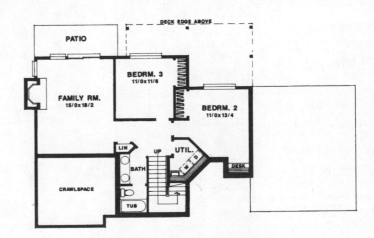

DAYLIGHT BASEMENT

High-Style Hillside Home

- This beautiful hillside home is loaded with stylish features.
- The inviting foyer leads guests into the vaulted Great Room, with its fabulous fireplace and sweeping views of a wide rear deck and the yard beyond.
- The U-shaped kitchen includes a walk-in pantry, a greenhouse window, an eating bar and an adjoining nook.
- The vaulted master bedroom offers access to a relaxing hot tub on the deck. The skylighted master bath also has a vaulted ceiling, and boasts a whirlpool tub and a separate shower.
- The versatile den could be used as a media room or as a bedroom.
- Two bedrooms downstairs share a full bath. The central bedroom would make a great guest room, with its walk-in closet and private patio.

Plan S-41892

Bedrooms: 3-4	Baths: 3
Living Area:	
Main floor	1,485 sq. ft.
Partial daylight basement	590 sq. ft.
Total Living Area:	**2,075 sq. ft.**
Mechanical room	30 sq. ft.
Garage	429 sq. ft.
Exterior Wall Framing:	2x6

Foundation Options:

Partial daylight basement

(Typical foundation & framing conversion diagram available—see order form.)

BLUEPRINT PRICE CODE: C

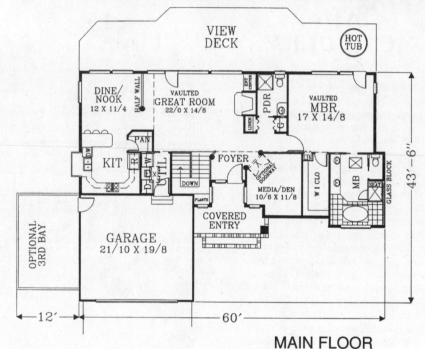

MAIN FLOOR

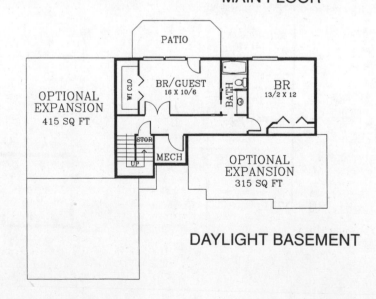

DAYLIGHT BASEMENT

TO ORDER THIS BLUEPRINT, **CALL TOLL-FREE 1-800-820-1283**

Plan S-41892

PRICES AND DETAILS ON PAGES 12-15

Sought-After Elegance

- Decorative corner quoins, copper accents and gorgeous windows take the brick and stucco facade of this home to the height of elegance.
- Luxurious appointments continue inside, with a sidelighted 11-ft.-high foyer leading to the formal living and dining rooms. The living room boasts a 14-ft. vaulted ceiling, while the dining room has an 11-ft. ceiling.
- Smoothly accessed from the dining room, the flow-through kitchen offers a serving counter to the breakfast nook. Bright windows light the two areas, which share an 11-ft. vaulted ceiling.

- Adjacent to the nook, the luxurious family room sports a handsome fireplace and access to a sprawling backyard deck. A fancy fan hangs from the soaring 14-ft. vaulted ceiling.
- Just off the family room, two roomy secondary bedrooms share a nice compartmentalized bath.
- The sumptuous master bedroom flaunts its own deck access, a quaint morning porch for quiet cups of coffee and a large walk-in closet.
- The master bath is highlighted by a plant shelf, a garden tub and a separate shower. An 11-ft. ceiling crowns the master bedroom and bath.
- Unless otherwise noted, all rooms have 9-ft. ceilings.
- A bonus room above the garage offers expansion possibilities.

Plan APS-2018	
Bedrooms: 3+	**Baths:** 2½
Living Area:	
Main floor	2,088 sq. ft.
Total Living Area:	**2,088 sq. ft.**
Bonus room (unfinished)	282 sq. ft.
Daylight basement	2,088 sq. ft.
Garage	460 sq. ft.
Storage	35 sq. ft.
Exterior Wall Framing:	2x4
Foundation Options:	
Daylight basement	

(All plans can be built with your choice of foundation and framing. A generic conversion diagram is available. See order form.)

BLUEPRINT PRICE CODE:	C

MAIN FLOOR

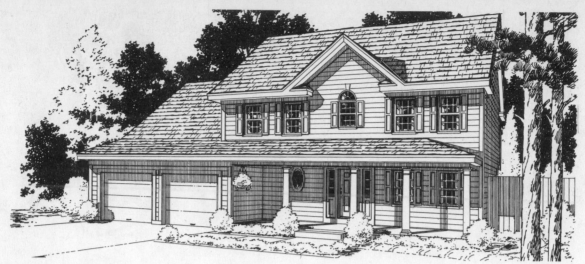

Comfortable Country Home

- A central gable and a wide, welcoming front porch with columns give this design comfortable country charm.
- The large living room is open to the dining room, which features a tray ceiling and views to the backyard.
- The kitchen offers an oversized island counter with a snack bar. The adjoining breakfast area has a sliding glass door to the backyard and a half-wall that separates it from the family room. This inviting room includes a fireplace and a bay window with a cozy seat.
- Upstairs, the master suite boasts three windows, including a lovely arched window, that overlook the front yard. The private bath offers a whirlpool tub and a separate shower.
- Three more bedrooms, a second full bath and a multipurpose den make this a great family-sized home.

Plan OH-165

Bedrooms: 4+	Baths: 2½
Living Area:	
Upper floor	1,121 sq. ft.
Main floor	1,000 sq. ft.
Total Living Area:	**2,121 sq. ft.**
Standard basement	1,000 sq. ft.
Garage	400 sq. ft.
Exterior Wall Framing:	2x4

Foundation Options:

Standard basement
(All plans can be built with your choice of foundation and framing. A generic conversion diagram is available. See order form.)

BLUEPRINT PRICE CODE: C

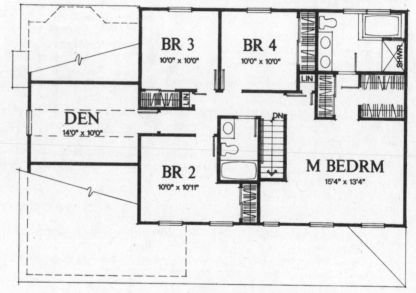

UPPER FLOOR

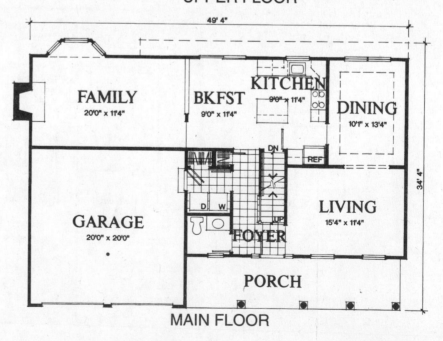

MAIN FLOOR

Plan OH-165

PRICES AND DETAILS ON PAGES 12-15

Visual Surprises

- The exterior of this home is accented with a dramatic roof cavity, while the inside uses angles to enhance the efficiency and variety of the floor plan.
- The double-door entry opens to a reception area, which unfolds to the spacious living room. A 16½-ft. sloped ceiling and an angled fireplace add drama to the living room and the adjoining bayed dining room, where sliding doors access a backyard terrace.
- The efficient kitchen easily serves both the formal dining room and the cheerful dinette, which offers sweeping outdoor views. A fireplace in the adjoining family room warms the entire area. A second terrace is accessible via sliding glass doors.
- The oversized laundry room could be finished as a nice hobby room.
- A skylighted stairway leads up to the sleeping areas. The master suite is fully equipped with a private bath, a separate dressing area, a walk-in closet and an exciting sun deck alcoved above the garage. Three additional bedrooms share another full bath.

Plan K-540-L

Bedrooms: 4	Baths: 2½
Living Area:	
Upper floor	884 sq. ft.
Main floor	1,238 sq. ft.
Total Living Area:	**2,122 sq. ft.**
Standard basement	1,106 sq. ft.
Garage	400 sq. ft.
Storage	122 sq. ft.
Exterior Wall Framing:	2x4 or 2x6

Foundation Options:

Standard basement

Slab

(All plans can be built with your choice of foundation and framing. A generic conversion diagram is available. See order form.)

BLUEPRINT PRICE CODE:	C

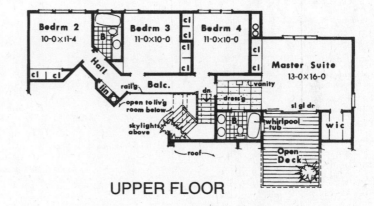

UPPER FLOOR

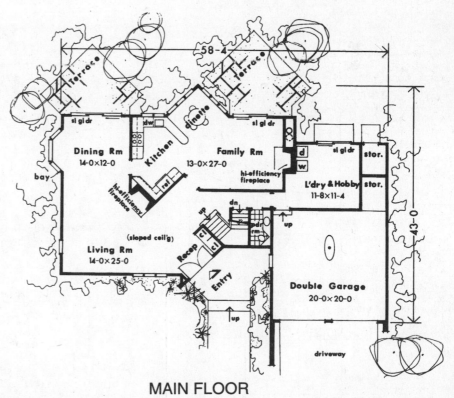

MAIN FLOOR

Great Gazebo!

- A wraparound porch with a striking gazebo adorns this traditional home.
- In from the covered porch, the front entry merges with the columned dining room and flows back to the living room.
- The bright living room boasts built-in shelves and a fabulous fireplace with flanking windows. This room also accesses a secluded office and an incredible backyard deck, which features a covered summer kitchen and an inviting spa out in the sun.
- The island kitchen offers a pantry closet and a sunny breakfast nook with a side door to the porch.
- The master bedroom has a boxed-out window and a luxurious bath with a large walk-in closet, a dual-sink vanity, a spa tub and a separate shower.
- The two upstairs bedrooms are brightened by dormered windows and share a full bath with a dual-sink vanity.
- An unfinished bonus space offers expansion possibilities.

Plan DD-2129

Bedrooms: 3+	Baths: 3
Living Area:	
Upper floor	569 sq. ft.
Main floor	1,560 sq. ft.
Total Living Area:	**2,129 sq. ft.**
Bonus space (unfinished)	140 sq. ft.
Standard basement	1,560 sq. ft.
Garage	531 sq. ft.
Exterior Wall Framing:	2x4

Foundation Options:
Standard basement
Crawlspace
Slab

(All plans can be built with your choice of foundation and framing. A generic conversion diagram is available. See order form.)

BLUEPRINT PRICE CODE: C

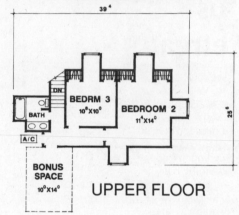

UPPER FLOOR

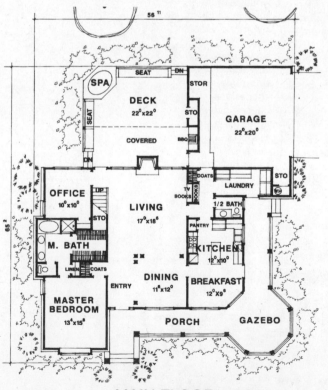

MAIN FLOOR

TO ORDER THIS BLUEPRINT, CALL TOLL-FREE 1-800-820-1283

Plan DD-2129

PRICES AND DETAILS ON PAGES 12-15

Luxurious Adult Retreat

- This rustic multi-level design is ideal for a gently sloping site. With its two levels of decks, the home is also great for lots with a view to the rear.
- A sumptuous adult retreat is secluded on the upper floor and includes a 13½-ft.-high cathedral-ceilinged bedroom, a private deck, an adjoining balcony loft, a walk-in closet and a deluxe bath.
- On the main floor, the high 17-ft. entry shows off the open stairway and looks into the sunken living areas ahead.
- The spacious living room's large bay window offers a panoramic view of the main-level wraparound deck. Next to a cozy woodstove is a wood bin that can be filled conveniently from the outside.
- Set off by a beautiful railing, the dining room gives formal occasions a unique flair. Atrium doors access the deck.
- Bright and efficient, the 12-ft.-high vaulted kitchen has lots of counter and storage space. A handy snack bar extends into a casual dining bay.
- Two secondary bedrooms, each with a boxed-out window, share a full bath on the main floor.

Plan NW-544-S

Bedrooms: 3	Baths: 2½
Living Area:	
Upper floor	638 sq. ft.
Main floor	1,500 sq. ft.
Total Living Area:	**2,138 sq. ft.**
Garage and shop	545 sq. ft.
Exterior Wall Framing:	2x6

Foundation Options:

Crawlspace

(All plans can be built with your choice of foundation and framing. A generic conversion diagram is available. See order form.)

BLUEPRINT PRICE CODE:	C

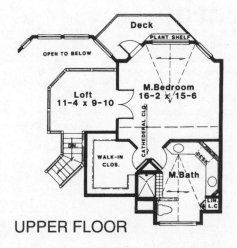

UPPER FLOOR

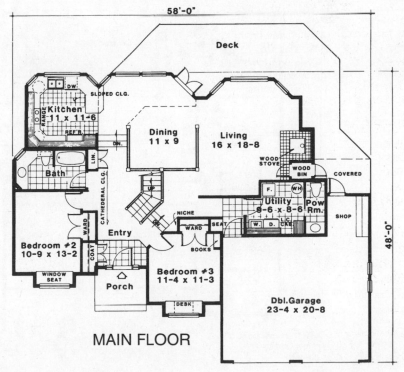

MAIN FLOOR

Arched Entry

- A beautiful arched entry introduces this grand Mediterranean home.
- Elegant double doors open into a tiled foyer, which is flanked by the home's formal living and dining rooms. Both rooms boast 12-ft. ceilings, and the dining room offers a tray ceiling.
- In the huge family room, sliding glass doors open to a covered patio. A fireplace flanked by built-in cabinets sets the stage for fun evenings at home.
- An 8-ft. wall separates the family room from the kitchen, which shares an

angled serving counter with the sunny bayed breakfast nook. A built-in desk nearby is a great spot to pay the bills.
- The secluded master suite includes a sprawling overhead plant shelf and sliding glass doors to the patio. A dramatic arch introduces the private bath, which includes a huge tub, a separate shower and a dual-sink vanity.
- Across the home, two more bedrooms share a hall bath. A quiet rear bedroom is serviced by another full bath. Each room boasts a neat plant shelf.
- Unless otherwise noted, a 10-ft. ceiling enhances every room in the home.

Plan HDS-99-233	
Bedrooms: 4	**Baths:** 3
Living Area:	
Main floor	2,140 sq. ft.
Total Living Area:	**2,140 sq. ft.**
Garage	430 sq. ft.
Exterior Wall Framing:	8-in. concrete block

Foundation Options:

Slab
(All plans can be built with your choice of foundation and framing. A generic conversion diagram is available. See order form.)

BLUEPRINT PRICE CODE:	**C**

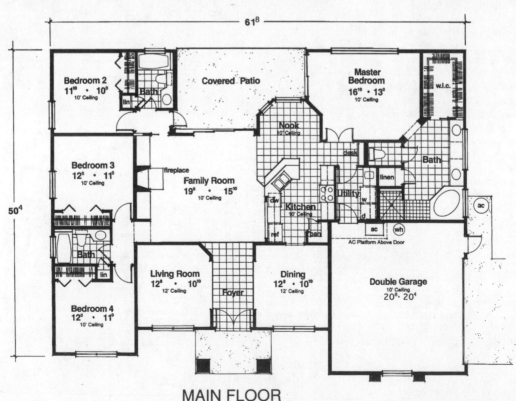

MAIN FLOOR

TO ORDER THIS BLUEPRINT, CALL TOLL-FREE 1-800-820-1283

Plan HDS-99-233

PRICES AND DETAILS ON PAGES 12-15

Colonial for Today

- Designed for a growing family, this handsome traditional home offers four bedrooms plus a den and three complete baths. The Colonial exterior is updated by a covered front entry porch with a fanlight window above.
- The dramatic tiled foyer is two stories high and provides direct access to all of the home's living areas. The spacious living room has an inviting brick fireplace and sliding pocket doors to the adjoining dining room.
- Overlooking the backyard, the huge combination kitchen/family room is the home's hidden charm. The kitchen features a peninsula breakfast bar with seating for six.
- The family room includes a window wall with sliding glass doors that open to an enticing terrace. A built-in entertainment center and bookshelves line another wall.
- The adjacent mudroom houses a pantry closet and the washer/dryer. A full bath and a big den complete the main floor.
- The upper floor is highlighted by a beautiful balcony that overlooks the foyer below. The luxurious master suite boasts a skylighted dressing area and two closets, including an oversized walk-in closet. The private master bath offers a whirlpool tub and a dual-sink vanity.

Plan AHP-7050	
Bedrooms: 4+	**Baths:** 3
Living Area:	
Upper floor	998 sq. ft.
Main floor	1,153 sq. ft.
Total Living Area:	**2,151 sq. ft.**
Standard basement	1,067 sq. ft.
Garage and storage	439 sq. ft.
Exterior Wall Framing:	2x6
Foundation Options:	
Standard basement	
Crawlspace	
Slab	

(All plans can be built with your choice of foundation and framing. A generic conversion diagram is available. See order form.)

BLUEPRINT PRICE CODE: C

MAIN FLOOR

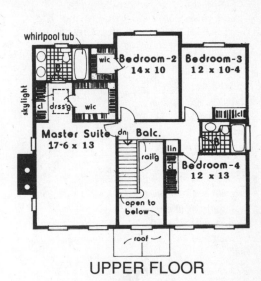

UPPER FLOOR

Colonial Calm

- This Colonial home introduces a rare measure of calm with its elegant, unique facade and welcoming interior.
- When you're up for entertaining, there's no better space than the living room, where a regal fireplace resides. Pocket doors open to the formal dining room.
- The family room is designed for casual fun, with a TV nook and shelving for board games and photographs. A big eating bar quickly serves rambunctious young ones and if the day gets too hectic, you can shoo everyone to the backyard terrace!
- At the front of the home, a den gives you enough room for those home business ventures. The private entrance to a full bath could make this a nice guest room or extra bedroom.
- Upstairs, a balcony overlook leads to the master suite, where a private, skylighted bath helps you unwind. The whirlpool tub is the perfect prescription for your tired muscles.

Plan AHP-9540

Bedrooms: 4+	Baths: 3
Living Area:	
Upper floor	998 sq. ft.
Main floor	1,153 sq. ft.
Total Living Area:	**2,151 sq. ft.**
Standard basement	1,067 sq. ft.
Garage and storage	439 sq. ft.
Exterior Wall Framing:	2x4 or 2x6

Foundation Options:
Standard basement
Crawlspace
Slab
(All plans can be built with your choice of foundation and framing. A generic conversion diagram is available. See order form.)

BLUEPRINT PRICE CODE:	C

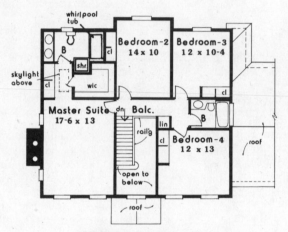

UPPER FLOOR

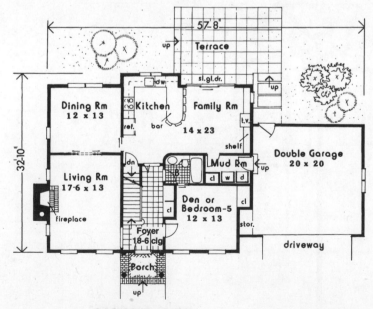

MAIN FLOOR

TO ORDER THIS BLUEPRINT, CALL TOLL-FREE 1-800-820-1283

Plan AHP-9540

PRICES AND DETAILS ON PAGES 12-15

A Taste of Europe

- This tasteful one-story home is characterized by a European exterior and an ultra-modern interior.
- High 10-ft. ceilings grace the central living areas, from the foyer to the Great Room, and from the nook through the kitchen to the dining room.
- The inviting Great Room showcases a fireplace framed by glass that overlooks the covered back porch.
- A snack bar unites the Great Room with the bayed nook and the galley-style kitchen. A spacious utility room is just off the kitchen and accessible from the two-car garage as well.
- The secluded master suite boasts a luxurious private bath and French doors that open to the covered backyard porch.
- The master bath features a raised garden spa tub set into an intimate corner, with a separate shower nearby. A large walk-in closet and two sinks separated by a built-in makeup table are also included.
- Two additional bedrooms, a second full bath and a front study or home office make up the remainder of this up-to-date design.

Plan VL-2162	
Bedrooms: 3	**Baths:** 2
Living Area:	
Main floor	2,162 sq. ft.
Total Living Area:	**2,162 sq. ft.**
Garage	498 sq. ft.
Exterior Wall Framing:	2x4

Foundation Options:

Crawlspace
Slab
(All plans can be built with your choice of foundation and framing. A generic conversion diagram is available. See order form.)

BLUEPRINT PRICE CODE: C

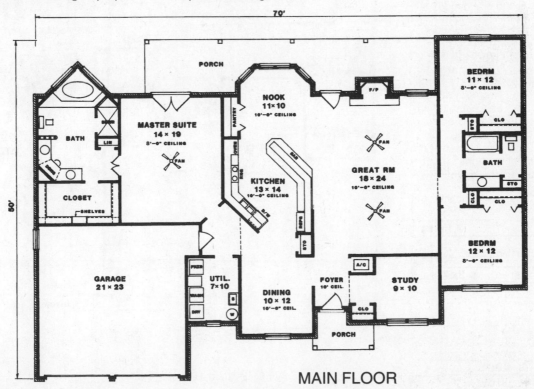

MAIN FLOOR

Captivating Facade

- This home attracts the eye with stately columns, half-round transoms and a sidelighted entry.
- A tall, barrel-vaulted foyer flows between the radiant formal areas at the front of the home.
- The barrel vault opens from the foyer to an overwhelming 14½-ft. vaulted family room, where a striking fireplace and a media center are captivating features.
- The central kitchen offers a dramatic 14½-ft. vaulted ceiling and a snack bar to the breakfast nook and family room. The nook's bay window overlooks a covered backyard patio.
- Formal occasions are hosted in the dining room, which boasts its own bay window and a 10½-ft. vaulted ceiling.
- The secluded master bedroom opens to the patio and flaunts an 11-ft. vaulted ceiling. A large walk-in closet and a posh bath with a step-up garden tub and a separate shower are also featured. On the other side of the home are three additional vaulted bedrooms and two more full baths.

Plan HDS-90-807

Bedrooms: 4	Baths: 3
Living Area:	
Main floor	2,171 sq. ft.
Total Living Area:	**2,171 sq. ft.**
Garage	405 sq. ft.

Exterior Wall Framing:
2x4 and 8-in. concrete block

Foundation Options:
Slab
(All plans can be built with your choice of foundation and framing. A generic conversion diagram is available. See order form.)

BLUEPRINT PRICE CODE:	C

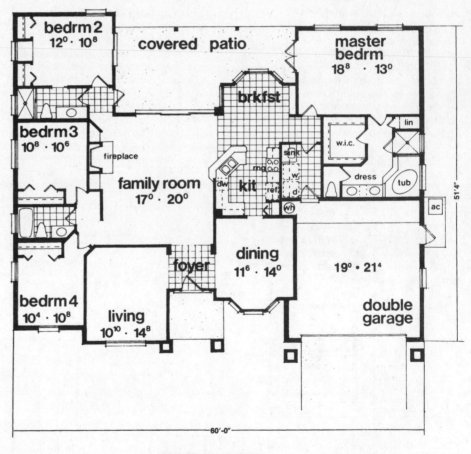

MAIN FLOOR

Plan HDS-90-807

*PRICES AND DETAILS
ON PAGES 12-15*

Family Matters

- This perfect home features many amenities to complement a family's quiet moments and festive celebrations.
- A wraparound porch sweetens the facade, which will draw compliments from the neighbors.
- The study's corner window seat beckons you to curl up with a good book.
- Beyond the dining room, the family room serves well as the activity hub. A 21-ft., 7-in. vaulted ceiling soars above a handsome fireplace, which is flanked by cabinets and bookshelves.
- The chef will love the island kitchen, where a boxed-out window is the perfect place to nurture an herb garden.
- French doors in the sunny nook provide access to an inviting deck.
- A 14-ft., 8-in. vaulted ceiling expands the master suite, which boasts a luxury bath and French doors to the porch.
- Upstairs, a bay-windowed bedroom with a 10½-ft. ceiling shares a full bath with a third bedroom.
- Unless otherwise noted, a 9-ft. ceiling adds a spacious feel to every room.

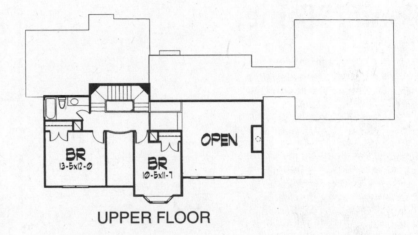

UPPER FLOOR

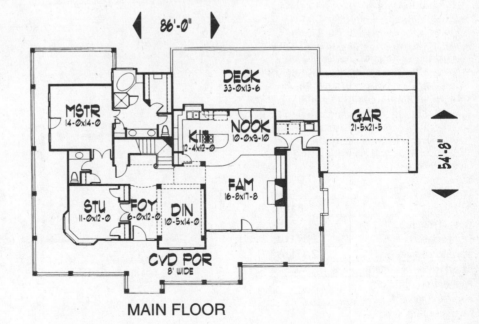

MAIN FLOOR

Plan DW-2175

Bedrooms: 3+	Baths: 2½
Living Area:	
Upper floor	479 sq. ft.
Main floor	1,696 sq. ft.
Total Living Area:	**2,175 sq. ft.**
Standard basement	1,696 sq. ft.
Garage	484 sq. ft.
Exterior Wall Framing:	2x4

Foundation Options:

Standard basement
Crawlspace
Slab

(All plans can be built with your choice of foundation and framing. A generic conversion diagram is available. See order form.)

BLUEPRINT PRICE CODE: C

Energy-Efficient Colonial Home

- This home combines classic Colonial styling with passive-solar energy efficiency. Insulated thermal flooring collects heat during the day to warm the home at night.
- An air-lock vestibule, which minimizes heat loss, leads into a spacious, elegant reception area.
- The bayed living room features optional folding doors to the family room, which offers a high-efficiency fireplace and two sets of sliding glass doors to a bright rear terrace.
- The expansive formal dining room leads into an efficient U-shaped kitchen, which boasts a pantry and a dinette with sliding glass doors to a glass-roofed sun room.
- The upper floor features an electrically operated skylight above the stairs.
- The master suite offers a walk-in closet and a private bath with a whirlpool tub.
- Three additional bedrooms share a second full bath.

Plan K-508-B

Bedrooms: 4	Baths: 2½
Living Area:	
Upper floor	1,003 sq. ft.
Main floor	1,072 sq. ft.
Sun room	101 sq. ft.
Total Living Area:	**2,176 sq. ft.**
Partial basement	633 sq. ft.
Garage and storage	458 sq. ft.
Exterior Wall Framing:	2x4 or 2x6

Foundation Options:
Partial basement
Slab
(Typical foundation & framing conversion diagram available–see order form.)

BLUEPRINT PRICE CODE: C

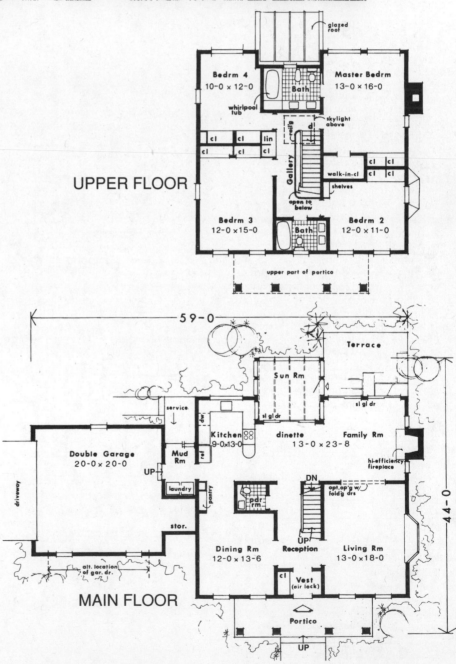

UPPER FLOOR

MAIN FLOOR

Spacious Country-Style

- This distinctive country-style home is highlighted by a wide front porch and multi-paned windows with shutters.
- Inside, the dining room is off the foyer and open to the living room, but is defined by elegant columns and beams above.
- The central living room boasts a 12-ft. cathedral ceiling, a fireplace and French doors to the rear patio.
- The delightful kitchen/nook area is spacious and well planned for both work and play.
- A handy utility room and a half-bath are on either side of a short hallway leading to the carport, which includes a large storage area.
- The master suite offers his-and-hers walk-in closets and an incredible bath that incorporates a plant shelf above the raised spa tub.
- The two remaining bedrooms share a hall bath that is compartmentalized to allow more than one user at a time.

Plan J-86140

Bedrooms: 3	Baths: 2½
Living Area:	
Main floor	2,177 sq. ft.
Total Living Area:	**2,177 sq. ft.**
Standard basement	2,177 sq. ft.
Carport	440 sq. ft.
Storage	120 sq. ft.
Exterior Wall Framing:	2x4

Foundation Options:

Standard basement

Crawlspace

Slab

(All plans can be built with your choice of foundation and framing. A generic conversion diagram is available. See order form.)

BLUEPRINT PRICE CODE:	C

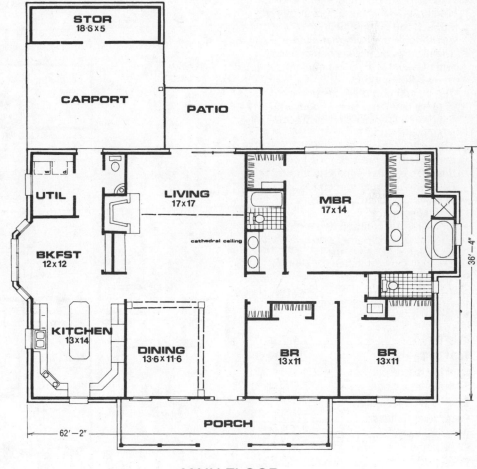

MAIN FLOOR

Country Kitchen

- A lovely front porch, dormers and shutters give this home a country-style exterior and complement its comfortable and informal interior.
- The roomy country kitchen connects with the sunny breakfast nook and the formal dining room.
- The central portion of the home consists of a large family room with a handsome fireplace and easy access to a backyard deck.
- The main-floor master suite, particularly impressive for a home of this size, features a majestic master bath with a corner garden tub, two walk-in closets and a dual-sink vanity with knee space.
- Upstairs, you will find two more good-sized bedrooms, a double bath and a large storage area.

Plan C-8645

Bedrooms: 3	Baths: 2½
Living Area:	
Upper floor	704 sq. ft.
Main floor	1,477 sq. ft.
Total Living Area:	**2,181 sq. ft.**
Standard basement	1,400 sq. ft.
Garage and storage	561 sq. ft.
Exterior Wall Framing:	2x4

Foundation Options:

Standard basement
Crawlspace
Slab
(All plans can be built with your choice of foundation and framing. A generic conversion diagram is available. See order form.)

BLUEPRINT PRICE CODE:	C

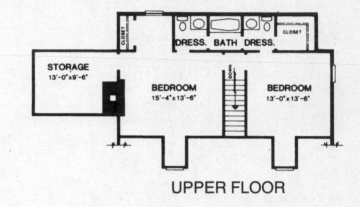

UPPER FLOOR

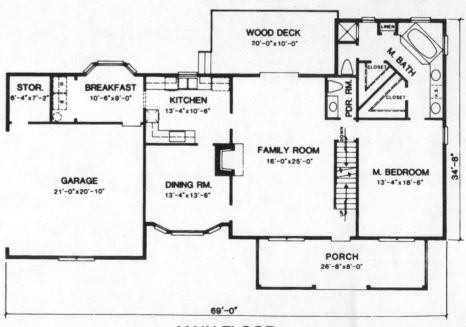

MAIN FLOOR

Plan C-8645

PRICES AND DETAILS
ON PAGES 12-15

Spacious Single-Story

- Vaulted ceilings distinguish this bright, open single-story home.
- Designed for both formal entertaining and casual family living, this airy home features an inviting stone-hearth fireplace in the living room and a dramatic woodstove in the corner of the family room.
- The living room flows into the formal dining room, which boasts a coffered ceiling and a built-in china hutch.
- The efficiently designed kitchen is positioned to serve both the formal and the informal areas. A functional island range, a pantry, a work desk and a serving bar to the large deck are featured in the kitchen.
- A skylight brightens the hallway to the sleeping wing, which includes three bedrooms, an oversized laundry room and two bathrooms. The sumptuous master suite offers a whirlpool garden tub, a double-basin vanity and a huge walk-in closet.

Plan LMB-9576-T

Bedrooms: 3+	Baths: 2
Living Area:	
Main floor	2,185 sq. ft.
Total Living Area:	**2,185 sq. ft.**
Garage	600 sq. ft.
Exterior Wall Framing:	2x6

Foundation Options:

Crawlspace
(All plans can be built with your choice of foundation and framing. A generic conversion diagram is available. See order form.)

BLUEPRINT PRICE CODE: C

MAIN FLOOR

Quiet Relaxation

- This elegant brick one-story home features a stunning master bedroom with a sunny morning porch for quiet relaxation. The bedroom's 11-ft. vaulted ceiling extends into the master bath, which boasts a corner garden tub and an attractive plant shelf.
- A few steps away, the open kitchen shares its 11-ft. ceiling and handy snack bar with the bright breakfast nook.
- A handsome fireplace warms the spacious family room, which is enhanced by a soaring 14-ft. ceiling. A striking French door provides access to a roomy deck that may also be reached from the master bedroom.
- The formal living areas flank the sidelighted foyer. The living room shows off a 14-ft. cathedral ceiling.
- Three secondary bedrooms with 9-ft. ceilings have easy access to a split bath. The center bedroom features a built-in desk with shelves above. Two of the bedrooms have walk-in closets.
- A convenient half-bath and a good-sized laundry room are located near the two-car garage, which offers additional storage space and excellent lighting from three bright windows.

Plan APS-2117	
Bedrooms: 4	**Baths:** 2½
Living Area:	
Main floor	2,187 sq. ft.
Total Living Area:	**2,187 sq. ft.**
Garage	460 sq. ft.
Exterior Wall Framing:	2x4
Foundation Options:	

Crawlspace
(All plans can be built with your choice of foundation and framing. A generic conversion diagram is available. See order form.)

| **BLUEPRINT PRICE CODE:** | C |

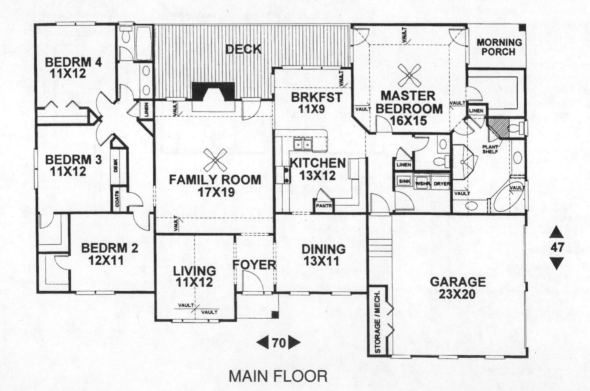

MAIN FLOOR

Plan APS-2117
PRICES AND DETAILS
ON PAGES 12-15

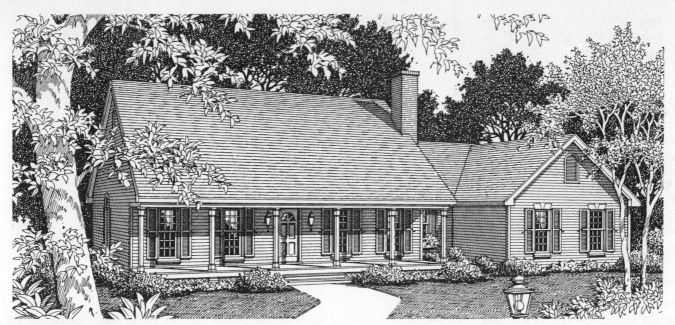

Versatile Sun Room

- This cozy country-style home offers an inviting front porch and an interior just as welcoming.
- The spacious living room features a warming fireplace and windows that overlook the porch.
- The living room opens to a dining area, where French doors access a covered porch and a sunny patio.
- The island kitchen has a sink view, plenty of counter space, and a handy pass-through to the adjoining sun room. The bright sun room is large enough to serve as a formal dining room, a family room or a hobby room.
- The private master suite is secluded to the rear. A garden spa tub, dual walk-in closets and separate dressing areas are nice features found in the master bath.

Plan J-90014

Bedrooms: 3	Baths: 2½
Living Area:	
Main floor	2,190 sq. ft.
Total Living Area:	**2,190 sq. ft.**
Standard basement	2,190 sq. ft.
Garage	465 sq. ft.
Storage	34 sq. ft.
Exterior Wall Framing:	2x6

Foundation Options:

Standard basement
Crawlspace
Slab

(All plans can be built with your choice of foundation and framing. A generic conversion diagram is available. See order form.)

BLUEPRINT PRICE CODE:	C

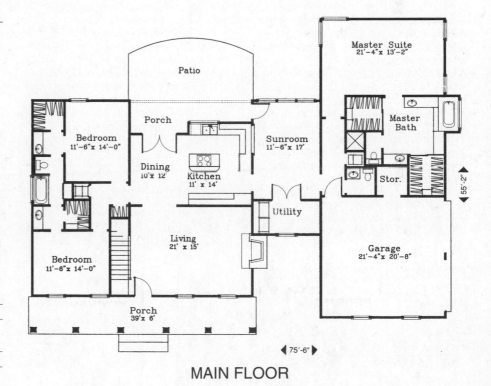

MAIN FLOOR

A Move Up

- Narrow lap siding and repeated round-top windows with divided panes give this traditional home a different look.
- The roomy interior offers space for the upwardly mobile family, with four to five bedrooms and large activity areas.
- The two-story foyer welcomes guests into a spacious formal area that combines the living and dining rooms. The rooms share a dramatic 13-ft. cathedral ceiling, while a handsome fireplace adds a peaceful glow.
- Behind double doors is a cozy study or fifth bedroom.
- A second fireplace and a media center make the family room a fun retreat. French doors open to a lovely terrace.
- Adjoining the family room is a well-designed kitchen with a bayed dinette.
- Double doors introduce the secluded master suite, which boasts a 12-ft. sloped ceiling and a quiet terrace. The private bath offers an invigorating whirlpool tub under a skylight.
- Three more bedrooms and another bath occupy the upper floor.

Plan AHP-9396

Bedrooms: 4+	Baths: 2½
Living Area:	
Upper floor	643 sq. ft.
Main floor	1,553 sq. ft.
Total Living Area:	**2,196 sq. ft.**
Standard basement	1,553 sq. ft.
Garage and storage	502 sq. ft.
Exterior Wall Framing:	2x4 or 2x6

Foundation Options:
Standard basement
Crawlspace
Slab
(All plans can be built with your choice of foundation and framing. A generic conversion diagram is available. See order form.)

BLUEPRINT PRICE CODE:	C

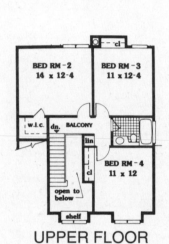

UPPER FLOOR

VIEW INTO LIVING AND DINING ROOMS

MAIN FLOOR

TO ORDER THIS BLUEPRINT, CALL TOLL-FREE 1-800-820-1283   Plan AHP-9396   **PRICES AND DETAILS ON PAGES 12-15**

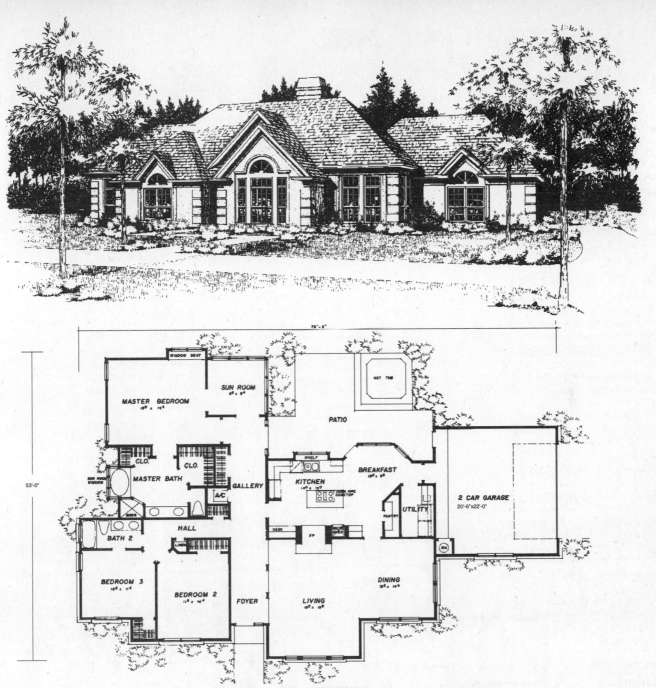

French Flair

- Quoins and semi-circular transoms give this French country home elegance and charm.
- The formal living areas at the front of the home combine for a huge entertainment center; a see-thru fireplace opens to the large island kitchen and bayed breakfast room, opposite.
- A rear patio offers a perfect spot for a hot tub.
- The foyer isolates the bedrooms; a gallery and luxury bath with garden tub and separate shower buffer the master suite and private sun room.

Plan DW-2198	
Bedrooms: 3	**Baths: 2**
Space:	
Main floor	2,198 sq. ft.
Total Living Area	**2,198 sq. ft.**
Basement	2,198 sq. ft.
Garage	451 sq. ft.
Exterior Wall Framing	2x4
Foundation options:	
Standard Basement	
Crawlspace	
Slab	
(Foundation & framing conversion diagram available—see order form.)	
Blueprint Price Code	C

Classic Styling

- This handsome one-story traditional would look great in town or in the country. The shuttered and paned windows, narrow lap siding and brick accents make it a classic.
- The sprawling design begins with the spacious, central living room, featuring a beamed ceiling that slopes up to 14 feet. A window wall overlooks the covered backyard porch, and an inviting fireplace includes an extra-wide hearth and built-in bookshelves.
- The galley-style kitchen features a snack bar to the sunny eating area and a raised-panel door to the dining room.
- The isolated master suite is a quiet haven offering a large walk-in closet, a dressing room and a spacious bath.
- Three more bedrooms, two with walk-in closets, and a compartmentalized bath are located at the opposite side of the home.

Plan E-2206	
Bedrooms: 4	**Baths:** 2
Living Area:	
Main floor	2,200 sq. ft.
Total Living Area:	**2,200 sq. ft.**
Standard basement	2,200 sq. ft.
Garage and storage	624 sq. ft.
Exterior Wall Framing:	2x6

Foundation Options:

Standard basement
Crawlspace
Slab

(All plans can be built with your choice of foundation and framing. A generic conversion diagram is available. See order form.)

BLUEPRINT PRICE CODE:	C

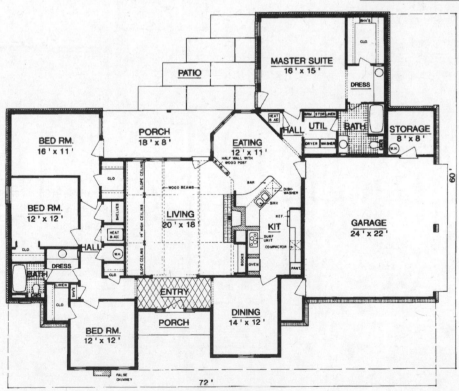

MAIN FLOOR

Plan E-2206

Tradition Recreated

- Classic traditional styling is recreated in this home with its covered porch, triple dormers and half-round windows.
- A central hall stems from the two-story-high foyer and accesses each of the main living areas.
- A large formal space is created with the merging of the living room and the dining room. The living room boasts a fireplace and a view of the front porch.
- The informal spaces merge at the rear of the home. The kitchen features an oversized cooktop island. The sunny dinette is enclosed with a circular glass wall. The family room boasts a media center and access to the rear terrace.
- A convenient main-floor laundry room sits near the garage entrance.
- The upper floor includes three secondary bedrooms that share a full bath, and a spacious master bedroom that offers dual walk-in closets and a large private bath.

Plan AHP-9393

Bedrooms: 4+	Baths: 3
Living Area:	
Upper floor	989 sq. ft.
Main floor	1,223 sq. ft.
Total Living Area:	**2,212 sq. ft.**
Standard basement	1,223 sq. ft.
Garage and storage	488 sq. ft.
Exterior Wall Framing:	2x4 or 2x6

Foundation Options:
Standard basement
Crawlspace
Slab
(Typical foundation & framing conversion diagram available—see order form.)

BLUEPRINT PRICE CODE: C

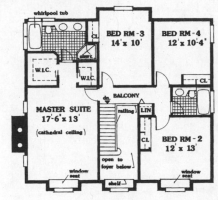

UPPER FLOOR

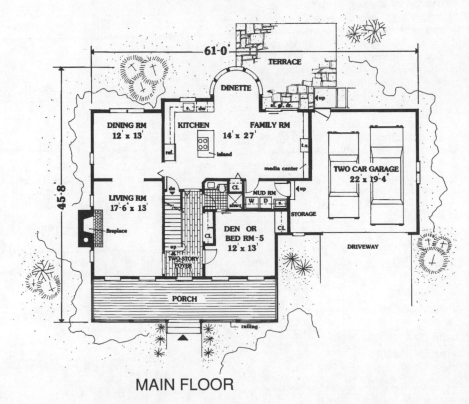

MAIN FLOOR

TO ORDER THIS BLUEPRINT,
CALL TOLL-FREE 1-800-820-1283

Plan AHP-9393

PRICES AND DETAILS
ON PAGES 12-15

103

Fantastic Floor Plan!

- Featured on "Hometime," the popular PBS television program, this unique design combines a dynamic exterior with a fantastic floor plan.
- The barrel-vaulted entry leads into the vaulted foyer, which is outlined by elegant columns. To the left, the living room features a 13-ft. vaulted ceiling, a curved wall and corner windows. To the right, the formal dining room is enhanced by a tray ceiling.
- Overlooking a large backyard deck, the island kitchen includes a corner pantry and a built-in desk. The breakfast room shares a columned snack bar with the family room, which has a fireplace and a 17-ft., 8-in. vaulted ceiling.
- The master suite boasts a 15-ft. vaulted ceiling and private access to a romantic courtyard. The sunken master bath features an enticing spa tub and a separate shower, both encased by a curved glass-block wall.
- The two upstairs bedrooms have private access to a large full bath.

Plan B-88015

Bedrooms: 3	Baths: 2½
Living Area:	
Upper floor	534 sq. ft.
Main floor	1,689 sq. ft.
Total Living Area:	**2,223 sq. ft.**
Standard basement	1,689 sq. ft.
Garage	455 sq. ft.
Exterior Wall Framing:	2x4

Foundation Options:

Standard basement

(All plans can be built with your choice of foundation and framing. A generic conversion diagram is available. See order form.)

BLUEPRINT PRICE CODE: C

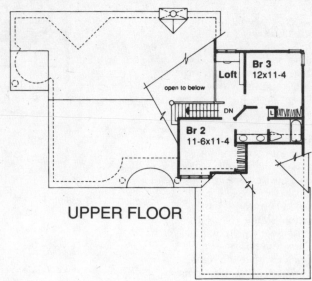

UPPER FLOOR

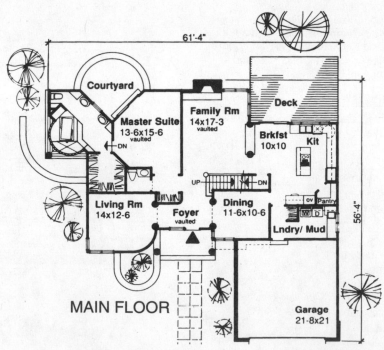

MAIN FLOOR

TO ORDER THIS BLUEPRINT, CALL TOLL-FREE 1-800-820-1283

Plan B-88015

PRICES AND DETAILS ON PAGES 12-15

Traditional Family

- A cute columned porch adds character to this traditional family home.
- A walk-in closet and a half-bath in the two-story foyer accommodate guests.
- To the right, the formal living and dining rooms make entertaining your guests a snap.
- The open kitchen includes a space-saving island and a windowed sink. Sliding glass doors in the bright dinette extend dining to an enormous patio that is perfect for a barbecue.
- A striking 11-ft. cathedral ceiling soars over the family room, where a cozy fireplace adds warmth.
- An open staircase leads up to the magnificent master bedroom, which is embellished with a 9½-ft. tray ceiling and a private whirlpool bath.
- Three secondary bedrooms share a conveniently located full bath.

Plan GL-2223	
Bedrooms: 4	**Baths: 2½**
Living Area:	
Upper floor	1,007 sq. ft.
Main floor	1,216 sq. ft.
Total Living Area:	**2,223 sq. ft.**
Standard basement	1,207 sq. ft.
Garage	484 sq. ft.
Exterior Wall Framing:	**2x6**
Foundation Options:	
Standard basement	

(All plans can be built with your choice of foundation and framing. A generic conversion diagram is available. See order form.)

| **BLUEPRINT PRICE CODE:** | **C** |

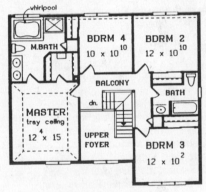

UPPER FLOOR

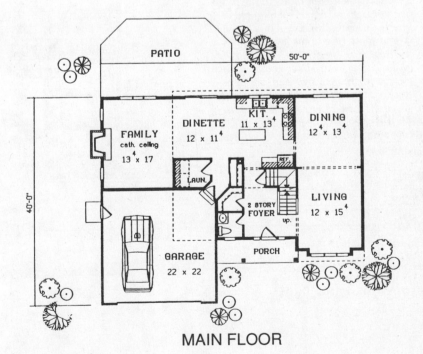

MAIN FLOOR

Peace of Mind

- Peace and privacy were the inspiration for this tranquil home.
- Past the inviting columned entry, the bright foyer flows into the spacious 13½-ft.-high vaulted living room, which includes a wet bar.
- The gourmet kitchen enjoys a 14-ft. vaulted ceiling and includes an angled snack counter and a large pantry. Sliding glass doors in the adjoining breakfast nook lead to a covered patio with a functional summer kitchen.
- The adjacent family room boasts a 15-ft. vaulted ceiling and a handsome window-flanked fireplace.
- The master suite offers an 11½-ft. vaulted ceiling, a windowed sitting area and patio access. His-and-hers walk-in closets flank the entrance to the plush master bath, which is highlighted by a garden tub overlooking a privacy yard.
- Three more bedrooms have vaulted ceilings that are at least 11½ ft. high. With a nearby full bath and back door entrance, the rear bedroom could be made into a great guest or in-law suite.

Plan HDS-99-157

Bedrooms: 4	Baths: 3

Living Area:	
Main floor	2,224 sq. ft.

Total Living Area:	**2,224 sq. ft.**
Garage	507 sq. ft.

Exterior Wall Framing:
2x4 and concrete block

Foundation Options:
Slab
(All plans can be built with your choice of foundation and framing. A generic conversion diagram is available. See order form.)

BLUEPRINT PRICE CODE: C

MAIN FLOOR

Plan HDS-99-157

PRICES AND DETAILS ON PAGES 12-15

Charming Chateau

- A two-story arched entry introduces this charming French chateau.
- To the left of the tiled foyer, the elegant formal dining room will impress friends when you entertain.
- In the kitchen, a handy island worktop and a step-in pantry take advantage of the unique space. The cheery breakfast nook is a great spot for family meals.
- A neat see-through fireplace and built-in bookshelves define the formal living

room and the casual family room. Lovely French doors open to a quiet covered porch in back.
- The secluded master suite on the main floor boasts two enormous walk-in closets and a lush private bath with an inviting marble tub, a separate shower and his-and-hers vanities.
- The kitchen and the nook have 9- and 8-ft. ceilings, respectively. All other main-floor rooms are enhanced by soaring 10-ft. ceilings.
- On the upper floor, two bedrooms share a unique bath. The front bedroom offers a 10-ft. ceiling. A bonus room can be adapted to fit your future needs.

Plan RD-2225	
Bedrooms: 3+	**Baths:** 2½
Living Area:	
Upper floor	547 sq. ft.
Main floor	1,678 sq. ft.
Total Living Area:	**2,225 sq. ft.**
Bonus room (unfinished)	136 sq. ft.
Garage and storage	519 sq. ft.
Exterior Wall Framing:	2x4
Foundation Options:	
Crawlspace	
Slab	

(All plans can be built with your choice of foundation and framing. A generic conversion diagram is available. See order form.)

BLUEPRINT PRICE CODE:	**C**

MAIN FLOOR

UPPER FLOOR

Appealing and Well-Appointed

- A feature-filled interior and a warm, appealing exterior are the keynotes of this spacious two-story home.

- Beyond the charming front porch, the foyer is brightened by sidelights and an octagonal window. To the right, a cased opening leads into the open living room and dining room. Plenty of windows, including a beautiful boxed-out window, bathe the formal area in light.

- The casual area consists of an extra-large island kitchen, a sizable breakfast area and a spectacular family room with a corner fireplace and a skylighted cathedral ceiling that slopes from 11 ft. to 17 ft. high.

- The upper floor hosts a superb master suite, featuring a skylighted bath with an 11-ft. sloped ceiling, a platform spa tub and a separate shower.

- A balcony hall leads to two more bedrooms, a full bath and an optional bonus room that would make a great loft, study or extra bedroom.

Plan AX-8923-A

Bedrooms: 3+	Baths: 2½
Living Area:	
Upper floor	853 sq. ft.
Main floor	1,199 sq. ft.
Optional loft/bedroom	180 sq. ft.
Total Living Area:	**2,232 sq. ft.**
Standard basement	1,184 sq. ft.
Garage	420 sq. ft.
Exterior Wall Framing:	**2x4**

Foundation Options:
Standard basement
Slab
(All plans can be built with your choice of foundation and framing. A generic conversion diagram is available. See order form.)

BLUEPRINT PRICE CODE: C

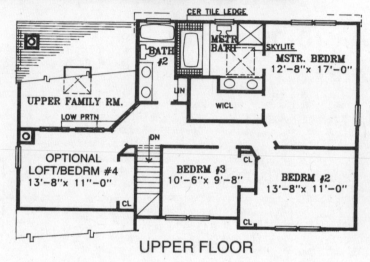

UPPER FLOOR

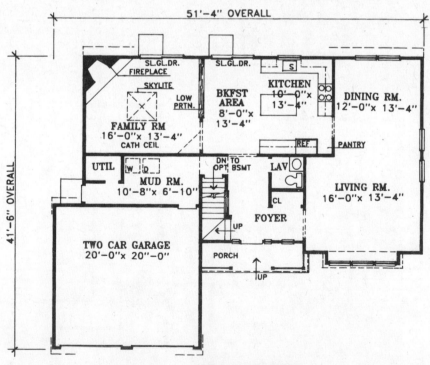

MAIN FLOOR

TO ORDER THIS BLUEPRINT, CALL TOLL-FREE 1-800-820-1283

Plan AX-8923-A

PRICES AND DETAILS ON PAGES 12-15

Sunny Comfort

- A covered wraparound porch and lovely arched windows give this home a comfortable country style.
- Inside, an elegant columned archway introduces the formal dining room.
- The huge Great Room features an 18-ft. vaulted ceiling, a dramatic wall of windows and two built-in wall units on either side of the fireplace.
- Ample counter space and a convenient work island allow maximum use of the roomy kitchen.
- The sunny breakfast nook opens to a porch through sliding glass doors.
- On the other side of the home, a dramatic bay window and a 10-ft. ceiling highlight the master bedroom. The enormous master bath features a luxurious whirlpool tub.
- Unless otherwise noted, all main-floor rooms have 9-ft. ceilings.
- Open stairs lead up to a balcony with a magnificent view of the Great Room. Two upstairs bedrooms, one with an 11-ft. vaulted ceiling, share a bath.

Plan AX-94317

Bedrooms: 3	Baths: 2½
Living Area:	
Upper floor	525 sq. ft.
Main floor	1,720 sq. ft.
Total Living Area:	**2,245 sq. ft.**
Standard basement	1,720 sq. ft.
Garage	502 sq. ft.
Storage/utility	51 sq. ft.
Exterior Wall Framing:	2x4

Foundation Options:

Standard basement

Crawlspace

Slab

(All plans can be built with your choice of foundation and framing. A generic conversion diagram is available. See order form.)

BLUEPRINT PRICE CODE: C

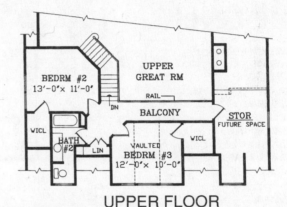

UPPER FLOOR

MAIN FLOOR

Luxurious Living on One Level

- The elegant exterior of this spacious one-story presents a classic air of quality and distinction.
- Three French doors brighten the inviting entry, which flows into the spacious living room. Boasting a 13-ft. ceiling, the living room enjoys a fireplace with a wide hearth and adjoining built-in bookshelves. A wall of glass, including a French door, provides views of the sheltered backyard porch.
- A stylish angled counter joins the spacious kitchen to the sunny bay-windowed eating nook.
- Secluded for privacy, the master suite features a nice dressing area, a large walk-in closet and private backyard access. A convenient laundry/utility room is adjacent to the master bath.
- At the opposite end of the home, double doors lead to three more bedrooms, a compartmentalized bath and lots of closet space.

Plan E-2208

Bedrooms: 4	**Baths:** 2
Living Area:	
Main floor	2,252 sq. ft.
Total Living Area:	**2,252 sq. ft.**
Standard basement	2,252 sq. ft.
Garage and storage	592 sq. ft.
Exterior Wall Framing:	2x6

Foundation Options:

Standard basement
Crawlspace
Slab
(All plans can be built with your choice of foundation and framing. A generic conversion diagram is available. See order form.)

BLUEPRINT PRICE CODE: C

Floor Plan

- BED RM. 16' x 11'
- BED RM. 12' x 12'
- BATH
- DRESS
- HALL
- BED RM 14' x 12'
- PORCH 18' x 8'
- LIVING 20' x 18'
- EATING 10' x 8'
- KIT
- ENTRY 16' x 6'
- PORCH 16' x 4'
- DINING 14' x 14'
- MASTER SUITE 16' x 15'
- CLO.
- DRESS
- UTIL
- BATH
- STORAGE 8' x 8'
- GARAGE 24' x 22'
- ATTIC STAIRS

60'

72'

MAIN FLOOR

Eye-Catching Hillside Design

Main floor: 1,010 sq. ft.
Upper floor: 958 sq. ft.
Lower level: 290 sq. ft.

Total living area: 2,258 sq. ft.
(Not counting garage)

PLAN P-6604-4D

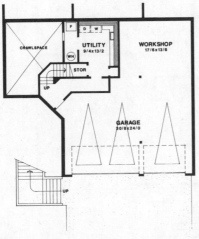

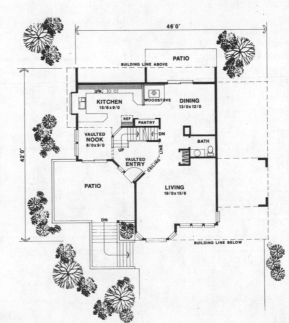

Blueprint Price Code C

**TO ORDER THIS BLUEPRINT,
CALL TOLL-FREE 1-800-820-1283**

Plan P-6604-4D

**PRICES AND DETAILS
ON PAGES 12-15**

111

At Home on the Farm

- With its magnificent wraparound covered porch, this classic country-style design would look at home nestled into green, rolling farmland.
- The airy foyer introduces the Great Room to the right, where a gorgeous fireplace resides.
- A central breakfast nook basks in the glow from a wide window arrangement. Porch access is immediate and laundry facilities are out of sight.
- Amenities in the kitchen include a tidy pantry and an oversized island for meal preparation. A door to the formal dining room muffles kitchen noise.
- Upstairs, the master bedroom flaunts a walk-in closet and a stunning bath that includes a spa tub, a separate shower and his-and-hers vanities.
- Along the hallway, two large secondary bedrooms share another full bath.
- A breathtaking Palladian window lights up a window seat in a restful sitting area off the balcony, making it a wonderful place to finish that novel or cross-stitch pattern.

Plan C-9430

Bedrooms: 3	Baths: 2½
Living Area:	
Upper floor	1,138 sq. ft.
Main floor	1,125 sq. ft.
Total Living Area:	**2,263 sq. ft.**
Daylight basement	1,125 sq. ft.
Exterior Wall Framing:	2x4

Foundation Options:

Daylight basement

Crawlspace

(All plans can be built with your choice of foundation and framing. A generic conversion diagram is available. See order form.)

BLUEPRINT PRICE CODE: **C**

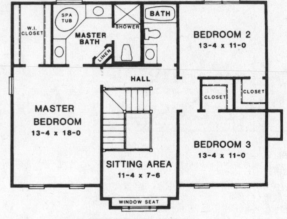

UPPER FLOOR

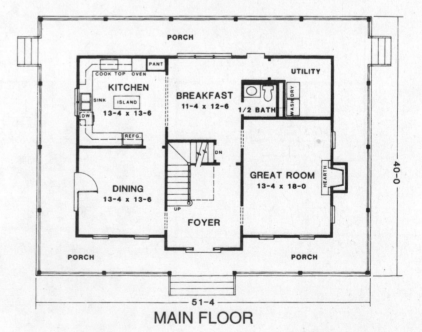

MAIN FLOOR

TO ORDER THIS BLUEPRINT, CALL TOLL-FREE 1-800-820-1283

Plan C-9430

PRICES AND DETAILS ON PAGES 12-15

A Palette of Pleasures

- This stylish traditional brick home has a palette of popular features that serves to enhance family living.
- The formal living spaces are located at the front of the home, flanking the foyer. The dining room is enhanced by a 9-ft. tray ceiling, while the living room boasts a 12-ft. cathedral ceiling.
- A combination kitchen, breakfast nook and family room is oriented to the rear of the home. A pass-through and a snack bar open to the family room, which features a fireplace, a 14-ft.-high vaulted ceiling and deck access.
- The secluded master bedroom offers a 9-ft. tray ceiling and private deck access. The posh master bath boasts a 13-ft. cathedral ceiling and his-and-hers walk-in closets. Dual vanities sit opposite a garden tub and a separate shower.
- Across the home, two secondary bedrooms have walk-in closets and share another full bath. A laundry/utility room and garage access are nearby.

Plan APS-2309

Bedrooms: 3	Baths: 2
Living Area:	
Main floor	2,275 sq. ft.
Total Living Area:	**2,275 sq. ft.**
Standard basement	2,275 sq. ft.
Garage	418 sq. ft.
Exterior Wall Framing:	2x4

Foundation Options:

Standard basement

(All plans can be built with your choice of foundation and framing. A generic conversion diagram is available. See order form.)

BLUEPRINT PRICE CODE: C

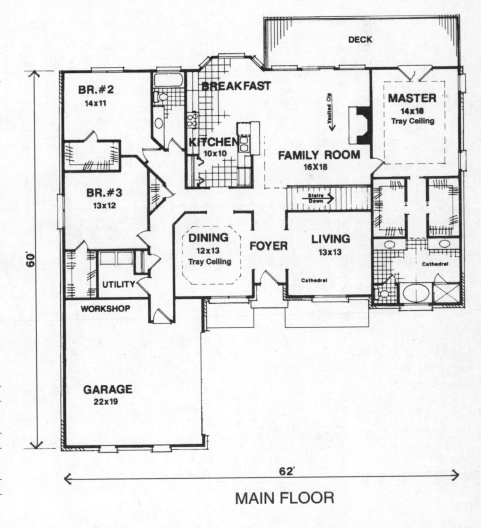

MAIN FLOOR

Stunning Windows

- This one-story design is enhanced by stunning window arrangements that brighten the formal areas and beyond.
- A step down from the skylighted foyer, the living room sparkles, with a tray ceiling, a striking fireplace and a turret-like bay with high arched windows.
- The island kitchen easily services the sunny bayed dining room and includes a built-in desk, a garden sink and an eating bar to the bright, vaulted nook.
- The adjoining vaulted family room is warmed by a corner woodstove and overlooks the rear patio.
- A decorative plant shelf introduces the bedroom wing. Double doors reveal the master bedroom, which boasts a tray ceiling, a rear window wall and access to the patio. The skylighted master bath includes a raised ceiling, a step-up garden spa tub and a separate shower.
- Across the hall, a den and a second bedroom share another full bath, while the utility room offers garage access.

Plans P-7754-3A & -3D

Bedrooms: 2+	Baths: 2
Living Area:	
Main floor (crawlspace version)	2,200 sq. ft.
Main floor (basement version)	2,288 sq. ft.
Total Living Area:	**2,200/2,288 sq. ft.**
Daylight basement	2,244 sq. ft.
Garage	722 sq. ft.
Exterior Wall Framing:	**2x4**
Foundation Options:	**Plan #**
Daylight basement	P-7754-3D
Crawlspace	P-7754-3A

(All plans can be built with your choice of foundation and framing. A generic conversion diagram is available. See order form.)

BLUEPRINT PRICE CODE:	**C**

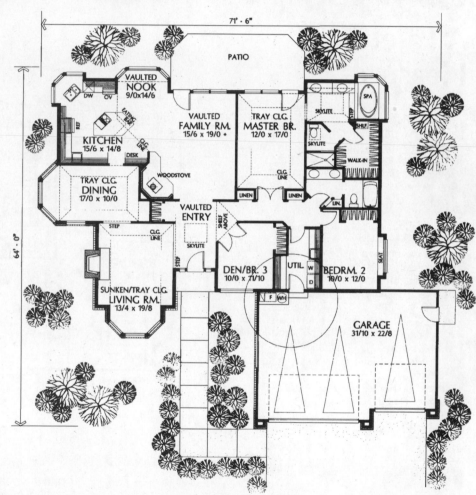

MAIN FLOOR

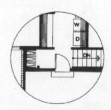

BASEMENT STAIRWAY LOCATION

Distinctive Two-Story

- The playful and distinctive exterior of this two-story encloses a functional, contemporary interior.
- The living areas unfold from the skylighted foyer, which is open to the upper-floor balcony. The formal sunken living room features a soaring 17-ft. cathedral ceiling. The adjoining step-down family room offers a fireplace and sliding glass doors to a wonderful deck.
- A low partition allows a view of the family room's fireplace from the breakfast area and the island kitchen.
- A luxurious master suite with a 13-ft. cathedral ceiling and room for three additional bedrooms are found on the upper floor, in addition to a dramatic view of the foyer below.

Plan AX-8922-A

Bedrooms: 3+	Baths: 2½
Living Area:	
Upper floor	840 sq. ft.
Main floor	1,213 sq. ft.
Fourth bedroom	240 sq. ft.
Total Living Area:	**2,293 sq. ft.**
Standard basement	1,138 sq. ft.
Garage	470 sq. ft.
Exterior Wall Framing:	2x4

Foundation Options:

Standard basement
Slab

(All plans can be built with your choice of foundation and framing. A generic conversion diagram is available. See order form.)

BLUEPRINT PRICE CODE: C

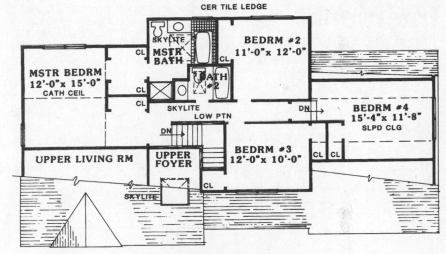

UPPER FLOOR

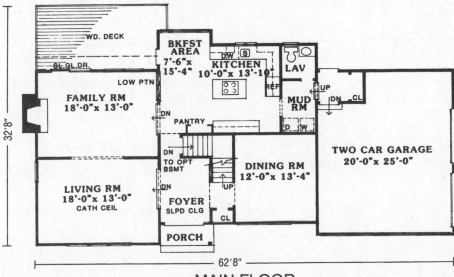

MAIN FLOOR

Gracious Traditional

- This traditional home is perfect for a corner lot, with a quaint facade and an attached garage around back.
- Tall windows, elegant dormers and a covered front porch welcome guests to the front entry and into the foyer.
- Just off the foyer, the formal dining room boasts a built-in hutch and views to the front porch.
- The expansive, skylighted Great Room features a wet bar, a 16-ft. vaulted

ceiling, a stunning fireplace and access to the screened back porch.
- The kitchen includes a large pantry and an eating bar to the bayed breakfast nook. A large utility room with garage access is nearby.
- The master bedroom offers a walk-in closet and a bath with a large corner tub and his-and-hers vanities.
- Two additional bedrooms have big walk-in closets, built-in desks and easy access to another full bath.
- Upstairs, a loft overlooks the Great Room and is perfect as an extra bedroom or a recreation area.

Plan C-8920

Bedrooms: 3+	Baths: 3
Living Area:	
Upper floor	305 sq. ft.
Main floor	1,996 sq. ft.
Total Living Area:	**2,301 sq. ft.**
Daylight basement	1,996 sq. ft.
Garage	469 sq. ft.
Exterior Wall Framing:	2x4

Foundation Options:

Daylight basement
Crawlspace
(All plans can be built with your choice of foundation and framing. A generic conversion diagram is available. See order form.)

BLUEPRINT PRICE CODE: C

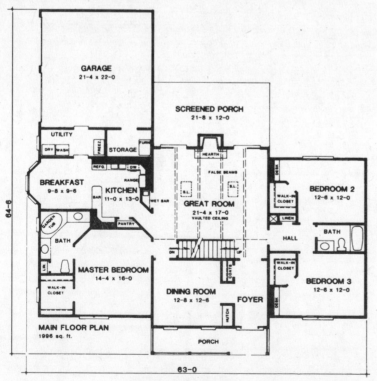

MAIN FLOOR

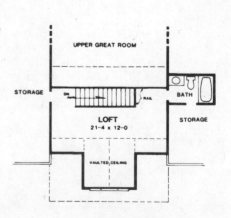

UPPER FLOOR

TO ORDER THIS BLUEPRINT, CALL TOLL-FREE 1-800-820-1283   Plan C-8920   *PRICES AND DETAILS ON PAGES 12-15*

Contemporary Elegance

- This striking contemporary design combines vertical siding with elegant traditional overtones.
- Inside, an expansive activity area is created with the joining of the vaulted living room, the family/dining room and the kitchen. The openness of the rooms creates a spacious, dramatic feeling, which extends to an exciting two-story sun space and a patio beyond.

- A convenient utility/service area near the garage includes a clothes-sorting counter, a deep sink and ironing space.
- Two bedrooms share a bright bath to round out the main floor.
- Upstairs, the master suite includes a sumptuous skylighted bath with two entrances. The tub is positioned on an angled wall, while the shower and toilet are secluded behind a pocket door. An optional overlook provides views down into the sun space, which is accessed by a spiral staircase.
- A versatile loft area and a large bonus room complete this design.

Plan LRD-1971	
Bedrooms: 3+	**Baths:** 2
Living Area:	
Upper floor	723 sq. ft.
Main floor	1,248 sq. ft.
Sun space	116 sq. ft.
Bonus room	225 sq. ft.
Total Living Area:	**2,312 sq. ft.**
Standard basement	1,248 sq. ft.
Garage	483 sq. ft.
Exterior Wall Framing:	2x6

Foundation Options:

Standard basement

Crawlspace

(All plans can be built with your choice of foundation and framing. A generic conversion diagram is available. See order form.)

BLUEPRINT PRICE CODE: **C**

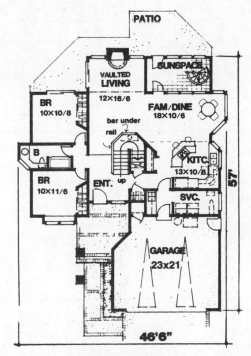

MAIN FLOOR

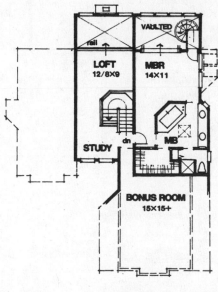

UPPER FLOOR

Triple Treat!

- With three exciting and distinctive front elevation options included, this ranch design is sure to please.
- The interior has something for everyone as well. The formal dining room, to the right of the foyer, is graced with an elegant transom window-wall.
- The formal living room has a vaulted ceiling and handsome columns to define its perimeter.
- The heart of the plan is the family room, which has a fireplace flanked by sliders which lead to the rear covered patio.
- The galley kitchen overlooks the family room and the sunny breakfast eating area.
- Two bedrooms lie on the left side of the plan, while the master suite lies on the right side with a den/fourth bedroom which can be privately used as a master sitting room.

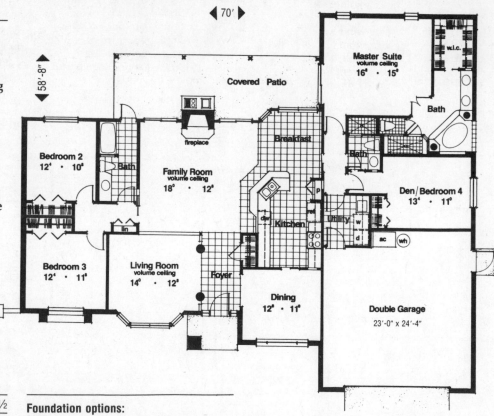

Plan HDS-90-804

Bedrooms: 3-4	Baths: 2½
Space:	
Total living area:	2,321 sq. ft.
Garage:	498 sq. ft.
Exterior Wall Framing:	2x4 and concrete

Foundation options:
Slab.
(Foundation & framing conversion diagram available — see order form.)

Blueprint Price Code: C

Plan HDS-90-804

Grand Colonial Home

- This grand Colonial home boasts a porch entry framed by bay windows and gable towers.
- The two-story foyer flows to the dining room on the left and adjoins the bayed living room on the right, with its warm fireplace and flanking windows.
- At the rear, the family room features a 17-ft. ceiling, a media wall, a bar and terrace access through French doors.
- Connected to the family room is a high-tech kitchen with an island work area, a pantry, a work desk and a circular dinette.
- A private terrace, a romantic fireplace, a huge walk-in closet and a lavish bath with a whirlpool tub are featured in the main-floor master suite.
- Three bedrooms and two full baths share the upper floor.

Plan AHP-9120

Bedrooms: 4	Baths: 3
Living Area:	
Upper floor	776 sq. ft.
Main floor	1,551 sq. ft.
Total Living Area:	**2,327 sq. ft.**
Standard basement	1,580 sq. ft.
Garage	440 sq. ft.
Exterior Wall Framing:	2x4 or 2x6

Foundation Options:

Standard basement

Crawlspace

Slab

(All plans can be built with your choice of foundation and framing. A generic conversion diagram is available. See order form.)

BLUEPRINT PRICE CODE: C

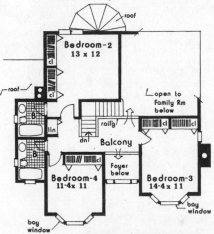

UPPER FLOOR

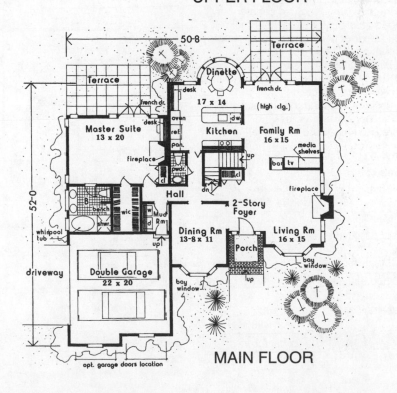

MAIN FLOOR

Impressive Columns

- Impressive columns and striking stucco give this home a distinguished look.
- Inside, a 14-ft. ceiling extends above the foyer, the formal living and dining rooms and the inviting family room.
- The stunning raised dining room is set off by decorative wood columns that support a wraparound overhead plant shelf. A two-way fireplace is shared with the family room, which also features built-in shelves and arched windows that overlook a large deck.
- The study includes built-in bookshelves and a ceiling that vaults to 13½ feet.
- The kitchen has an angled counter bar and a corner pantry while the breakfast nook provides deck access. Both rooms are enhanced by 10-ft. ceilings.
- The large master suite shows off a bayed sitting area and a roomy, private bath. Ceilings heights here are 10 ft. in the sleeping area and 9 ft. in the bath.
- Two secondary bedrooms with 12-ft. vaulted ceilings share a nice hall bath.

Plan DW-2342

Bedrooms: 3+	Baths: 2
Living Area:	
Main floor	2,342 sq. ft.
Total Living Area:	**2,342 sq. ft.**
Standard basement	2,342 sq. ft.
Garage	460 sq. ft.
Exterior Wall Framing:	2x4

Foundation Options:

Standard basement

Crawlspace

Slab

(All plans can be built with your choice of foundation and framing. A generic conversion diagram is available. See order form.)

BLUEPRINT PRICE CODE: C

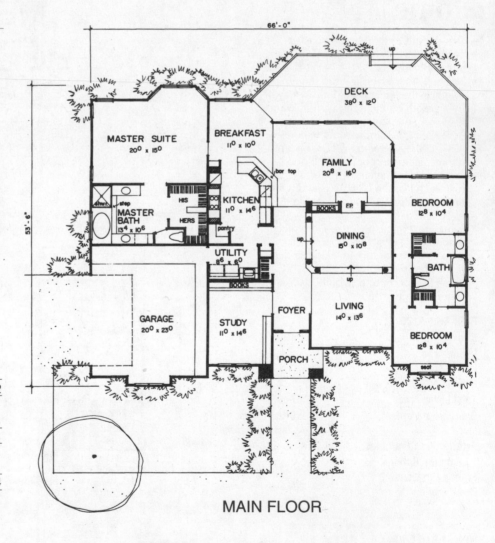

MAIN FLOOR

Plan DW-2342

PRICES AND DETAILS ON PAGES 12-15

Stately Colonial

- This stately Colonial features a covered front entry and a secondary entry near the garage and the utility room.
- The main foyer opens to a comfortable den with elegant double doors.
- The formal living areas adjoin to the left of the foyer and culminate in a lovely bay window overlooking the backyard.
- The open island kitchen has a great central location, easily accessed from each of the living areas. Informal dining can be extended to the outdoors through sliding doors in the dinette.
- A half-wall introduces the big family room, which boasts a high 16-ft., 9-in. vaulted ceiling, an inviting fireplace and optional built-in cabinets.
- The upper floor is shared by four bedrooms, including a spacious master bedroom with a large walk-in closet, a dressing area for two and a private bath. An alternate bath layout is included in the blueprints.
- A bonus room may be added above the garage for additional space.

Plan A-2283-DS

Bedrooms: 4+	Baths: 2½
Living Area:	
Upper floor	1,137 sq. ft.
Main floor	1,413 sq. ft.
Total Living Area:	**2,550 sq. ft.**
Optional bonus room	280 sq. ft.
Standard basement	1,413 sq. ft.
Garage	484 sq. ft.
Exterior Wall Framing:	2x6
Foundation Options:	

Standard basement
(All plans can be built with your choice of foundation and framing. A generic conversion diagram is available. See order form.)

BLUEPRINT PRICE CODE:	D

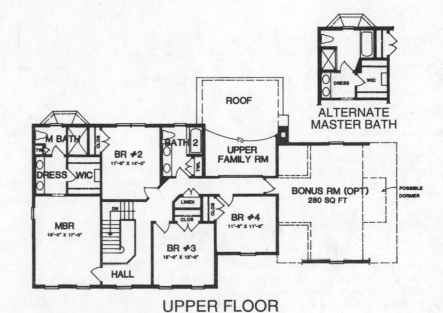

ALTERNATE MASTER BATH

UPPER FLOOR

MAIN FLOOR

One More Time!

- The character and excitement of our most popular plan in recent years, E-3000, have been recaptured in this smaller version of the design.
- The appealing facade is distinguished by a covered front porch and accented with decorative columns, triple dormers and rail-topped corner windows.
- Off the foyer, a central gallery leads to the spacious family room, where a corner fireplace and a 17-ft. vaulted ceiling are highlights. Columns in the gallery introduce the kitchen and the dining areas.
- The kitchen showcases a walk-in pantry, a built-in desk and a long snack bar that serves the eating nook and the dining room.
- The stunning main-floor master suite offers a quiet sitting area and a private angled bath with dual vanities, a corner garden tub and a separate shower.
- A lovely curved stairway leads to a balcony that overlooks the family room and the foyer. Two large bedrooms, a split bath and easily accessible attics are also found upstairs.

Plan E-2307-A

Bedrooms: 3	Baths: 2½
Living Area:	
Upper floor	595 sq. ft.
Main floor	1,765 sq. ft.
Total Living Area:	**2,360 sq. ft.**
Standard basement	1,765 sq. ft.
Garage	484 sq. ft.
Storage	44 sq. ft.
Exterior Wall Framing:	2x6

Foundation Options:

Standard basement
Crawlspace
Slab

(All plans can be built with your choice of foundation and framing. A generic conversion diagram is available. See order form.)

BLUEPRINT PRICE CODE:	C

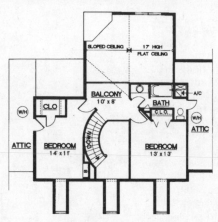

UPPER FLOOR

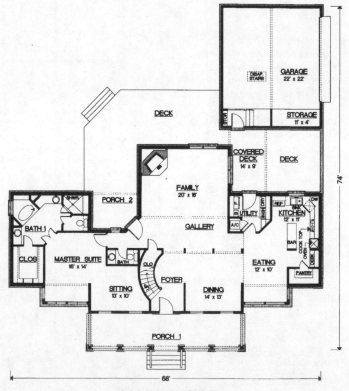

MAIN FLOOR

Plan E-2307-A

PRICES AND DETAILS
ON PAGES 12-15

Arched Accents

- Elegant arches add drama to the covered porch of this lovely home.
- Interior arches flank the two-story-high foyer, offering eye-catching entrances to the formal dining and living rooms.
- A dramatic window-framed fireplace and a 17-ft. ceiling enhance the spacious family room. A columned archway leads into the island kitchen, which offers a convenient serving bar.
- The adjoining breakfast area features a pantry closet, open shelves and a French door to the backyard. A half-bath and a laundry room are close by.
- The ceilings in all main-floor rooms are 9 ft. high unless otherwise specified.
- Upstairs, a balcony overlooks the family room and the foyer. The master suite flaunts a 10-ft. tray ceiling, a beautiful window showpiece and a private bath with a 13-ft. vaulted ceiling and a garden tub. The bedroom may be extended to include a sitting area.
- Boasting its own dressing vanity, the rear-facing bedroom offers private access to a compartmentalized bath that also serves the two remaining bedrooms.

Plan FB-2368

Bedrooms: 4	Baths: 2½
Living Area:	
Upper floor	1,168 sq. ft.
Main floor	1,200 sq. ft.
Total Living Area:	**2,368 sq. ft.**
Daylight basement	1,200 sq. ft.
Garage	504 sq. ft.
Exterior Wall Framing:	2x4

Foundation Options:

Daylight basement

Slab

(All plans can be built with your choice of foundation and framing. A generic conversion diagram is available. See order form.)

BLUEPRINT PRICE CODE: **C**

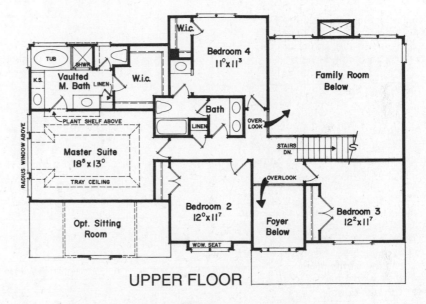

UPPER FLOOR

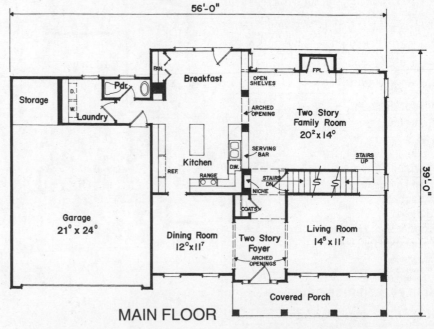

MAIN FLOOR

Classic Lines, Elegant Flair

- The rich brick arches and classic lines of this home lend an elegant look that will never become outdated.
- Inside, graceful archways lead from the two-story-high entry to the living and dining rooms, both of which feature 10-ft., 9-in. ceilings.
- The kitchen offers abundant counter space, an expansive window over the sink, a large island cooktop, a desk and a pantry. The adjoining nook has sliding glass doors to a backyard deck or patio, while the entire area is warmed by the fireplace in the family room.
- A nice study with a bay window is entered through double doors.
- Upstairs, the master suite is a real treat, with a luxurious whirlpool tub and his-and-hers walk-in closets.
- Two more bedrooms, a full bath and a storage room are also included. The storage room could be used as an exercise or hobby room.

Plan R-2083

Bedrooms: 3+	Baths: 2½
Living Area:	
Upper floor	926 sq. ft.
Main floor	1,447 sq. ft.
Total Living Area:	**2,373 sq. ft.**
Garage	609 sq. ft.
Storage	138 sq. ft.
Exterior Wall Framing:	2x6

Foundation Options:

Crawlspace
(All plans can be built with your choice of foundation and framing. A generic conversion diagram is available. See order form.)

BLUEPRINT PRICE CODE: C

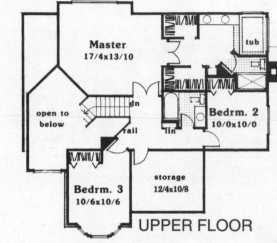

UPPER FLOOR

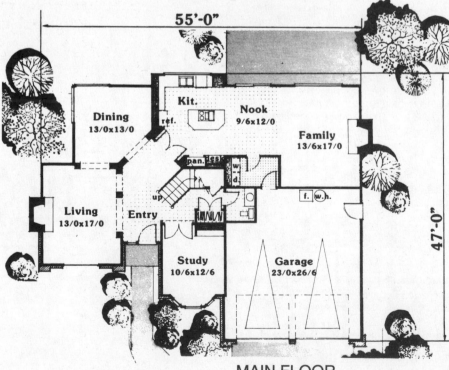

MAIN FLOOR

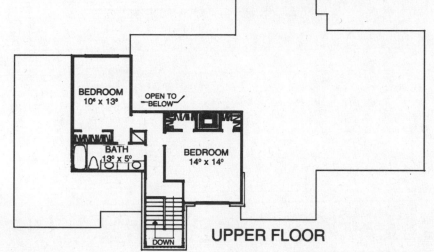

UPPER FLOOR

BEDROOM 10⁸ x 13⁸

OPEN TO BELOW

BATH 13⁰ x 5⁵

BEDROOM 14⁰ x 14⁰

DOWN

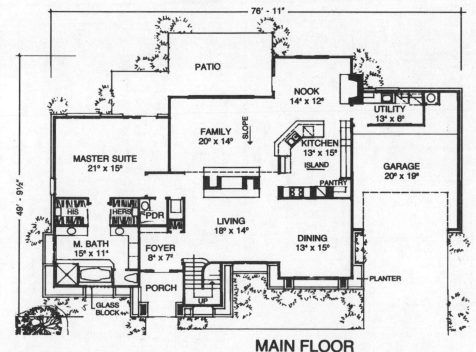

MAIN FLOOR

76' - 11"

49' - 9½"

PATIO

NOOK 14⁴ x 12⁶

UTILITY 13⁴ x 6⁰

FAMILY 20⁰ x 14⁰

SLOPE

KITCHEN 13⁴ x 15⁶

ISLAND

GARAGE 20⁰ x 19⁶

MASTER SUITE 21⁰ x 15⁰

PANTRY

HIS HERS PDR

LIVING 18⁰ x 14⁰

DINING 13⁴ x 15⁰

M. BATH 15⁸ x 11⁴

FOYER 8⁴ x 7²

PORCH

PLANTER

GLASS BLOCK

UP

A Horizontal Emphasis

- A metal roof with 4' overhangs offer this unique home energy savings and distinction; a horizontal emphasis is created with the use of blocks.
- The foyer opens to a spacious living and dining room arrangement with see-thru fireplace.
- The family room, on the other side, has vaulted ceiling and rear window wall overlooking the patio.
- The island kitchen is open to the family room and breakfast nook, which offers a second fireplace.
- The main-floor master suite features his 'n her walk-in closets, access to the adjoining patio and a luxury bath.
- Two additional bedrooms share the upper level.

Plan DW-2394	
Bedrooms: 3	**Baths:** 2 ½
Space:	
Upper floor	501 sq. ft.
Main floor	1,893 sq. ft.
Total Living Area	**2,394 sq. ft.**
Basement	1,893 sq. ft.
Garage	390 sq. ft.
Exterior Wall Framing	2x4
Foundation options:	
Standard Basement	
Crawlspace	
Slab	
(Foundation & framing conversion diagram available—see order form.)	
Blueprint Price Code	C

Emotional Connection

- With radiant windows adorning much of the rear facade, this home promises an emotional connection with the rolling landscape surrounding it.
- Imagine the view from the bayed hearth room, which basks in the warmth from a cheery peninsula fireplace. An eating bar introduces the island kitchen, which boasts a tidy step-in pantry and plenty

of counter space. You can serve breakfast with ease in the corner nook.
- Dazzle your neighbors by displaying the Christmas tree in the windowed corner of the family room. There's plenty of space to gather around for a little family bonding.
- The master suite pampers you with an opulent bath that includes two walk-in closets, twin sinks, a corner whirlpool tub and a sit-down shower.
- For the family on the go, the single garage bay makes a great home for a boat, a snowmobile or a golf cart!

Plan KLF-955	
Bedrooms: 3+	**Baths:** 2
Living Area:	
Main floor	2,394 sq. ft.
Total Living Area:	**2,394 sq. ft.**
Split 3-car garage/storage	818 sq. ft.
Exterior Wall Framing:	2x4
Foundation Options:	
Slab	

(All plans can be built with your choice of foundation and framing. A generic conversion diagram is available. See order form.)

BLUEPRINT PRICE CODE: **C**

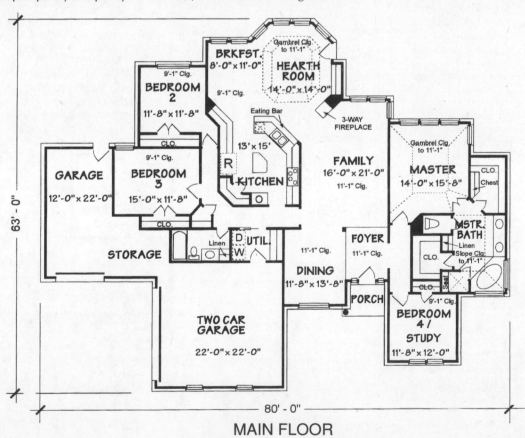

MAIN FLOOR

TO ORDER THIS BLUEPRINT, CALL TOLL-FREE 1-800-820-1283   Plan KLF-955   *PRICES AND DETAILS ON PAGES 12-15*

High Luxury in One Story

- Beautiful arched windows lend a luxurious feeling to the exterior of this one-story home.
- Soaring 12-ft. ceilings add volume to both the wide entry area and the central living room, which boasts a large fireplace and access to a covered porch and the patio beyond.
- Double doors separate the formal dining room from the corridor-style kitchen. Features of the kitchen include a pantry and an angled eating bar. The sunny, bayed eating area is perfect for casual family meals.
- The plush master suite has amazing amenities: a walk-in closet, a skylighted, angled whirlpool tub, a separate shower and private access to the laundry/utility room and the patio.
- Three good-sized bedrooms and a full bath are situated across the home.

Plan E-2302

Bedrooms: 4	Baths: 2
Living Area:	
Main floor	2,396 sq. ft.
Total Living Area:	**2,396 sq. ft.**
Standard basement	2,396 sq. ft.
Garage	484 sq. ft.
Exterior Wall Framing:	2x6

Foundation Options:

Standard basement
Crawlspace
Slab

(All plans can be built with your choice of foundation and framing. A generic conversion diagram is available. See order form.)

BLUEPRINT PRICE CODE:	C

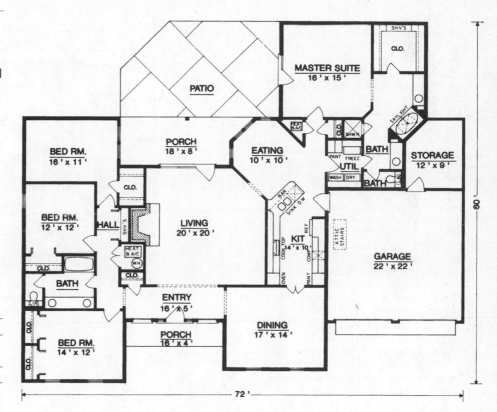

MAIN FLOOR

Captivating Design

- This captivating and award-winning design is introduced by a unique entry landscape that includes striking columns, an exciting fountain courtyard and a private garden.
- The beautiful, open interior commands attention with expansive glass and ceilings at least 10 ft. high throughout.
- The foyer's 15-ft. ceiling extends into the adjoining dining room, which is set off by a decorative glass-block wall.
- A step-down soffit frames the spacious central living room with its dramatic entry columns and 13-ft. ceiling. A rear bay overlooks a large covered patio.
- The gourmet kitchen shows off an oversized island cooktop and snack bar. A pass-through above the sink provides easy service to the patio's summer kitchen, while indoor dining is offered in the sunny, open breakfast area.
- A warm fireplace and flanking storage shelves adorn an exciting media wall in the large adjacent family room.
- The secondary bedrooms share a full bath near the laundry room and garage.
- Behind double doors on the other side of the home, the romantic master suite is bathed in sunlight. A private garden embraces an elegant oval tub.

Plan HDS-99-185

Bedrooms: 3+	Baths: 2½
Living Area:	
Main floor	2,397 sq. ft.
Total Living Area:	**2,397 sq. ft.**
Garage	473 sq. ft.
Exterior Wall Framing:	2x4

Foundation Options:

Slab

(All plans can be built with your choice of foundation and framing. A generic conversion diagram is available. See order form.)

BLUEPRINT PRICE CODE: C

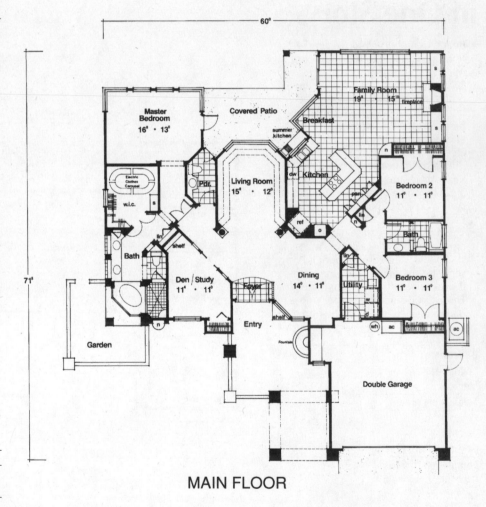

MAIN FLOOR

Plan HDS-99-185

PRICES AND DETAILS
ON PAGES 12-15

Open Country

- With its covered porch and shutters, this home exudes country styling outside and offers an open, expansive interior.
- The two-story entry flows between the formal spaces, and an open-railed stairway overlooks the family room.
- The raised ceiling extends into the central family room, where windows flank a soothing fireplace.
- The open kitchen is a chef's dream, with its central work island, storage room and pantry. Its angled counter allows service to the family room and the breakfast nook. The nook includes a corner window seat and backyard access.
- Nearby, a door opens from the garage, and a utility area has room for a freezer.
- The main-floor master suite boasts a huge, divided walk-in closet, dual vanities and a garden tub.
- The upper floor includes two more bedrooms and a second full bath. A bonus room allows space for another bedroom or a home studio.

Plan RD-2168

Bedrooms: 3+	Baths: 2½
Living Area:	
Upper floor	521 sq. ft.
Main floor	1,647 sq. ft.
Bonus room	240 sq. ft.
Total Living Area:	**2,408 sq. ft.**
Standard basement	1,639 sq. ft.
Garage and storage	576 sq. ft.
Exterior Wall Framing:	2x4

Foundation Options:

Standard basement

Crawlspace

Slab

(All plans can be built with your choice of foundation and framing. A generic conversion diagram is available. See order form.)

BLUEPRINT PRICE CODE:	C

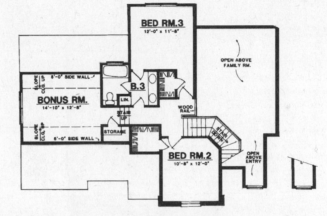

UPPER FLOOR

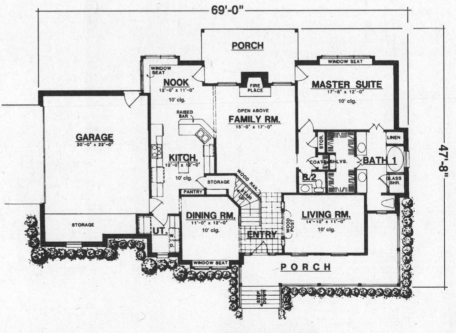

MAIN FLOOR

TO ORDER THIS BLUEPRINT,
CALL TOLL-FREE 1-800-820-1283

Plan RD-2168

PRICES AND DETAILS
ON PAGES 12-15

129

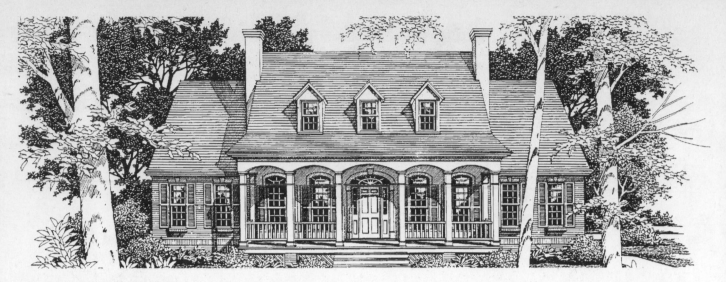

Wonderful Detailing

- The wonderfully detailed front porch, with its graceful arches, columns and railings, gives this home a character all its own. Dormer windows and arched transoms further accentuate the porch.
- The floor plan features a central living room with a 10-ft.-high ceiling and a fireplace framed by French doors. These doors open to a covered porch or a sun room, and a sheltered deck beyond.
- Just off the living room, the island kitchen and breakfast area provide a spacious place for family or guests. The nearby formal dining room has arched transom windows and a 10-ft. ceiling, as does the bedroom off the foyer. All of the remaining rooms have 9-ft. ceilings.
- The unusual master suite includes a window alcove, access to the porch and a fantastic bath with a garden tub.
- A huge utility room, a storage area off the garage and a 1,000-sq.-ft. attic space are other bonuses of this design.

Plan J-90019

Bedrooms: 3	Baths: 2½
Living Area:	
Main floor	2,410 sq. ft.
Total Living Area:	**2,410 sq. ft.**
Standard basement	2,410 sq. ft.
Garage	512 sq. ft.
Storage	86 sq. ft.
Exterior Wall Framing:	2x6

Foundation Options:

Standard basement
Crawlspace
Slab

(All plans can be built with your choice of foundation and framing. A generic conversion diagram is available. See order form.)

BLUEPRINT PRICE CODE: C

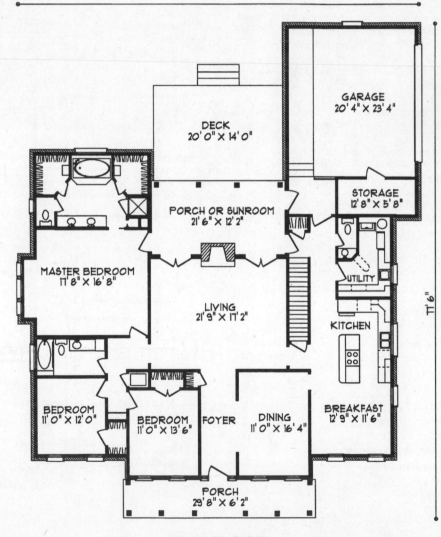

64' 4"

71' 6"

GARAGE
20' 4" X 23' 4"

DECK
20' 0" X 14' 0"

STORAGE
12' 8" X 5' 8"

PORCH OR SUNROOM
21' 6" X 12' 2"

UTILITY

MASTER BEDROOM
17' 8" X 16' 8"

LIVING
21' 9" X 17' 2"

KITCHEN

BEDROOM
11' 0" X 12' 0"

BEDROOM
11' 0" X 13' 6"

FOYER

DINING
11' 0" X 16' 4"

BREAKFAST
12' 9" X 11' 6"

PORCH
29' 8" X 6' 2"

MAIN FLOOR

TO ORDER THIS BLUEPRINT,
CALL TOLL-FREE 1-800-820-1283

Plan J-90019

PRICES AND DETAILS
ON PAGES 12-15

Five-Bedroom Traditional

- This sophisticated traditional home makes a striking statement both inside and out.
- The dramatic two-story foyer is flanked by the formal living spaces. The private dining room overlooks the front porch, while the spacious living room has outdoor views on two sides.
- A U-shaped kitchen with a snack bar, a sunny dinette area and a large family room flow together at the back of the home. The family room's fireplace warms the open, informal expanse, while sliding glass doors in the dinette access the backyard terrace.
- The second floor has five roomy bedrooms and two skylighted bathrooms. The luxurious master suite has a high ceiling with a beautiful arched window, a dressing area and a huge walk-in closet. The private bath offers dual sinks, a whirlpool tub and a separate shower.
- Attic space is located above the garage.

Plan AHP-9392

Bedrooms: 5	Baths: 2½
Living Area:	
Upper floor	1,223 sq. ft.
Main floor	1,193 sq. ft.
Total Living Area:	**2,416 sq. ft.**
Standard basement	1,130 sq. ft.
Garage	509 sq. ft.
Storage	65 sq. ft.
Exterior Wall Framing:	2x4 or 2x6

Foundation Options:

Standard basement
Crawlspace
Slab
(Typical foundation & framing conversion diagram available—see order form.)

BLUEPRINT PRICE CODE: **C**

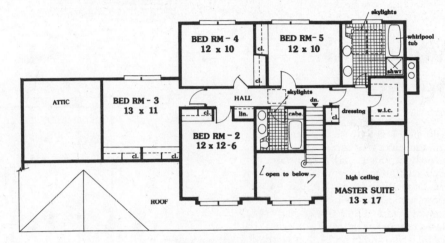

UPPER FLOOR

MAIN FLOOR

Old-Fashioned Charm

- A trio of dormers add old-fashioned charm to this modern design.
- Both the living room and the dining room offer 12-ft.-high vaulted ceilings and flow together to create a sense of even more spaciousness.
- The open kitchen/nook/family room features a sunny alcove, a walk-in pantry and a woodstove.
- A first-floor den and a walk-through utility room are other big bonuses.
- Upstairs, the master suite includes a walk-in closet and a deluxe bath with a spa tub and a separate shower and water closet.
- Two more bedrooms, each with a window seat, and a bonus room complete this stylish design.

Plan CDG-2004

Bedrooms: 3+	Baths: 2½
Living Area:	
Upper floor	928 sq. ft.
Main floor	1,317 sq. ft.
Bonus area	192 sq. ft.
Total Living Area:	**2,437 sq. ft.**
Partial daylight basement	780 sq. ft.
Garage	537 sq. ft.
Exterior Wall Framing:	2x6

Foundation Options:

Partial daylight basement
Crawlspace
(All plans can be built with your choice of foundation and framing. A generic conversion diagram is available. See order form.)

BLUEPRINT PRICE CODE:	**C**

UPPER FLOOR

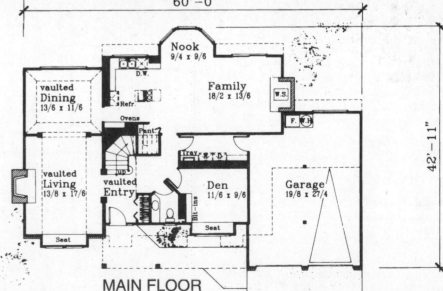

MAIN FLOOR

TO ORDER THIS BLUEPRINT, CALL TOLL-FREE 1-800-820-1283   Plan CDG-2004   *PRICES AND DETAILS ON PAGES 12-15*

Regal Poise

- With its stately brick facade, gorgeous half-round transoms and striking gables, this regal home will grace the most upscale neighborhood.

- A warmly appointed family room anchors the home, boasting a prominent fireplace flanked by built-in cabinets. French doors lead to a covered porch that is suitable for neighborly barbecue parties. Transom windows add dazzle.

- The exciting wraparound kitchen boasts an angled bar and stacked ovens with cookie sheet storage above. The adjoining bayed breakfast nook nestles between two porches.

- Shielded from kitchen noise by double doors, the formal dining room provides an intimate space for special meals.

- Natural light floods the master suite through a brilliant bayed window arrangement. In the master bath, a lush plant shelf overlooks a whirlpool tub and a neat split vanity with knee space.

- In the opposite wing of the home, two good-sized secondary bedrooms share a compartmentalized bath, allowing the kids an extra measure of privacy.

- To the right of the sidelighted foyer, French doors introduce a peaceful study that may also be used as a bedroom.

Plan KLF-941

Bedrooms: 3+	Baths: 2½
Living Area:	
Main floor	2,437 sq. ft.
Total Living Area:	**2,437 sq. ft.**
Garage and storage	589 sq. ft.
Exterior Wall Framing:	2x4

Foundation Options:

Slab
(All plans can be built with your choice of foundation and framing. A generic conversion diagram is available. See order form.)

BLUEPRINT PRICE CODE: C

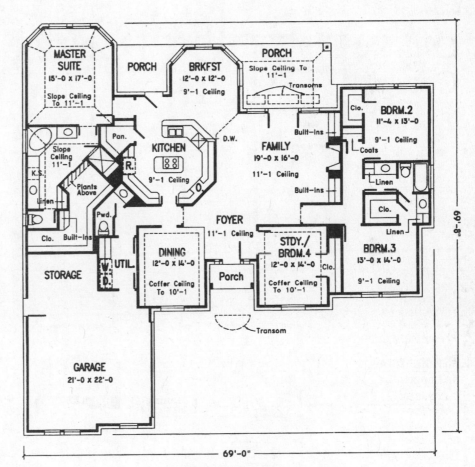

MAIN FLOOR

TO ORDER THIS BLUEPRINT,
CALL TOLL-FREE 1-800-820-1283

Plan KLF-941

PRICES AND DETAILS
ON PAGES 12-15

133

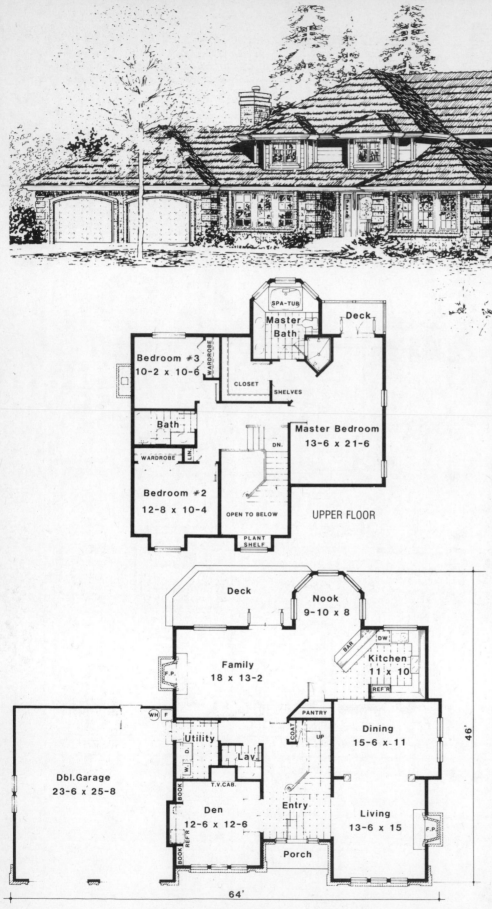

UPPER FLOOR

MAIN FLOOR

Family Style Two-Story

● Modern design with traditional touches is at home in any neighborhood.
● Main floor presents plenty of space for an active, growing family and guests as well.
● Large family room flows together with sunny breakfast nook and large deck.
● Efficient kitchen includes eating bar.
● Dining and living room areas combine to create big space for gatherings of friends and family.
● Spacious master suite includes a private balcony and a spectacular bath with spa tub and unique five-sided shower.

Plan NW-618

Bedrooms: 3	Baths: 2½
Space:	
Upper floor:	974 sq. ft.
Main floor:	1,467 sq. ft.
Total living area:	2,441 sq. ft.
Garage:	603 sq. ft.
Exterior Wall Framing:	2x4

Foundation options:
Crawlspace only.
(Foundation & framing conversion diagram available — see order form.)

Blueprint Price Code:	C

Plan NW-618

PRICES AND DETAILS ON PAGES 12-15

Dramatic Interior Spaces

- This home's design utilizes unique shapes and angles to create a dramatic and dynamic interior.
- Skylights brighten the impressive two-story entry from high above, as it flows to the formal living areas.
- The sunken Great Room features a massive stone-hearthed fireplace with flanking windows, plus a 19-ft. vaulted ceiling. Sliding glass doors open the formal dining room to a backyard patio.
- The spacious kitchen features an oversized island, plenty of counter space and a sunny breakfast nook.
- A den or third bedroom shares a full bath with another secondary bedroom to complete the main floor.
- An incredible bayed master suite takes up the entire upper floor of the home. The skylighted master bath features a bright walk-in closet, a dual-sink vanity, a sunken tub and a separate shower.

Plans P-6580-3A & -3D

Bedrooms: 2+	Baths: 2
Living Area:	
Upper floor	705 sq. ft.
Main floor	1,738 sq. ft.
Total Living Area:	**2,443 sq. ft.**
Daylight basement	1,738 sq. ft.
Garage	512 sq. ft.
Exterior Wall Framing:	2x4
Foundation Options:	**Plan #**
Daylight basement	P-6580-3D
Crawlspace	P-6580-3A

(All plans can be built with your choice of foundation and framing. A generic conversion diagram is available. See order form.)

BLUEPRINT PRICE CODE:	**C**

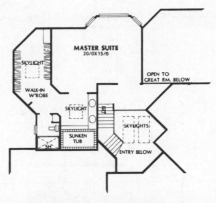

UPPER FLOOR

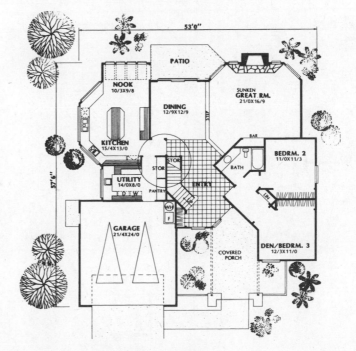

MAIN FLOOR

BASEMENT STAIRWAY LOCATION

Bold and Beautiful

- An angled garage adds a unique touch to the bold exterior of this brick-trimmed ranch.
- Inside, an open, vaulted foyer allows a view to the vaulted living room with brilliant front window wall, a den or study with elegant double doors and the kitchen and nook straight ahead.
- Double doors can close off the kitchen from the foyer if desired; but, you'll want to show off the modern island cooktop and huge bay window that surrounds the nook.
- A massive wood stove warms the adjoining vaulted family room that offers access to one of three rear patios.
- Double doors access both the master bedroom and private bath; a skylight and spa tub, vaulted ceiling and patio are exciting extras.

Plan CDG-1008

Bedrooms: 3-4	Baths: 2
Space:	
Main floor	2,445 sq. ft.
Total Living Area	**2,445 sq. ft.**
Garage	763 sq. ft.
Exterior Wall Framing	2x6
Foundation options:	
Crawlspace	
(Foundation & framing conversion diagram available—see order form.)	
Blueprint Price Code	C

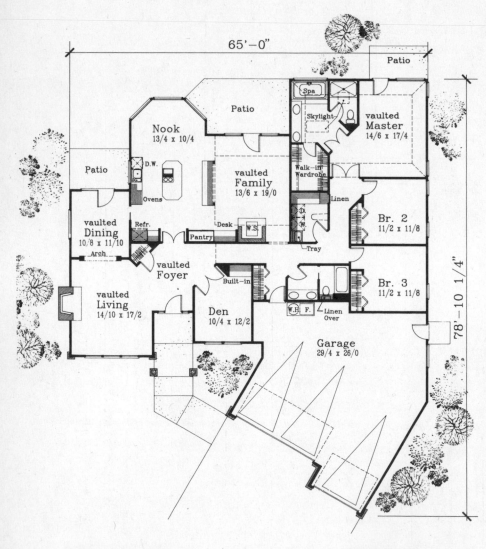

Plan CDG-1008

Tasteful Style

- Traditional lines and a contemporary floor plan combine to make this home a perfect choice for the '90s.
- The two-story-high entry introduces the formal living room, which is warmed by a fireplace and brightened by a round-top window arrangement. The living room's ceiling rises to 13 ft., 9 inches.
- A handy pocket door separates the formal dining room from the kitchen for special occasions. The U-shaped kitchen features an eating bar, a work desk and a bayed nook with access to an outdoor patio.
- The spacious family room includes a second fireplace and outdoor views.
- Ceilings in all main-floor rooms are at least 9 ft. high for added spaciousness.
- Upstairs, the master suite features a 12-ft. vaulted ceiling, two walk-in closets and a compartmentalized bath with a luxurious tub in a window bay.
- Two additional bedrooms share a split bath. A versatile bonus room could serve as an extra bedroom or as a sunny area for hobbies or paperwork.

Plan S-8389

Bedrooms: 3+	Baths: 2½
Living Area:	
Upper floor	932 sq. ft.
Main floor	1,290 sq. ft.
Bonus room	228 sq. ft.
Total Living Area:	**2,450 sq. ft.**
Standard basement	1,290 sq. ft.
Garage	429 sq. ft.
Exterior Wall Framing:	2x6

Foundation Options:
Standard basement
Crawlspace
Slab
(All plans can be built with your choice of foundation and framing. A generic conversion diagram is available. See order form.)

BLUEPRINT PRICE CODE: C

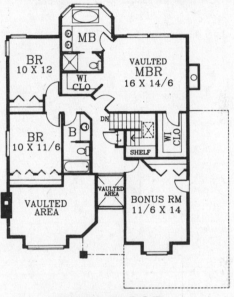

UPPER FLOOR

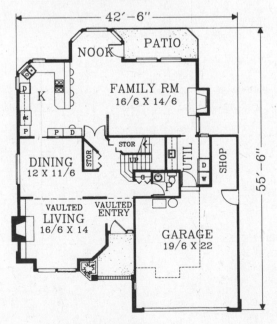

MAIN FLOOR

TO ORDER THIS BLUEPRINT,
CALL TOLL-FREE 1-800-820-1283

Plan S-8389

PRICES AND DETAILS
ON PAGES 12-15

137

Panoramic Porch

- A gracious, ornately rounded front porch and a two-story turreted bay lend Victorian charm to this home.
- A two-story foyer with round-top transom windows and a plant ledge above greets guests at the entry.
- The living room enjoys a 13-ft.-high ceiling and a panoramic view overlooking the front porch and yard.
- The formal dining room and den each feature a bay window for added style.
- The sunny kitchen incorporates an angled island cooktop with a eating bar to the bayed breakfast room.
- A step down, the family room offers a corner fireplace that may be enjoyed throughout the casual living spaces.
- The upper floor is highlighted by a stunning master suite, which flaunts an octagonal sitting area with a 10-ft. tray ceiling and turreted bay. The master bath offers a corner spa tub and a separate shower. Two additional bedrooms share another full bath.

Plan AX-90307

Bedrooms: 3+	Baths: 3
Living Area:	
Upper floor	956 sq. ft.
Main floor	1,499 sq. ft.
Total Living Area:	**2,455 sq. ft.**
Standard basement	1,499 sq. ft.
Garage	410 sq. ft.
Exterior Wall Framing:	2x4

Foundation Options:

Standard basement
Slab

(All plans can be built with your choice of foundation and framing. A generic conversion diagram is available. See order form.)

BLUEPRINT PRICE CODE: C

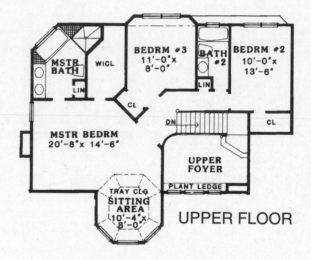

UPPER FLOOR

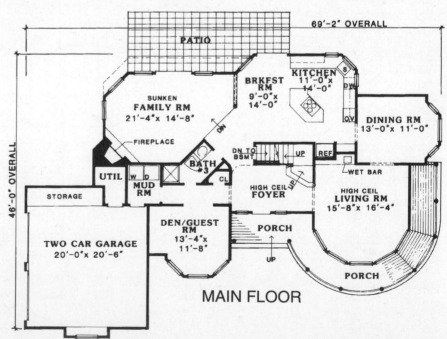

MAIN FLOOR

TO ORDER THIS BLUEPRINT, CALL TOLL-FREE 1-800-820-1283

Plan AX-90307

PRICES AND DETAILS ON PAGES 12-15

Sophisticated One-Story

- Beautiful windows accentuated by elegant keystones highlight the exterior of this sophisticated one-story design.
- An open floor plan is the hallmark of the interior, beginning with the foyer that provides instant views of the study as well as the dining and living rooms.
- The spacious living room boasts a fireplace with built-in bookshelves and a rear window wall that stretches into the morning room.
- The sunny morning room has a snack bar to the kitchen. The island kitchen includes a walk-in pantry, a built-in desk and easy access to the utility room and the convenient half-bath.
- The master suite features private access to a nice covered patio, plus an enormous walk-in closet and a posh bath with a spa tub and glass-block shower.
- A hall bath serves the two secondary bedrooms. These three rooms, plus the utility area, have standard 8-ft. ceilings. Other ceilings are 10 ft. high.

Plan DD-2455

Bedrooms: 3+	Baths: 2½
Living Area:	
Main floor	2,457 sq. ft.
Total Living Area:	**2,457 sq. ft.**
Standard basement	2,457 sq. ft.
Garage	585 sq. ft.
Exterior Wall Framing:	2x4

Foundation Options:
Standard basement
Crawlspace
Slab
(All plans can be built with your choice of foundation and framing. A generic conversion diagram is available. See order form.)

BLUEPRINT PRICE CODE:	C

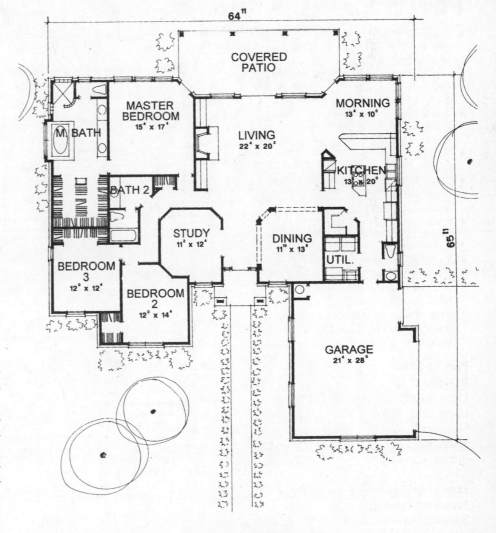

MAIN FLOOR

PLANS H-3711-1 & -1A
WITH GARAGE

All-American Country Home

- The covered wraparound porch of this popular all-American home creates an old-fashioned country appeal.
- Off the entryway is the generous-sized living room, which offers a fireplace and French doors that open to the porch.
- The large adjoining dining room further expands the entertaining area.
- The country kitchen has a handy island and flows into the cozy family room, which is enhanced by exposed beams. A handsome fireplace warms the entire informal area, while windows overlook the porch.
- The quiet upper floor hosts four good-sized bedrooms and two baths. The master suite includes a walk-in closet, a dressing area and a private bath with a sit-down shower.
- This home is available with or without a basement and with or without a garage.

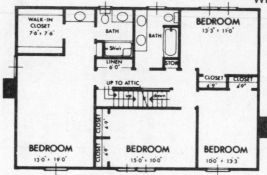

PLANS H-3711-2 & -2A
WITHOUT GARAGE

UPPER FLOOR

Plans H-3711-1, -1A, -2 & -2A

Bedrooms: 4	Baths: 2½
Living Area:	
Upper floor	1,176 sq. ft.
Main floor	1,288 sq. ft.
Total Living Area:	**2,464 sq. ft.**
Standard basement	1,176 sq. ft.
Garage	505 sq. ft.
Exterior Wall Framing:	2x6
Foundation Options:	**Plan #**
Basement with garage	H-3711-1
Basement without garage	H-3711-2
Crawlspace with garage	H-3711-1A
Crawlspace without garage	H-3711-2A

(All plans can be built with your choice of foundation and framing. A generic conversion diagram is available. See order form.)

BLUEPRINT PRICE CODE: C

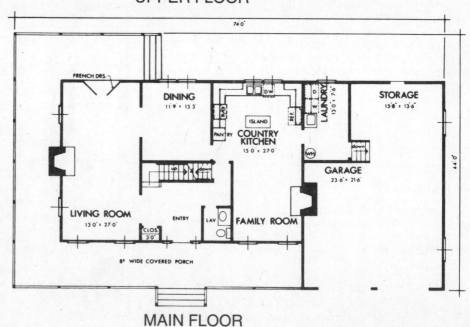

MAIN FLOOR

TO ORDER THIS BLUEPRINT, CALL TOLL-FREE 1-800-820-1283 Plans H-3711-1, -1A, -2 & -2A **PRICES AND DETAILS ON PAGES 12-15**

Light-Hearted, Open Elegance

- Tradition takes a few twists with arched brickwork and a two-story-high foyer in this transitional three-bedroom home.
- Large windows and a 10½-ft. vaulted ceiling add light and drama to the formal living room. A warm fireplace is the focal point.
- A 9-ft. vaulted ceiling expands the dining room, which offers easy access to the outdoors.
- Skylights, a windowed nook, a handy pantry and an angled island make the sunny kitchen perfect for both family cooking and formal entertaining.
- Off the kitchen, the generous-sized family room with a practical wood-stove is the center of family activity.
- A secluded study provides a quiet work retreat or extra bedroom.
- Upstairs, all three bedrooms are enhanced by 9½-ft. ceilings. The elegant master suite features an octagonal sitting area to capture the view, plus a large walk-in closet and a skylighted bath with a step-up tub.

Plan R-2117

Bedrooms: 3+	Baths: 3
Living Area:	
Upper floor	1,005 sq. ft.
Main floor	1,460 sq. ft.
Total Living Area:	**2,465 sq. ft.**
Garage	626 sq. ft.
Exterior Wall Framing:	2x6

Foundation Options:

Crawlspace

(All plans can be built with your choice of foundation and framing. A generic conversion diagram is available. See order form.)

BLUEPRINT PRICE CODE:	C

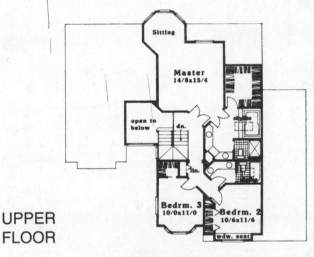

UPPER FLOOR

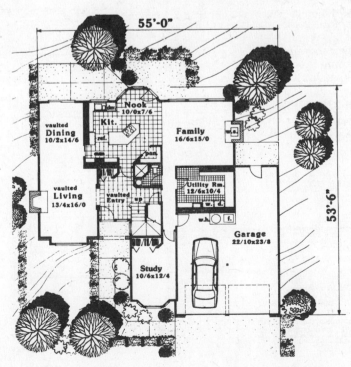

MAIN FLOOR

Heavenly!

- One look at this magnificent home's facade and interior will prove its celestial standing!
- Anchoring the home is the fabulous family room, where a handsome fireplace resides. A nearby wet bar easily serves both the family room and the billiards room. A cozy alcove gives way to a pool bath for summer fun.
- A long, covered deck will prove its worth the first time you invite over the in-laws! Fire up the barbecue!
- In the island kitchen, there's room for more than one cook. Makes you want to teach the kids the fine art of apple pie baking, doesn't it?
- The richly appointed master bedroom includes a roomy sitting area and a bath that will knock your socks off! It delivers huge, twin walk-in closets and a beautiful garden tub. Light a few candles and soak away your cares!
- A sophisticated, curved stairway angles up to the sprawling game room, where there's plenty of room for a Foosball table and even a few full-size video games. A big-screen TV would look superb in the media center.

Plan DD-4767

Bedrooms: 4	Baths: 5½
Living Area:	
Upper floor	1,315 sq. ft.
Main floor	3,452 sq. ft.
Total Living Area:	**4,767 sq. ft.**
Garage	752 sq. ft.
Storage	80 sq. ft.
Exterior Wall Framing:	2x4
Foundation Options:	
Slab	
(All plans can be built with your choice of foundation and framing. A generic conversion diagram is available. See order form.)	
BLUEPRINT PRICE CODE:	H

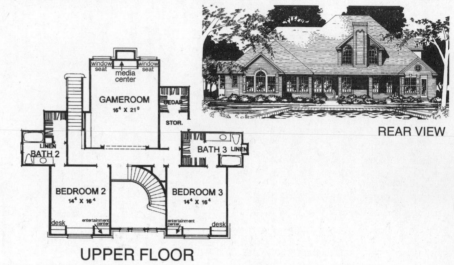

REAR VIEW

UPPER FLOOR

MAIN FLOOR

Plan DD-4767

PRICES AND DETAILS
ON PAGES 12-15

Design Excellence

- This stunning one-story home features dramatic detailing and an exceptionally functional floor plan.
- The brick exterior and exciting window treatments beautifully hint at the spectacular interior design.
- High ceilings, a host of built-ins and angled window walls are just some of the highlights.
- The family room showcases a curved wall of windows and a three-way fireplace that can be enjoyed from the adjoining kitchen and breakfast room.
- The octagonal breakfast room offers access to a lovely porch and a handy half-bath. The large island kitchen boasts a snack bar and a unique butler's pantry that connects with the dining room. The sunken living room includes a second fireplace and a window wall.
- The master suite sports a coffered ceiling, a private sitting area and a luxurious bath with a gambrel ceiling.
- Each of the four possible bedrooms has private access to a bath.

Plan KLF-922

Bedrooms: 3+	Baths: 3½
Living Area:	
Main floor	3,450 sq. ft.
Total Living Area:	**3,450 sq. ft.**
Garage	698 sq. ft.
Exterior Wall Framing:	2x4

Foundation Options:

Slab

(All plans can be built with your choice of foundation and framing. A generic conversion diagram is available. See order form.)

BLUEPRINT PRICE CODE:	E

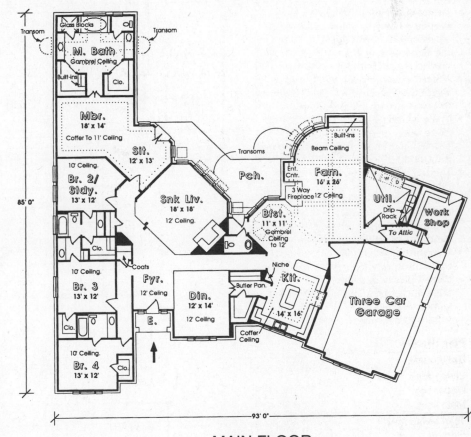

MAIN FLOOR

Stunning and Sophisticated

- A well-balanced blend of brick, stucco, and glass gives this stunning one-story home a sophisticated look.
- Past the recessed entry, the 16-ft.-high foyer is highlighted by a round-topped transom window. An arched opening introduces the formal dining room.
- The spectacular living room boasts an elegant 16-ft. coffered ceiling and is brightened by a trio of tall windows topped by a radius transom.
- The spacious island kitchen includes a roomy corner pantry and a built-in desk. A serving bar is convenient to the family room and the sunny breakfast area.
- A window-flanked fireplace is the focal point of the family room, which features a 16-ft. vaulted ceiling.
- A tray ceiling adorns the luxurious master suite. The vaulted master bath has a 16-ft. ceiling and includes a garden tub, a separate shower and his-and-hers vanities and walk-in closets.

Plan FB-5074-ARLI

Bedrooms: 3+	Baths: 2½
Living Area:	
Main floor	2,492 sq. ft.
Total Living Area:	**2,492 sq. ft.**
Daylight basement	2,492 sq. ft.
Garage	400 sq. ft.
Exterior Wall Framing:	2x4

Foundation Options:

Daylight basement
Crawlspace
(All plans can be built with your choice of foundation and framing. A generic conversion diagram is available. See order form.)

BLUEPRINT PRICE CODE: C

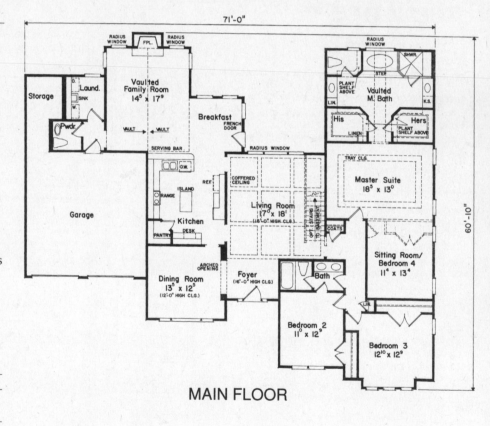

MAIN FLOOR

Plan FB-5074-ARLI

PRICES AND DETAILS ON PAGES 12-15

Picture-Perfect

- Those tall, cold glasses of summertime lemonade will taste even better when enjoyed on the shady front porch of this picture-perfect home.
- Inside, the two-story, sidelighted foyer unfolds to the formal living areas and the Great Room beyond.
- Fireplaces grace the living room and the Great Room, which are separated by French pocket doors. A TV nook borders the fireplace in the Great Room, letting the kids catch their favorite show while Mom and Dad fix dinner in the kitchen. Two sets of French doors swing wide to reveal a backyard deck.
- A glassy dinette with an 8-ft. ceiling makes breakfasts cozy and comfortable.
- Restful nights will be the norm in the master suite, which boasts a 14-ft. cathedral ceiling. Next to the walk-in closet, the private bath has a whirlpool tub in a fabulous boxed-out window.
- Unless otherwise noted, all main-floor rooms are topped by 9-ft. ceilings.
- At day's end, guests and children may retire to the upper floor, where four big bedrooms and a full bath await them.

Plan AHP-9512

Bedrooms: 5	Baths: 2½
Living Area:	
Upper floor	928 sq. ft.
Main floor	1,571 sq. ft.
Total Living Area:	**2,499 sq. ft.**
Standard basement	1,571 sq. ft.
Garage and storage	420 sq. ft.
Exterior Wall Framing:	2x4 or 2x6

Foundation Options:

Standard basement

Crawlspace

Slab

(All plans can be built with your choice of foundation and framing. A generic conversion diagram is available. See order form.)

BLUEPRINT PRICE CODE: C

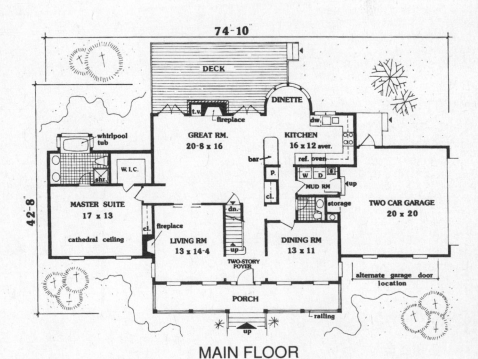

UPPER FLOOR

MAIN FLOOR

TO ORDER THIS BLUEPRINT,
CALL TOLL-FREE 1-800-820-1283

Plan AHP-9512

PRICES AND DETAILS
ON PAGES 12-15

145

Soaring Gables

- Majestic arched windows and soaring gables adorn the exterior of this incredible brick home.
- Inside, the two-story entry provides breathtaking views into the open Great Room, which showcases a wet bar and a handsome fireplace flanked by picture windows and high arched transoms.
- Lovely columns define the sun-drenched dining room, which includes hutch space and a lovely bay window.
- The spacious kitchen features access to the upper floor, plus a columned island that serves the breakfast nook and adjoining hearth room.
- French doors open to the luxurious master suite. Amenities here include two huge walk-in closets and a glamorous whirlpool bath.
- A curved stairway climbs gracefully to the upper floor, which overlooks the entry below.
- Three bedrooms are housed on this level, one of which boasts a private balcony and bi-fold doors that look out over the breakfast nook.

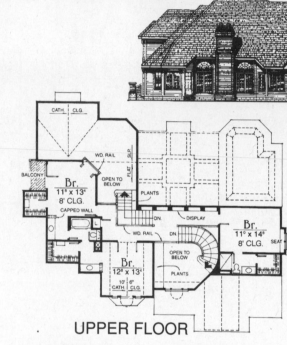

REAR VIEW

UPPER FLOOR

Plan CC-3505-M

Bedrooms: 4+	Baths: 3½
Living Area:	
Upper floor	1,013 sq. ft.
Main floor	2,492 sq. ft.
Total Living Area:	**3,505 sq. ft.**
Standard basement	2,492 sq. ft.
Garage	769 sq. ft.
Exterior Wall Framing:	2x4

Foundation Options:

Standard basement

(All plans can be built with your choice of foundation and framing. A generic conversion diagram is available. See order form.)

BLUEPRINT PRICE CODE:	F

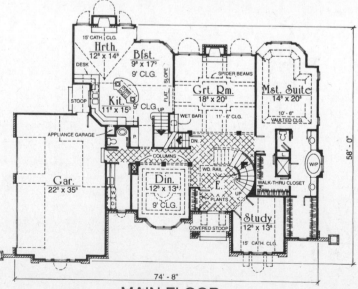

MAIN FLOOR

Plan CC-3505-M

Enjoyable Porch

- This stylish home offers an exciting four-season porch and a large deck. Transom windows adorn the exterior and allow extra light into the interior.
- The airy 17-ft., 4-in.-high foyer provides views into all of the living areas.
- The sunken Great Room boasts a see-through fireplace, a Palladian window and a 13-ft., 4-in. cathedral ceiling.
- An island cooktop highlights the corner kitchen, which is open to both the formal dining room and the casual dinette. Double doors access the porch, with its 12-ft. vaulted ceiling and French door to the inviting deck.
- The master bedroom is enhanced by a 10-ft., 3-in. tray ceiling and the see-through fireplace. The master bath has a whirlpool tub and a separate shower, each with striking glass-block walls.
- The front bedroom boasts an arched window under an 11-ft., 9-in. ceiling.
- The den off the foyer may be used to accommodate overnight guests.
- Unless otherwise noted, all rooms have 9-ft. ceilings.

Plan PI-92-535

Bedrooms: 2+	Baths: 2½
Living Area:	
Main floor	2,302 sq. ft.
Four-season porch	208 sq. ft.
Total Living Area:	**2,510 sq. ft.**
Daylight basement	2,302 sq. ft.
Garage	912 sq. ft.
Exterior Wall Framing:	2x6

Foundation Options:

Daylight basement
(All plans can be built with your choice of foundation and framing. A generic conversion diagram is available. See order form.)

BLUEPRINT PRICE CODE:	D

MAIN FLOOR

Formal Meets Informal

- The charming, columned front porch of this appealing home leads visitors into a two-story-high foyer with a beautiful turned staircase.
- The gracious formal living room shares a 15-ft. cathedral ceiling and a dramatic see-through fireplace with the adjoining family room.
- A railing separates the family room from the spacious breakfast area and the island kitchen. A unique butler's pantry joins the kitchen to the dining room, which is enhanced by a tray ceiling.
- A convenient laundry room is located between the kitchen and the entrance to the garage .
- All four bedrooms are located on the upper level. The master suite boasts an 11-ft. cathedral ceiling, a walk-in closet and a large, luxurious bath.

Plan OH-132

Bedrooms: 4	Baths: 2½
Living Area:	
Upper floor	1,118 sq. ft.
Main floor	1,396 sq. ft.
Total Living Area:	**2,514 sq. ft.**
Standard basement	1,396 sq. ft.
Garage	413 sq. ft.
Storage/workshop	107 sq. ft.
Exterior Wall Framing:	2x4

Foundation Options:

Standard basement

(All plans can be built with your choice of foundation and framing. A generic conversion diagram is available. See order form.)

BLUEPRINT PRICE CODE: D

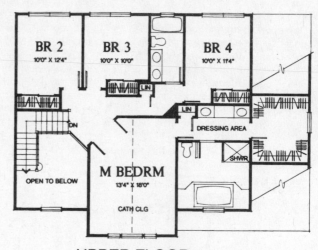

UPPER FLOOR

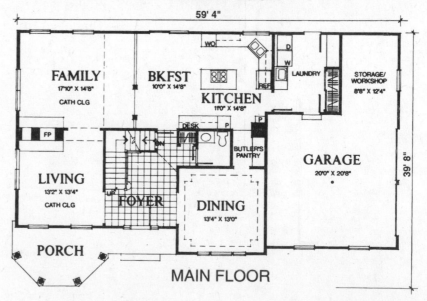

MAIN FLOOR

TO ORDER THIS BLUEPRINT, CALL TOLL-FREE 1-800-820-1283   Plan OH-132   **PRICES AND DETAILS ON PAGES 12-15**

Traditional Theme

- A variety of unusual window, siding and trim treatments lends a traditional theme to this playful home. Inside, volume ceilings, angular rooms and lots of glass make the floor plan an attention-getter.
- The foyer offers an immediate view of the vaulted dining room straight ahead, which has French doors opening to a covered patio. To the right of the foyer is the formal living room, which has a cupola extension in its vaulted ceiling.
- The combination of kitchen, breakfast room and family room is sure to be a hit. The island kitchen overlooks the octagonal breakfast area and the family room, which includes a fireplace flanked by built-ins and French doors to the patio.
- The spectacular main-floor master suite also has vaulted ceilings and access to the patio. In addition, it offers a plush private bath. Note the pool bath that borders the master bedroom!
- The upper floor hosts three bedrooms, a full bath and a loft.

Plan HDS-90-827

Bedrooms: 4		**Baths:** 2 full, 2 half	
Living Area:			
Upper floor			690 sq. ft.
Main floor			1,830 sq. ft.
Total Living Area:			**2,520 sq. ft.**
Garage			470 sq. ft.
Exterior Wall Framing:			2x4

Foundation Options:

Slab
(All plans can be built with your choice of foundation and framing. A generic conversion diagram is available. See order form.)

BLUEPRINT PRICE CODE: D

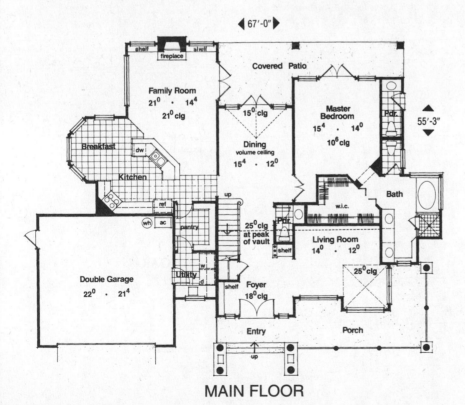

MAIN FLOOR

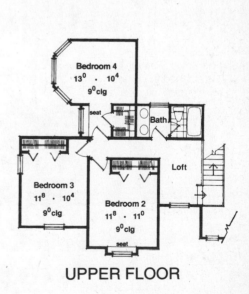

UPPER FLOOR

Plan HDS-90-827

PRICES AND DETAILS
ON PAGES 12-15

Family Ties

- This grand French-style home will serve well as the focal point of family activities for years to come.
- The dignified brick exterior presents an elegant image that retains an inviting, comfortable feel. The striking entry sits under a two-story arch and a beautiful window arrangement, as it whispers a quiet welcome to guests.
- Inside, the living room and formal dining room occupy the heart of the home. Separated by a stylish round column, these rooms await holiday galas and other grand affairs throughout the year.
- A see-through fireplace adds warm cheer to both the living room and the

family room. In the family room, bookshelves store audio/video equipment, CDs, books and videos.
- Meal preparation becomes a fun chore in the gourmet kitchen. Here, an island workstation and a walk-in pantry give you space to store countless sundries. A counter between the kitchen and the breakfast nook can hold a pitcher of milk, an assortment of cereals and a pot of coffee.
- Across the home, the master suite beckons you to relax there at day's end. Hectic mornings will take on a luxurious feel in the master bath.
- The loft upstairs would be a fine library or computer nook for the kids. Three more bedrooms complete the floor.

Plan RD-2540	
Bedrooms: 4	**Baths:** 3½
Living Area:	
Upper floor	844 sq. ft.
Main floor	1,696 sq. ft.
Total Living Area:	**2,540 sq. ft.**
Garage and storage	519 sq. ft.
Exterior Wall Framing:	2x4

Foundation Options:
Crawlspace
Slab
(All plans can be built with your choice of foundation and framing. A generic conversion diagram is available. See order form.)

BLUEPRINT PRICE CODE:	D

MAIN FLOOR

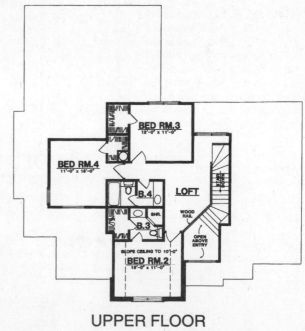

UPPER FLOOR

Plan RD-2540

Mystical Airs

- Exquisite detailings of arches and copper give this home's stucco facade a mystical air.
- Inside, you can escape to your own world in the spacious yet intimate den.
- Your entertainment options are numerous in the living room, where a boxed-out window lets in cheery light. An arched opening framed by columns leads to the formal dining room.
- During the holidays, what better place to gather your loved ones than the family room? If it's not too cold out, you could even step onto your backyard deck for a breath of brisk air!
- An island in the kitchen aids food preparation immensely it you're planning on feeding a large number. The breakfast nook features a bayed view of the world outside your window.
- A private retreat room adjoining the upper-floor master bedroom lets you unwind and finish off that new novel or maybe put the finishing touches on a watercolor. Young parents may choose to use the retreat room as a nursery.

Plan B-95002

Bedrooms: 3+	Baths: 2½
Living Area:	
Upper floor	1,080 sq. ft.
Main floor	1,463 sq. ft.
Total Living Area:	**2,543 sq. ft.**
Standard basement	1,463 sq. ft.
Garage and storage	455 sq. ft.
Exterior Wall Framing:	**2x6**

Foundation Options:

Standard basement
(All plans can be built with your choice of foundation and framing. A generic conversion diagram is available. See order form.)

BLUEPRINT PRICE CODE:	D

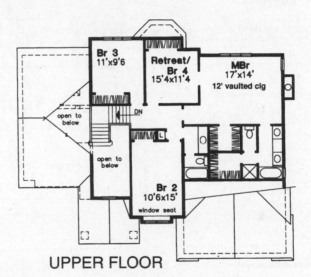

UPPER FLOOR

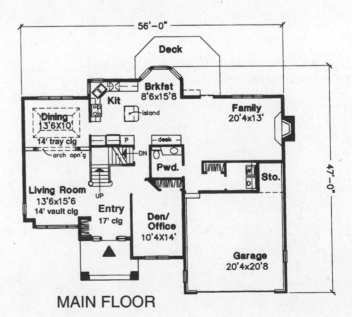

MAIN FLOOR

Bright Design

- Sweeping rooflines, arched transom windows and a stucco exterior give this exciting design a special flair.
- Inside the high, dramatic entry, guests are greeted with a stunning view of the living room, which is expanded by a 12-ft. volume ceiling. This formal expanse is augmented by an oversized bay that looks out onto a covered patio and possible pool area.
- To the left of the foyer is the formal dining room, accented by columns and a 14-ft. receding tray ceiling.
- The island kitchen overlooks a sunny breakfast nook and a large family room, each with 12-ft.-high ceilings. A handy pass-through transports food to the patio, which offers a summer kitchen.
- The master wing includes a large bedroom with a 10-ft.-high coffered ceiling, a sitting area with patio access, a massive walk-in closet and a sun-drenched garden bath.
- The private den/study could also serve as an extra bedroom.
- Two to three more bedrooms share two full baths. The front bedrooms boast 12-ft. ceilings and the rear bedroom is accented by a 10-ft. ceiling.

Plan HDS-90-814

Bedrooms: 3+	Baths: 3½
Living Area:	
Main floor	3,743 sq. ft.
Total Living Area:	**3,743 sq. ft.**
Garage	725 sq. ft.

Exterior Wall Framing:
2x4 and 8-in. concrete block

Foundation Options:
Slab
(All plans can be built with your choice of foundation and framing. A generic conversion diagram is available. See order form.)

BLUEPRINT PRICE CODE:	F

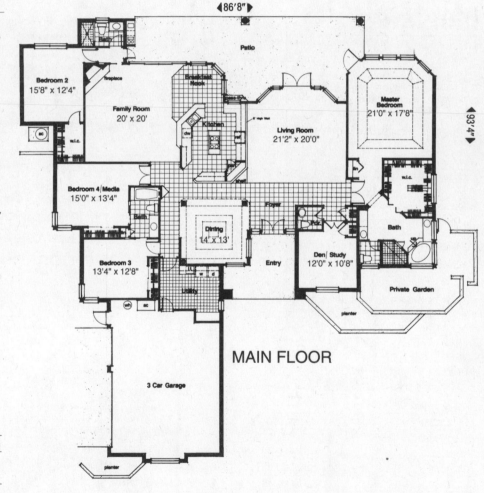

MAIN FLOOR

TO ORDER THIS BLUEPRINT,
CALL TOLL-FREE 1-800-820-1283

Plan HDS-90-814

*PRICES AND DETAILS
ON PAGES 12-15*

Ultimate Elegance

- The ultimate in elegance and luxury, this home begins with an impressive foyer that reveals a sweeping staircase and a direct view of the backyard.
- The centrally located parlor, perfect for receiving guests, has a two-story-high ceiling, a spectacular wall of glass, a fireplace and a unique ale bar. French doors open to a covered veranda with a relaxing spa and a summer kitchen.
- The gourmet island kitchen boasts an airy 10-ft. ceiling, a menu desk and a walk-in pantry. The octagonal morning room has a vaulted ceiling and access to a second stairway to the upper level.
- A pass-through snack bar in the kitchen overlooks the gathering room, which hosts a cathedral ceiling, French doors to the veranda and a second fireplace.
- Bright and luxurious, the master suite has a 10-ft. ceiling and features a unique morning kitchen, a sunny sitting area and a lavish private bath.
- The curved staircase leads to three bedroom suites upstairs. The rear suites share an enchanting deck.

Plan EOF-3

Bedrooms: 4+	Baths: 5½
Living Area:	
Upper floor	1,150 sq. ft.
Main floor	3,045 sq. ft.
Total Living Area:	**4,195 sq. ft.**
Garage	814 sq. ft.
Exterior Wall Framing:	2x6

Foundation Options:

Slab

(All plans can be built with your choice of foundation and framing. A generic conversion diagram is available. See order form.)

BLUEPRINT PRICE CODE: **G**

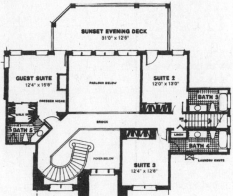

UPPER FLOOR

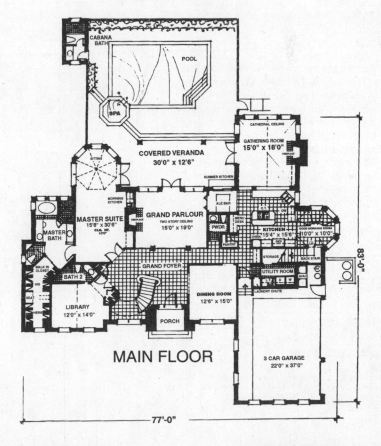

MAIN FLOOR

TO ORDER THIS BLUEPRINT,
CALL TOLL-FREE 1-800-820-1283

Plan EOF-3

PRICES AND DETAILS
ON PAGES 12-15

153

Design Leaves Out Nothing

- This design has it all, from the elegant detailing of the exterior to the exciting, luxurious spaces of the interior.
- High ceilings, large, open rooms and lots of glass are found throughout the home. Nearly all of the main living areas, as well as the master suite, overlook the veranda.
- Unusual features include a built-in ale bar in the formal dining room, an art niche in the Grand Room and a TV niche in the Gathering Room. The Gathering Room also features a fireplace framed by window seats, a wall of windows facing the backyard and a half-wall open to the morning room. The cooktop-island kitchen is conveniently accessible from all of the living areas.
- The delicious master suite includes a raised lounge, a three-sided fireplace and French doors that open to the veranda. The spiral stairs nearby lead to the "evening deck" above. The master bath boasts two walk-in closets, a sunken shower and a Roman tub.
- The upper floor hosts two complete suites and a loft, plus a vaulted bonus room reached via a separate stairway.

Plan EOF-61

Bedrooms: 3+	Baths: 4½
Living Area:	
Upper floor	877 sq. ft.
Main floor	3,094 sq. ft.
Bonus room	280 sq. ft.
Total Living Area:	**4,251 sq. ft.**
Garage	774 sq. ft.
Exterior Wall Framing:	2x6

Foundation Options:

Slab

(All plans can be built with your choice of foundation and framing. A generic conversion diagram is available. See order form.)

BLUEPRINT PRICE CODE:	**G**

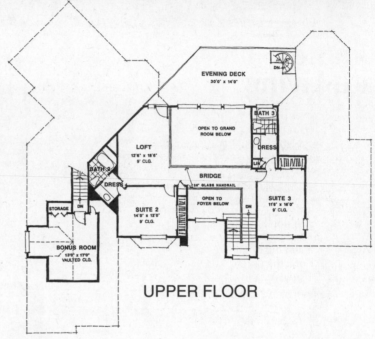

UPPER FLOOR

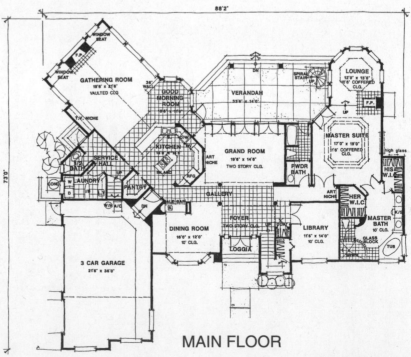

MAIN FLOOR

Plan EOF-61

PRICES AND DETAILS ON PAGES 12-15

Estate Living

- This grand estate is as big and beautiful on the inside as it is on the outside.
- The formal dining room and parlor, each with a tall window, flank the entry's graceful curved staircase.
- The sunken family room is topped by a two-story-high ceiling and wrapped in floor-to-ceiling windows. A patio door opens to the covered porch, which features a nifty built-in barbecue.
- The island kitchen and the bright breakfast area also overlook the porch, with access through the deluxe utility room.

- The master suite has it all, including a romantic fireplace framed by bookshelves. The opulent bath offers a raised spa tub, a separate shower, his-and-hers walk-in closets and a dual-sink vanity. The neighboring bedroom, which also has a private bath, would make an ideal nursery.
- The upper floor hosts a balcony hall that provides a breathtaking view of the family room below. Each of the two bedrooms here has its own bath.
- The main floor is expanded by 10-ft. ceilings, while 9-ft. ceilings grace the upper floor.

Plan DD-4300-B	
Bedrooms: 4	**Baths:** 4½
Living Area:	
Upper floor	868 sq. ft.
Main floor	3,416 sq. ft.
Total Living Area:	**4,284 sq. ft.**
Standard basement	3,416 sq. ft.
Garage and storage	633 sq. ft.
Exterior Wall Framing:	2x4 or 2x6

Foundation Options:
Standard basement
Crawlspace
Slab
(All plans can be built with your choice of foundation and framing. A generic conversion diagram is available. See order form.)

BLUEPRINT PRICE CODE: G

MAIN FLOOR

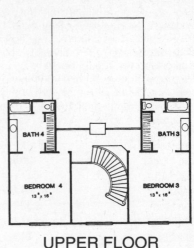

UPPER FLOOR

Extraordinary!

- For a home that is truly outstanding in style and size, this design is hard to beat! From the entry's spectacular curved stairways and 19-ft. ceiling, to the master suite's luxurious skylighted bath, elegance is found throughout.
- The spacious central living room is set off with decorative entry columns and boasts a dramatic fireplace, a 14-ft. vaulted ceiling and outdoor access.
- The gourmet kitchen is concealed behind double doors. The kitchen offers a great windowed sink area, a cooktop island, a walk-in pantry and a snack bar. The octagonal breakfast nook has a patio door to the backyard and adjoins a sunken family room with a 12-ft. ceiling and another cozy fireplace.
- Up one flight of stairs is a quiet den and an extravagant master suite. Behind dramatic double doors, the master bedroom has a romantic sitting bay and panoramic views. The skylighted bath shows off an exciting garden tub, a separate shower, a huge walk-in closet and a toilet room with a bidet.
- Up one more flight are two secondary bedrooms, each with a private bath.

UPPER FLOOR

Plan R-4029

Bedrooms: 3+	Baths: 4½
Living Area:	
Upper floor	972 sq. ft.
Main floor	3,346 sq. ft.
Total Living Area:	**4,318 sq. ft.**
Partial basement	233 sq. ft.
Garage	825 sq. ft.
Exterior Wall Framing:	2x6
Foundation Options:	

Partial basement
(All plans can be built with your choice of foundation and framing. A generic conversion diagram is available. See order form.)

BLUEPRINT PRICE CODE: G

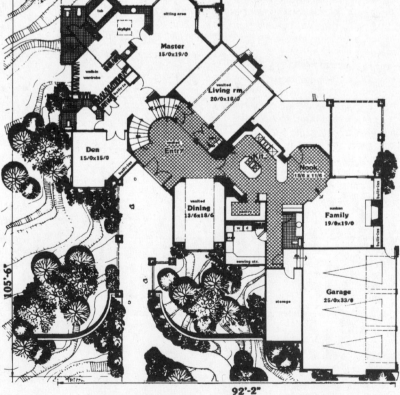

MAIN FLOOR

TO ORDER THIS BLUEPRINT, CALL TOLL-FREE 1-800-820-1283 Plan R-4029 *PRICES AND DETAILS ON PAGES 12-15*

Elegance Perfected

- The grand style of this luxurious home brings elegance and grace to perfection.
- The contemporary architecture exudes an aura of grandeur, drawing the eye to its stately 2½-story entry portico.
- The interior is equally stunning with open, flowing spaces, high ceilings and decorative, room-defining columns.
- The formal zone is impressive, with a vast foyer and a sunken living room highlighted by dramatic window walls and a 20½-ft. ceiling. Round columns set off a stunning octagonal dining room with a 19-ft., 4-in. ceiling. A curved wet bar completes the effect!
- The informal areas consist of an island kitchen, a breakfast nook, a large family room and an octagonal media room. Activities can be extended to the covered back patio through doors in the breakfast nook and the family room.
- The fabulous master suite shows off a romantic fireplace, a 12-ft. ceiling, an enormous walk-in closet and a garden bath with a circular shower!
- Two more main-floor bedrooms, an upper-floor bedroom and loft area, plus two more baths complete the plan.

Plan HDS-90-819

Bedrooms: 4+	Baths: 3½
Living Area:	
Upper floor	765 sq. ft.
Main floor	3,770 sq. ft.
Total Living Area:	**4,535 sq. ft.**
Garage	750 sq. ft.
Exterior Wall Framing:	2x4

Foundation Options:

Slab

(All plans can be built with your choice of foundation and framing. A generic conversion diagram is available. See order form.)

BLUEPRINT PRICE CODE: **H**

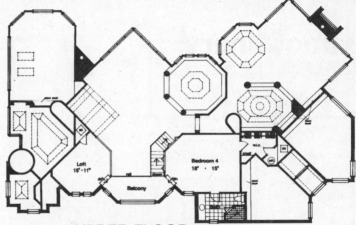

UPPER FLOOR

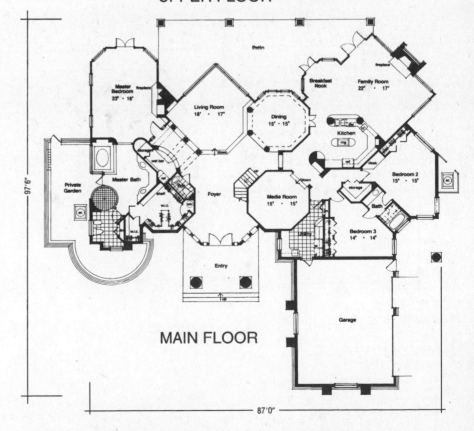

MAIN FLOOR

Trendy Transitional Design

UPPER FLOOR

Sitting

Master Br.
15x20-6

Open to below

Br. 2
11x11-6

Open to below

Plant Shelf

Br. 3
11x10

Plant Shelf

Br. 4
13-6x11-6

MAIN FLOOR

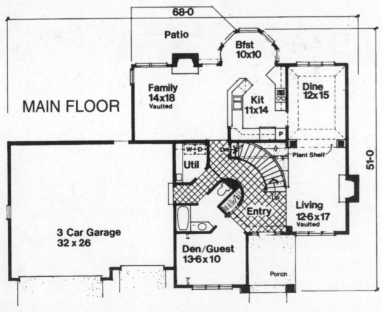

68-0

Patio

Bfst
10x10

Family
14x18
Vaulted

Kit
11x14

Dine
12x15

Plant Shelf

W+D

Util

Entry

Living
12-6x17
Vaulted

3 Car Garage
32 x 26

Den/Guest
13-6x10

Porch

51-0

- This striking transitional design offers a combination of staggered hip and gable rooflines, arched transoms, brick trim and a three-car garage with decorative facade.
- The dramatic vaulted entry focuses on circular walls and a curved staircase.
- To the right, a large, vaulted living room with fireplace combines with a formal dining room for a spacious setting. The two rooms are separated by a decorative plant shelf and columns.
- Open to the walk-through kitchen are a gazebo breakfast area and a vaulted family room with corner window and second fireplace.
- The main-floor guest room can be used as a den or library.
- The upper-level master bedroom is separated from the three other bedrooms. A private master bath and octagonal sitting area are featured.

Plan AG-9104	
Bedrooms: 4-5	**Baths:** 3
Living Area:	
Upper floor:	1,128 sq. ft.
Main floor	1,456 sq. ft.
Total Living Area:	**2,584 sq. ft.**
Standard basement	1,456 sq. ft.
Garage	832 sq. ft.
Exterior Wall Framing:	2x6
Foundation Options:	
Standard basement	
(Typical foundation & framing conversion diagram available—see order form.)	
BLUEPRINT PRICE CODE:	D

Sunny Entry

- A dramatic columned entry highlighted by a sunny window arrangement greets visitors to this glorious home.
- Double doors open to the tiled foyer, which shares a 12-ft. ceiling with the formal living and dining rooms. A tray ceiling tops the dining room, and sliding glass doors in the living room open to a tranquil covered patio.
- The secluded family room boasts a fireplace flanked by bookshelves, plus sliding glass doors to the backyard.
- An island serving bar links the family room to the kitchen and the breakfast nook. A desk and a walk-in pantry are some of the kitchen's features. A wall of windows bathes the nook in sunlight.
- Two bedrooms nearby include private access to a separated bath.
- Across the home, beautiful French doors open to the master suite, which flaunts patio access and two walk-in closets. The master bath boasts a garden tub and two vanities.
- A quiet study off the foyer could accommodate overnight guests. A hall bath nearby features patio access.
- All rooms are enhanced by 10-ft. ceilings, unless otherwise noted.

Plan HDS-99-207

Bedrooms: 3+	Baths: 3
Living Area:	
Main floor	2,593 sq. ft.
Total Living Area:	**2,593 sq. ft.**
Garage	508 sq. ft.

Exterior Wall Framing:

2x4 and 8-in. concrete block

Foundation Options:

Slab

(All plans can be built with your choice of foundation and framing. A generic conversion diagram is available. See order form.)

BLUEPRINT PRICE CODE: D

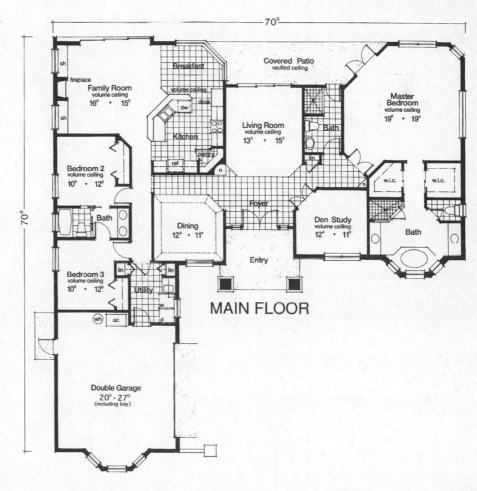

MAIN FLOOR

Elegant Arches

- Gracious arched windows and an entry portico create rhythm and style for this home's brick-clad exterior.
- An elegant curved staircase lends interest to the raised, two-story foyer.
- Two steps down to the left of the foyer lies the living room, with its dramatic 14-ft. cathedral ceiling. Lovely columns define the adjoining dining room. A cozy fireplace warms the entire area.
- The island kitchen overlooks the bayed breakfast room and offers a handy pass-through to the adjoining family room.
- The two-story-high family room boasts a second fireplace and a wall of windows topped by large transoms.
- The quiet master bedroom features a bay window and an 11-ft. sloped ceiling. The master bath shows off a garden tub and a separate shower.
- A sizable deck is accessible from both the breakfast room and the master suite.
- Three more bedrooms and two baths share the upper floor. A balcony bridge overlooks the foyer and family room.

Plan DD-3639

Bedrooms: 4+	Baths: 3½
Living Area:	
Upper floor	868 sq. ft.
Main floor	2,771 sq. ft.
Total Living Area:	**3,639 sq. ft.**
Standard basement	2,771 sq. ft.
Garage	790 sq. ft.
Exterior Wall Framing:	2x4

Foundation Options:

Standard basement
Crawlspace
Slab

(All plans can be built with your choice of foundation and framing. A generic conversion diagram is available. See order form.)

BLUEPRINT PRICE CODE: F

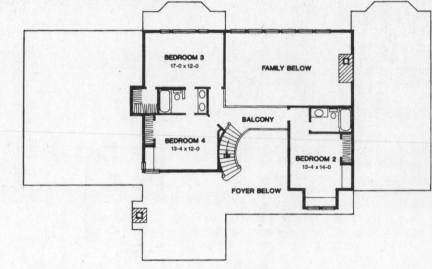

UPPER FLOOR

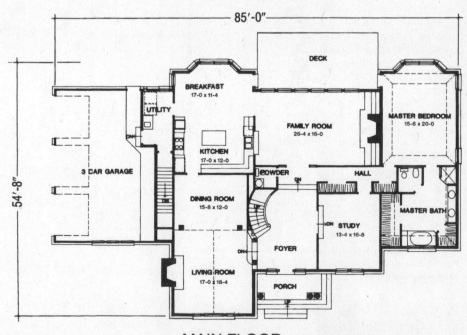

MAIN FLOOR

TO ORDER THIS BLUEPRINT, CALL TOLL-FREE 1-800-820-1283 Plan DD-3639 **PRICES AND DETAILS ON PAGES 12-15**

Photo courtesy of Breland and Farmer Designers, Inc.

Shaded Kiss

- Columned porches give this brick and stucco home a shaded kiss of Old World charm and grace. Dormer windows and a soaring roofline complete the facade.

- The magic continues inside, with a massive living room that boasts a cozy fireplace to satisfy your passion for romance. French doors grant passage to a secluded porch.

- Privacy reigns in the isolated master suite, which offers a sitting area and a built-in desk. Double doors introduce the luxurious bath with style. There, you'll find a marvelous oval tub, a separate shower, and a walk-in closet and vanity for each of you.

- Like to entertain? Give your meals that personal touch in the formal dining room! For casual cuisine, try the eating nook at the other end of the kitchen, or gather around the island for munchies.

- Upstairs, a balcony hall lets the kids enjoy the porch before heading to bed. The upper porch is railed for their safety and your peace of mind.

Plan E-2604

Bedrooms: 4	Baths: 2½
Living Area:	
Upper floor	855 sq. ft.
Main floor	1,750 sq. ft.
Total Living Area:	**2,605 sq. ft.**
Standard basement	1,655 sq. ft.
Garage and storage	569 sq. ft.
Exterior Wall Framing:	2x6

Foundation Options:

Standard basement
Crawlspace
Slab

(All plans can be built with your choice of foundation and framing. A generic conversion diagram is available. See order form.)

BLUEPRINT PRICE CODE: D

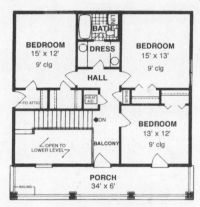

NOTE:
The above photographed home may have been modified by the homeowner. Please refer to floor plan and/or drawn elevation shown for actual blueprint details.

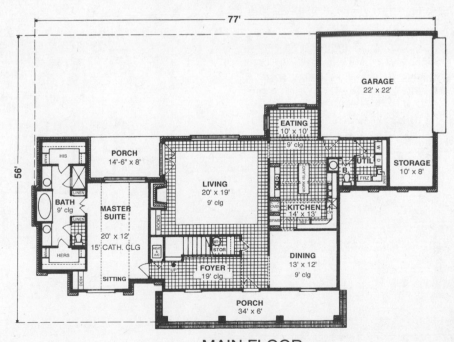

UPPER FLOOR

MAIN FLOOR

REAR VIEW

Fantastic Facade, Stunning Spaces

- Matching dormers and a generous covered front porch give this home its fantastic facade. Inside, the open living spaces are just as stunning.
- A two-story foyer bisects the formal living areas. The living room offers three bright windows, an inviting fireplace and sliding French doors to the Great Room. The formal dining room overlooks the front porch and has easy access to the kitchen.
- The Great Room is truly grand, featuring a fireplace and a TV center flanked by French doors that lead to a large deck.
- A circular dinette connects the Great Room to the kitchen, which is handy to a mudroom and a powder room.
- The main-floor master suite boasts a 14-ft. cathedral ceiling, a walk-in closet and a private bath with a whirlpool tub.
- Upstairs, four large bedrooms share another whirlpool bath. One bedroom offers a 12-ft. sloped ceiling.

Plan AHP-9397

Bedrooms: 5	Baths: 2½
Living Area:	
Upper floor	928 sq. ft.
Main floor	1,545 sq. ft.
Total Living Area:	**2,473 sq. ft.**
Standard basement	1,545 sq. ft.
Garage and storage	432 sq. ft.
Exterior Wall Framing:	2x4 or 2x6

Foundation Options:

Standard basement
Crawlspace
Slab

(All plans can be built with your choice of foundation and framing. A generic conversion diagram is available. See order form.)

BLUEPRINT PRICE CODE:	C

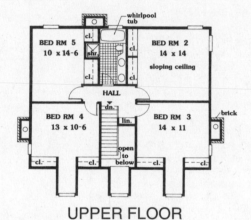

UPPER FLOOR

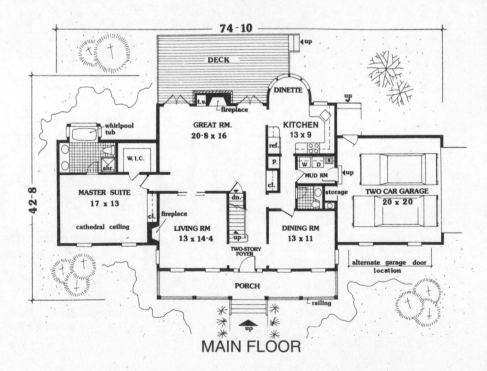

MAIN FLOOR

TO ORDER THIS BLUEPRINT, CALL TOLL-FREE 1-800-820-1283   Plan AHP-9397   *PRICES AND DETAILS ON PAGES 12-15*

Full of Surprises

- While dignified and reserved on the outside, this plan presents intriguing angles, vaulted ceilings and surprising spaces throughout the interior.
- The elegant, vaulted living room flows from the expansive foyer and includes a striking fireplace and a beautiful bay.
- The spacious island kitchen offers wide corner windows above the sink and easy service to both the vaulted dining room and the skylighted nook.
- The adjoining vaulted family room features a warm corner woodstove and sliding doors to the backyard patio.
- The superb master suite includes a vaulted sleeping area and an exquisite private bath with a skylighted dressing area, a large walk-in closet, a step-up spa tub and a separate shower.
- Three secondary bedrooms are located near another full bath and a large laundry room with garage access.

Plans P-7711-3A & -3D

Bedrooms: 4	Baths: 2
Living Area:	
Main floor (crawlspace version)	2,510 sq. ft.
Main floor (basement version)	2,580 sq. ft.
Total Living Area:	**2,510/2,580 sq. ft.**
Daylight basement	2,635 sq. ft.
Garage	806 sq. ft.
Exterior Wall Framing:	2x6
Foundation Options:	**Plan #**
Daylight basement	P-7711-3D
Crawlspace	P-7711-3A

(All plans can be built with your choice of foundation and framing. A generic conversion diagram is available. See order form.)

BLUEPRINT PRICE CODE:	D

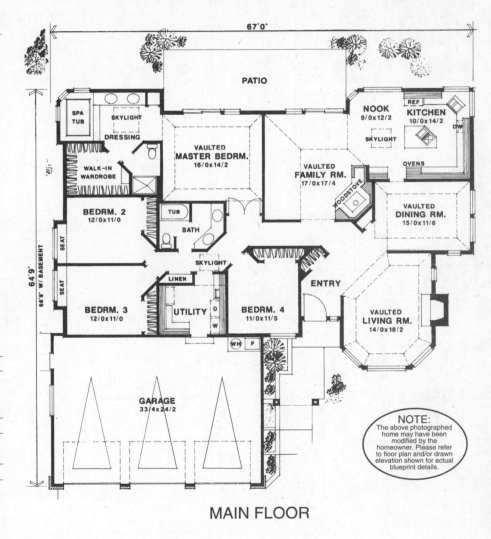

NOTE:
The above photographed home may have been modified by the homeowner. Please refer to floor plan and/or drawn elevation shown for actual blueprint details.

MAIN FLOOR

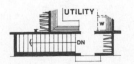

BASEMENT STAIRWAY LOCATION

Outdoor Orientation

- Courtyards, patios and a sun room orient this multi-level home to the outdoors and let the sun shine in.
- The soaring two-story-high entry leads visitors to the vaulted living room, which is warmed by a fireplace.
- The living room's 12-ft. ceiling is shared with the dining room, which offers views of the backyard.

- The expansive kitchen includes a large island, plenty of counter space and a bright, airy sun room for casual dining.
- The sun room overlooks the sunken family room, which boasts a woodstove and sliding glass doors to both a back patio and a private courtyard.
- A den or fourth bedroom has private access to a full bath.
- The upper floor includes two full baths and three bedrooms. The master bath has dramatic angles and a large walk-in closet, plus a separate tub and shower.

Plans P-7659-3A & -3D	
Bedrooms: 3+	**Baths:** 3
Living Area:	
Upper floor	1,050 sq. ft.
Main floor	1,498 sq. ft.
Total Living Area:	**2,548 sq. ft.**
Daylight basement	1,490 sq. ft.
Garage	583 sq. ft.
Exterior Wall Framing:	2x4
Foundation Options:	**Plan #**
Daylight basement	P-7659-3D
Crawlspace	P-7659-3A

(All plans can be built with your choice of foundation and framing. A generic conversion diagram is available. See order form.)

| **BLUEPRINT PRICE CODE:** | **D** |

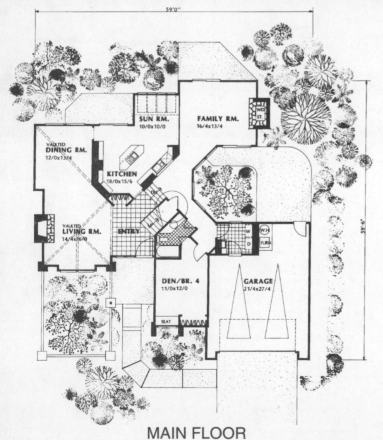

MAIN FLOOR

**NOTE: The above photographed home may have been modified by the homeowner. Please refer to floor plan and/or drawn elevation shown for actual blueprint details.

BASEMENT STAIRWAY LOCATION

UPPER FLOOR

TO ORDER THIS BLUEPRINT, CALL TOLL-FREE 1-800-820-1283

Plans P-7659-3A & -3D

PRICES AND DETAILS ON PAGES 12-15

You Asked for It!

- Our most popular plan in recent years, E-3000, has now been downsized for affordability, without sacrificing character or excitement.
- Exterior appeal is created with a covered front porch with decorative columns, triple dormers and rail-topped bay windows.
- The floor plan has combined the separate living and family rooms available in E-3000 into one spacious family room with corner fireplace, which flows into the dining room through a columned gallery.
- The kitchen serves the breakfast room over an angled snack bar, and features a huge pantry.
- The stunning main-floor master suite offers a private sitting area, a walk-in closet and a dramatic, angled bath.
- There are two large bedrooms upstairs accessible via a curved staircase with bridge balcony.

Plan E-2307

Bedrooms: 3	Baths: 2½
Living Area:	
Upper floor	595 sq. ft.
Main floor	1,765 sq. ft.
Total Living Area:	**2,360 sq. ft.**
Standard basement	1,765 sq. ft.
Garage	484 sq. ft.
Storage	44 sq. ft.
Exterior Wall Framing:	2x6

Foundation Options:

Standard basement

Crawlspace

Slab

(All plans can be built with your choice of foundation and framing. A generic conversion diagram is available. See order form.)

BLUEPRINT PRICE CODE:	C

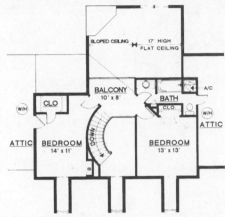

UPPER FLOOR

MAIN FLOOR

Dynamic Design

- Angled walls, vaulted ceilings and lots of glass set the tempo for this dynamic home.
- The covered front entry opens to a raised foyer and a beautiful staircase with a bayed landing.
- One step down, a spectacular see-through fireplace with a raised hearth and built-in wood storage is visible from both the bayed dining room and the stunning Great Room.
- The Great Room also showcases an 18-ft.-high vaulted ceiling, wraparound windows and access to a deck or patio.
- The adjoining nook has a door to the deck and is served by the kitchen's snack bar. The kitchen is enhanced by a 9-ft. ceiling, corner windows and a pass-through to the dining room.
- Upstairs, the master suite offers a 10-ft.-high coved ceiling, a splendid bath, a large walk-in closet and a private deck.

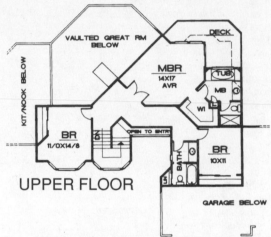

UPPER FLOOR

Plan S-41587

Bedrooms: 3+	Baths: 3
Living Area:	
Upper floor	1,001 sq. ft.
Main floor	1,550 sq. ft.
Total Living Area:	**2,551 sq. ft.**
Basement	1,550 sq. ft.
Garage (three-car)	773 sq. ft.
Exterior Wall Framing:	2x6

Foundation Options:
Daylight basement
Standard basement
Crawlspace
Slab
(All plans can be built with your choice of foundation and framing. A generic conversion diagram is available. See order form.)

BLUEPRINT PRICE CODE: D

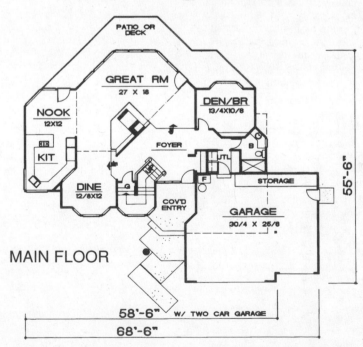

MAIN FLOOR

Plan S-41587

Hot Tub, Deck Highlighted

- Designed for indoor/outdoor living, this home features a skylighted spa room with a hot tub and a backyard deck that spans the width of the home.
- A central hall leads to the sunny kitchen and nook, which offer corner windows, a snack bar and a pantry.
- Straight ahead, the open dining and living rooms form one huge space, further pronounced by expansive windows. The 16-ft. vaulted living room also features a fireplace and sliding glass doors to the deck.
- The master suite includes a cozy window seat, a large walk-in closet, a private bath and access to the tiled spa room. The spa may also be entered from the deck and an inner hall.
- Upstairs, two more bedrooms share a full bath and a balcony that overlooks the living room below.
- The optional daylight basement offers a deluxe sauna, a fourth bedroom, a laundry room and a wide recreation room with a fireplace. A large game room and storage are also included.

REAR VIEW

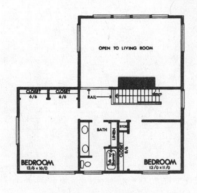

UPPER FLOOR

DAYLIGHT BASEMENT

Plans H-2114-1A & -1B

Bedrooms: 3+	Baths: 2½-3½
Living Area:	
Upper floor	732 sq. ft.
Main floor	1,682 sq. ft.
Spa room	147 sq. ft.
Daylight basement	1,386 sq. ft.
Total Living Area:	**2,561/3,947 sq. ft.**
Garage	547 sq. ft.
Exterior Wall Framing:	2x6
Foundation Options:	**Plan #**
Daylight basement	H-2114-1B
Crawlspace	H-2114-1A

(All plans can be built with your choice of foundation and framing. A generic conversion diagram is available. See order form.)

BLUEPRINT PRICE CODE:	**D/F**

MAIN FLOOR

STAIRWAY AREA IN CRAWLSPACE VERSION

Photo by Felice Photographers

Classic Country-Style

- Almost completely surrounded by an expansive porch, this classic plan exudes warmth and grace.
- The foyer is liberal in size and leads guests to a formal dining room to the left or the large living room to the right.
- The open country kitchen includes a sunny, bay-windowed breakfast nook. A utility area, a full bath and garage access are nearby.
- Upstairs, the master suite is impressive, with its large sleeping area, walk-in closet and magnificent garden bath.
- Three secondary bedrooms share a full bath with a dual-sink vanity.
- Also note the stairs leading up to an attic, which is useful for storage space.

Plan J-86134

Bedrooms: 4	Baths: 3
Living Area:	
Upper floor	1,195 sq. ft.
Main floor	1,370 sq. ft.
Total Living Area:	**2,565 sq. ft.**
Standard basement	1,370 sq. ft.
Garage	576 sq. ft.
Exterior Wall Framing:	2x4

Foundation Options:

Standard basement
Crawlspace
Slab
(All plans can be built with your choice of foundation and framing. A generic conversion diagram is available. See order form.)

BLUEPRINT PRICE CODE: D

NOTE:
The above photographed home may have been modified by the homeowner. Please refer to floor plan and/or drawn elevation shown for actual blueprint details.

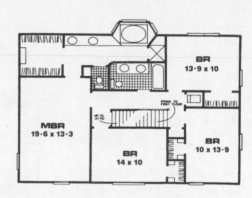

UPPER FLOOR

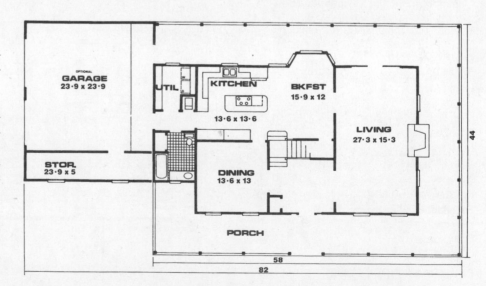

MAIN FLOOR

TO ORDER THIS BLUEPRINT, CALL TOLL-FREE 1-800-820-1283

Plan J-86134

PRICES AND DETAILS ON PAGES 12-15

Dramatic Western Contemporary

- Dramatic and functional building features contribute to the comfort and desire of this family home.
- Master suite offers a spacious private bath and luxurious hydro spa.
- Open, efficient kitchen accommodates modern appliances, a large pantry, and a snack bar.
- Skylights shed light on the entryway, open staircase, and balcony.
- Upper level balcony area has private covered deck, and may be used as a guest room or den.

REAR VIEW

UPPER FLOOR

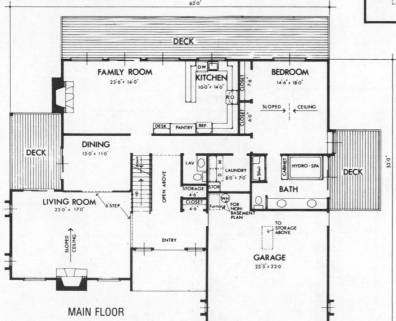

MAIN FLOOR

Plans H-3708-1 & -1A

Bedrooms: 4	Baths: 2½

Space:	
Upper floor:	893 sq. ft.
Main floor:	2,006 sq. ft.
Total living area:	**2,899 sq. ft.**
Basement:	approx. 2,006 sq. ft.
Garage:	512 sq. ft.

Exterior Wall Framing:	2x6

Foundation options:
Daylight basement (Plan H-3708-1).
Crawlspace (Plan H-3708-1A).
(Foundation & framing conversion diagram available — see order form.)

Blueprint Price Code:	D

Photo by Mark Englund/HomeStyles

Stately Elegance

- The elegant interior of this home is introduced by a dramatic barrel-vaulted entry with stately columns.
- Double doors open to the 19-ft.-high foyer, where a half-round transom window brightens an attractive open-railed stairway.
- Off the foyer, the living room is separated from the sunny dining room by impressive columns.
- The island kitchen offers a bright corner sink, a walk-in pantry and a bayed breakfast area with backyard views.
- The adjoining family room offers a door to a backyard patio, while a wet bar and a fireplace enhance the whole area.
- Upstairs, the master suite boasts a private bath with two walk-in closets, a garden spa tub and a separate shower.
- Three secondary bedrooms have private bathroom access.
- Ceilings in all rooms are 9 ft. high for added spaciousness.

Plan DD-2968-A

Bedrooms: 4+	Baths: 3½
Living Area:	
Upper floor	1,382 sq. ft.
Main floor	1,586 sq. ft.
Total Living Area:	**2,968 sq. ft.**
Standard basement	1,586 sq. ft.
Garage	521 sq. ft.
Exterior Wall Framing:	2x4

Foundation Options:

Standard basement
Crawlspace
Slab

(All plans can be built with your choice of foundation and framing. A generic conversion diagram is available. See order form.)

BLUEPRINT PRICE CODE:	D

NOTE:
The above photographed home may have been modified by the homeowner. Please refer to floor plan and/or drawn elevation shown for actual blueprint details.

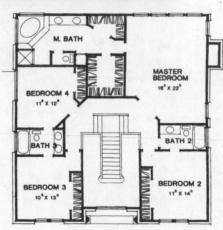

UPPER FLOOR

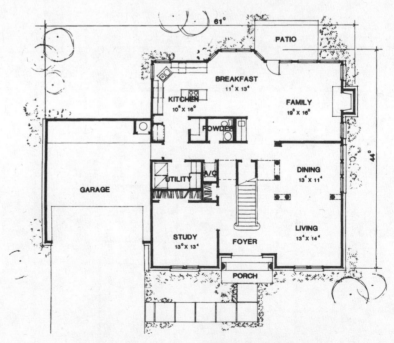

MAIN FLOOR

Plan DD-2968-A

Elegant Interior

- An inviting covered porch welcomes guests into the elegant interior of this spectacular country home.
- Just past the entrance, the formal dining room boasts a stepped ceiling and a nearby server with a sink.
- The adjoining island kitchen has an eating bar that serves the breakfast room, which is enhanced by a 12-ft. cathedral ceiling and a bayed area of 8- and 9-ft.-high windows. Sliding glass doors lead to a covered side porch.
- Brightened by a row of 8-ft.-high windows and a glass door to the backyard, the spacious Great Room features a stepped ceiling, a built-in media center and a corner fireplace.
- The master bedroom has a tray ceiling and a cozy sitting area. The skylighted master bath boasts a whirlpool tub, a separate shower and a walk-in closet.
- A second main-floor bedroom, or optional study, offers private access to a compartmentalized bath. Two more bedrooms share a third bath on the upper floor. Generous storage space is also included.

Plan AX-3305-B

Bedrooms: 3+	Baths: 3
Living Area:	
Upper floor	550 sq. ft.
Main floor	2,017 sq. ft.
Total Living Area:	**2,567 sq. ft.**
Upper-floor storage	377 sq. ft.
Standard basement	2,017 sq. ft.
Garage	415 sq. ft.
Exterior Wall Framing:	2x4
Foundation Options:	
Standard basement	
Crawlspace	
Slab	

(All plans can be built with your choice of foundation and framing. A generic conversion diagram is available. See order form.)

BLUEPRINT PRICE CODE: D

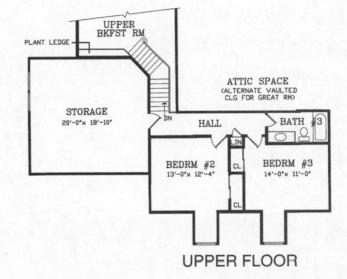

UPPER FLOOR

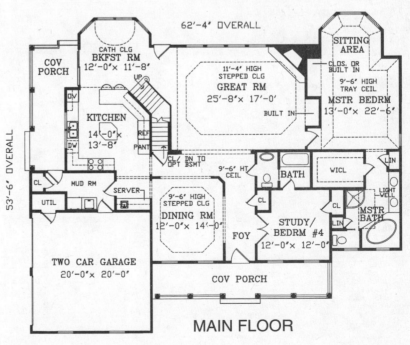

MAIN FLOOR

Photo by Gil Ford

Spacious and Stately

- This popular home design boasts a classic Creole exterior and a symmetrical layout, with 9-ft.-high ceilings on the main floor.
- French doors lead from the formal living and dining rooms to the large family room. The central fireplace is flanked by French doors that open to a covered rear porch and an open-air deck.
- The kitchen is reached easily from the family room, the dining room and the rear entrance. An island cooktop and a window-framed eating area are other features found here.
- The real seller, though, is the main-floor master suite with its spectacular bath. Among its many extras are a built-in vanity, a spa tub and a 16-ft. sloped ceiling with a skylight.
- Three upstairs bedrooms, each with double closets and private bath access, make this the perfect family-sized home.

Plan E-3000

Bedrooms: 4	**Baths:** 3½
Living Area:	
Upper floor	1,027 sq. ft.
Main floor	2,008 sq. ft.
Total Living Area:	**3,035 sq. ft.**
Standard basement	2,008 sq. ft.
Garage	484 sq. ft.
Storage	96 sq. ft.
Exterior Wall Framing:	2x6

Foundation Options:

Standard basement

Crawlspace

Slab

(All plans can be built with your choice of foundation and framing. A generic conversion diagram is available. See order form.)

BLUEPRINT PRICE CODE: **E**

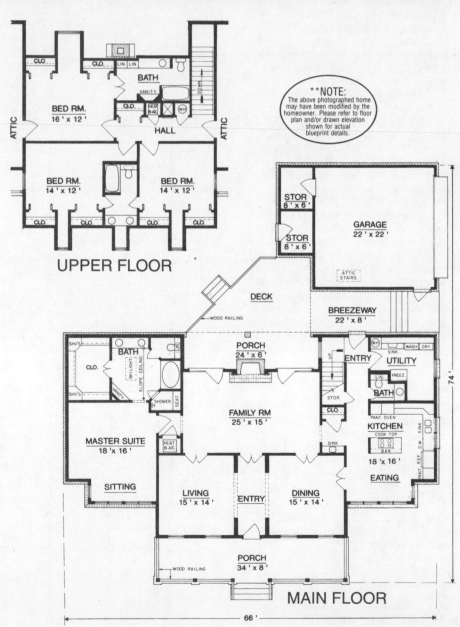

NOTE:
The above photographed home may have been modified by the homeowner. Please refer to floor plan and/or drawn elevation shown for actual blueprint details.

UPPER FLOOR

MAIN FLOOR

Victorian Farmhouse

- Fish-scale shingles and horizontal siding team up with the detailed front porch to create a look of yesterday. Brickwork enriches the sides and rear of the home.
- The main level features 10-ft.-high ceilings throughout the central living space. The front-oriented formal areas merge with the family room via three sets of French doors.

- The island kitchen and skylighted eating area have 16-ft. sloped ceilings.
- A breezeway off the deck connects the house to a roomy workshop. A two-car garage is located under the workshop and a large utility room is just inside the rear entrance.
- The main-floor master suite offers an opulent skylighted bath with a garden vanity, a spa tub, a separate shower and an 18-ft.-high sloped ceiling.
- The upper floor offers three more bedrooms, two full baths and a balcony that looks to the backyard.

Plan E-3103

Bedrooms: 4	Baths: 3½
Living Area:	
Upper floor	1,113 sq. ft.
Main floor	2,040 sq. ft.
Total Living Area:	**3,153 sq. ft.**
Daylight basement	2,040 sq. ft.
Tuck-under garage and storage	580 sq. ft.
Workshop and storage	580 sq. ft.
Exterior Wall Framing:	2x6

Foundation Options:
Daylight basement
Crawlspace
Slab
(All plans can be built with your choice of foundation and framing. A generic conversion diagram is available. See order form.)

BLUEPRINT PRICE CODE:	E

MAIN FLOOR

UPPER FLOOR

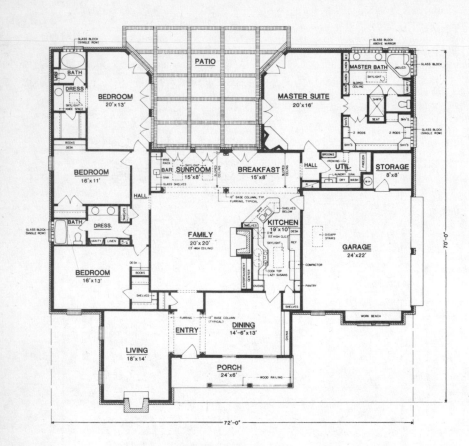

PLAN E-3102
WITHOUT BASEMENT

Exterior walls are 2x6 construction.
Specify crawlspace or slab foundation.

Ranch-Style Designed for Entertaining

- This all-brick home offers both formal living and dining rooms.

- The family room is large scale with 13' ceilings, formal fireplace and an entertainment center. An adjoining sun room reveals a tucked away wet bar.

- The master suite has private patio access and its own fireplace. An adjoining bath offers abundant closet and linen storage, a separate shower and garden tub with glass block walls.

- The home contains three additional bedrooms and two baths. Each bath has glass block above the tubs and separate dressing rooms.

- The master bedroom ceiling is sloped to 14' high. Both the sun room and the breakfast room have sloped ceilings with skylights. Typical ceiling heights are 9'.

- The home is energy efficient.

Heated area:	3,158 sq. ft.
Unheated area:	767 sq. ft.
Total area:	3,925 sq. ft.

174 **TO ORDER THIS BLUEPRINT,**
CALL TOLL-FREE 1-800-820-1283

Blueprint Price Code E
Plan E-3102

*PRICES AND DETAILS
ON PAGES 12-15*

Photo by Mark Englund/HomeStyles

Extraordinary Estate Living

- Extraordinary estate living is at its best in this palatial beauty.
- The double-doored entry opens to a large central living room that overlooks a covered patio with a vaulted ceiling. Volume 14-ft. ceilings are found in the living room, in the formal dining room and in the den or study, which may serve as a fourth bedroom.
- The gourmet chef will enjoy the spacious kitchen, which flaunts a

cooktop island, a walk-in pantry and a peninsula snack counter shared with the breakfast room and family room.
- This trio of informal living spaces also shares a panorama of glass and a corner fireplace centered between TV and media niches.
- Isolated at the opposite end of the home is the spacious master suite, which offers private patio access. Dual walk-in closets define the entrance to the adjoining master bath, complete with a garden Jacuzzi and separate dressing areas.
- The hall bath also opens to the outdoors for use as a pool bath.

Plan HDS-99-177	
Bedrooms: 3+	**Baths:** 3
Living Area:	
Main floor	2,597 sq. ft.
Total Living Area:	**2,597 sq. ft.**
Garage	761 sq. ft.
Exterior Wall Framing:	2x4
Foundation Options:	
Slab	

(All plans can be built with your choice of foundation and framing. A generic conversion diagram is available. See order form.)

BLUEPRINT PRICE CODE: **D**

NOTE:
The above photographed home may have been modified by the homeowner. Please refer to floor plan and/or drawn elevation shown for actual blueprint details.

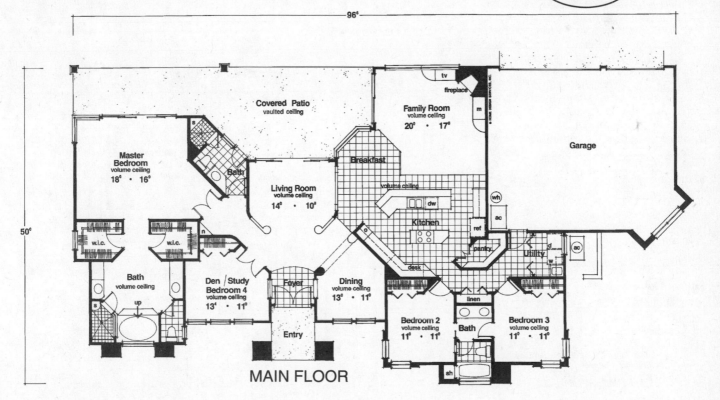

MAIN FLOOR

TO ORDER THIS BLUEPRINT,
CALL TOLL-FREE 1-800-820-1283

Plan HDS-99-177

PRICES AND DETAILS
ON PAGES 12-15

175

Large-Scale Living

- Eye-catching windows and an appealing wraparound porch highlight the exterior of this outstanding home.
- Inside, high ceilings and large-scale living spaces prevail, beginning with the foyer, which has an 18-ft. ceiling.
- The spacious living room flows into the formal dining room, which opens to the porch and to an optional rear deck.
- The island kitchen extends to a bright breakfast room with deck access. The family room offers an 18-ft. vaulted ceiling and a corner fireplace.
- Unless otherwise noted, every main-floor room boasts a 9-ft. ceiling.
- Upstairs, the lush master bedroom boasts an 11-ft. vaulted ceiling and two walk-in closets. The skylighted master bath features a spa tub, a separate shower and a dual-sink vanity.
- Three more bedrooms are reached by a balcony, which overlooks the family room. In one bedroom, the ceiling jumps to 10 ft. at the beautiful window.

Plan AX-93309

Bedrooms: 4	Baths: 2½
Living Area:	
Upper floor	1,180 sq. ft.
Main floor	1,290 sq. ft.
Total Living Area:	**2,470 sq. ft.**
Basement	1,290 sq. ft.
Garage and storage	421 sq. ft.
Exterior Wall Framing:	2x4

Foundation Options:

Daylight basement
Standard basement
Slab

(All plans can be built with your choice of foundation and framing. A generic conversion diagram is available. See order form.)

BLUEPRINT PRICE CODE:	C

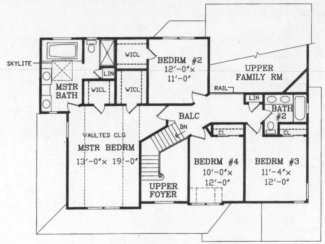

UPPER FLOOR

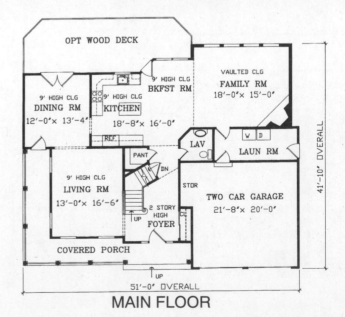

MAIN FLOOR

TO ORDER THIS BLUEPRINT, CALL TOLL-FREE 1-800-820-1283   Plan AX-93309   *PRICES AND DETAILS ON PAGES 12-15*

Large Deck Wraps Home

- A full deck and an abundance of windows surround this exciting two-level contemporary.
- The brilliant living room boasts a huge fireplace and a 14-ft.-high cathedral ceiling, plus a stunning prow-shaped window wall.

- Skywalls brighten the island kitchen and the dining room. A pantry closet and laundry facilities are nearby.
- The master bedroom offers private access to the deck. The master bath includes a dual-sink vanity, a large tub and a separate shower. A roomy hall bath serves a second bedroom.
- A generous-sized family room, another full bath and two additional bedrooms share the lower level with a two-car garage and a shop area.

Plan NW-579	
Bedrooms: 4	**Baths:** 3
Living Area:	
Main floor	1,707 sq. ft.
Daylight basement	901 sq. ft.
Total Living Area:	**2,608 sq. ft.**
Tuck-under garage	588 sq. ft.
Shop	162 sq. ft.
Exterior Wall Framing:	2x6
Foundation Options:	

Daylight basement
(All plans can be built with your choice of foundation and framing. A generic conversion diagram is available. See order form.)

BLUEPRINT PRICE CODE:	D

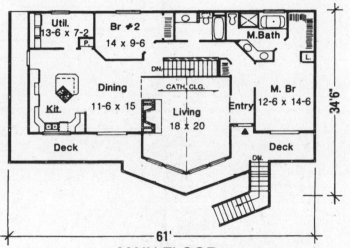

MAIN FLOOR

VIEW INTO LIVING ROOM

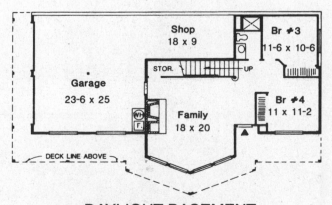

DAYLIGHT BASEMENT

TO ORDER THIS BLUEPRINT,
CALL TOLL-FREE 1-800-820-1283

Plan NW-579

PRICES AND DETAILS
ON PAGES 12-15

177

Half-Round Highlights

- The formal exterior look of this stately home is highlighted by repeated front-projecting gables and dormers with half-round transoms.
- Guests enter through a charming covered front porch into a bright foyer that opens to a vaulted living room. The formal dining room features a see-through fireplace linking it with the living room.
- The island kitchen overlooks a spacious bay-windowed breakfast room.
- The main-floor master suite features a vaulted ceiling, large walk-in closet and long, open master bath with corner tub under glass.
- Upstairs there are two more bedrooms, a full bath and a large family room.
- Ceilings are an impressive 9 ft. on the main floor, with standard 8-ft. ceilings upstairs.

Plan DD-2626

Bedrooms: 3	Baths: 2½
Living Area:	
Upper floor	975 sq. ft.
Main floor	1,651 sq. ft.
Total Living Area:	**2,626 sq. ft.**
Standard basement	1,651 sq. ft.
Garage	528 sq. ft.
Exterior Wall Framing:	2x4

Foundation Options:

Standard basement
Crawlspace
Slab
(Typical foundation & framing conversion diagram available—see order form.)

BLUEPRINT PRICE CODE:	D

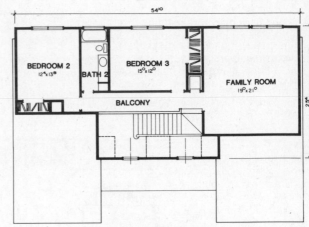

UPPER FLOOR

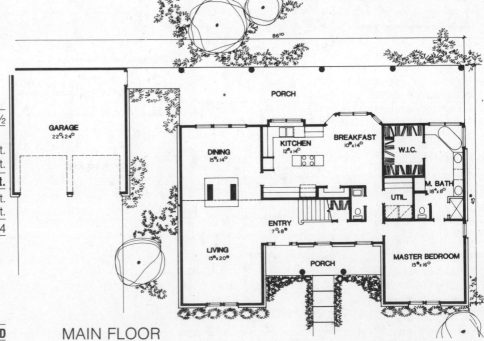

MAIN FLOOR

Plan DD-2626

PRICES AND DETAILS
ON PAGES 12-15

Full of Promise

- An open floor plan and beautiful adornments promise comfortable living within this appealing one-story.
- Beyond the sidelighted entry, the massive living room is bordered on two sides by exotic arched openings. A 12-ft. ceiling rises over the entry and the living room, while the focal point at eye level is a rustic, two-sided fireplace with a brick hearth.
- The formal dining room is efficiently served from the spacious kitchen, which boasts an island cooktop, a nifty serving bar and a refreshing wet bar that is open to the living room.
- The bayed eating nook overlooks and accesses a covered backyard porch with stately brick columns.
- Respite can be found in the secluded master suite, with its relaxing sitting area. Double doors open to the master bath, where enjoyable amenities like a skylighted whirlpool tub and a separate shower await.
- Two secondary bedrooms along the hall boast walk-in closets and share a unique compartmentalized bath.
- Unless otherwise noted, all rooms are crowned with 9-ft. ceilings.

Plan LS-94041-E

Bedrooms: 3	Baths: 3
Living Area:	
Main floor	2,637 sq. ft.
Total Living Area:	**2,637 sq. ft.**
Standard basement	2,637 sq. ft.
Garage	704 sq. ft.
Exterior Wall Framing:	2x4

Foundation Options:

Standard basement
(All plans can be built with your choice of foundation and framing. A generic conversion diagram is available. See order form.)

BLUEPRINT PRICE CODE: D

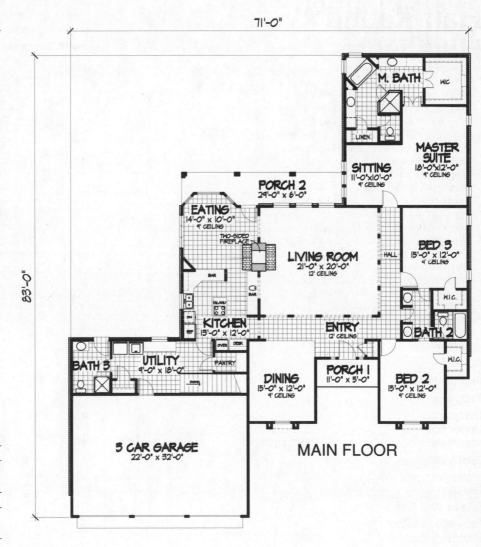

MAIN FLOOR

Well-Planned Walk-Out

- A handsome exterior, combined with an excellent interior design, makes this plan a popular and smart choice.
- The tiled entry opens to the formal dining room and the Great Room, which are separated by stylish columns and heightened by vaulted ceilings.
- A see-through fireplace with an adjacent wet bar highlights the Great Room. A window wall offers wonderful views of the expansive backyard deck.
- The fantastic kitchen, which is also warmed by the fireplace, offers a built-in desk, a walk-in pantry and an angled snack bar that faces an octagonal breakfast bay.
- The spacious main-floor master suite includes a raised ceiling, a huge walk-in closet and a lavish bath.
- An elegant den, a handy half-bath and a roomy laundry complete the main floor.
- A dramatic, open stairway overlooking an eye-catching planter leads to the walk-out basement. Included are two bedrooms and a full bath, plus an optional bonus room or family room.

Plan AG-9105

Bedrooms: 3+	Baths: 2½
Living Area:	
Main floor	1,838 sq. ft.
Daylight basement (finished)	800 sq. ft.
Total Living Area:	**2,638 sq. ft.**
Daylight basement (unfinished)	1,038 sq. ft.
Garage	462 sq. ft.
Exterior Wall Framing:	2x6

Foundation Options:

Daylight basement

(All plans can be built with your choice of foundation and framing. A generic conversion diagram is available. See order form.)

BLUEPRINT PRICE CODE: D

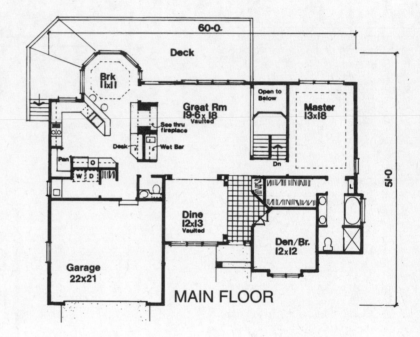

MAIN FLOOR

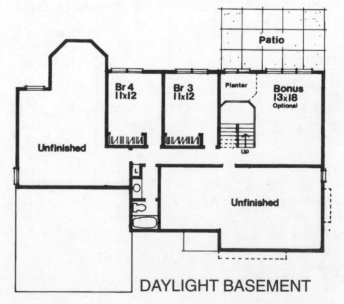

DAYLIGHT BASEMENT

TO ORDER THIS BLUEPRINT, CALL TOLL-FREE 1-800-820-1283   Plan AG-9105   *PRICES AND DETAILS ON PAGES 12-15*

Home at Last!

- Whether you're returning from a business trip or a personal vacation, you'll never get tired of coming home to this spectacular stucco delight.
- Breezy outdoor spaces parade around the home, starting with a nostalgic front porch and ending at a relaxing spa tub on a sprawling backyard deck.
- The spacious interior is bright and open. Past the entry, a gallery with French doors leads to the superb kitchen.
- The family can discuss the day's news over breakfast at the big snack bar or in the sunny bayed morning room.
- For activities of a larger scale, the living room offers an engaging fireplace, exciting views and enough space to house your entertainment equipment.
- A two-sided fireplace adds a romantic glow to the master bedroom and private sitting area. The elegant, skylighted master bath promises luxury for two!
- All main-floor rooms have 9-ft. ceilings.
- The upper-floor bedrooms are furnished with a shared bath and their own walk-in closets and sunny sitting spaces.

Plan DD-2617

Bedrooms: 4	Baths: 3
Living Area:	
Upper floor	609 sq. ft.
Main floor	2,034 sq. ft.
Total Living Area:	**2,643 sq. ft.**
Standard basement	2,034 sq. ft.
Garage and storage	544 sq. ft.
Exterior Wall Framing:	2x4

Foundation Options:

Standard basement

Crawlspace

Slab

(All plans can be built with your choice of foundation and framing. A generic conversion diagram is available. See order form.)

BLUEPRINT PRICE CODE: D

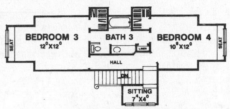

UPPER FLOOR

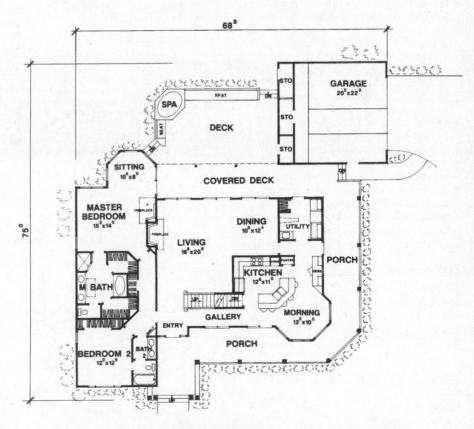

MAIN FLOOR

Patio Living

- A well-executed floor plan sets this impeccable design apart from the ordinary. Rooms of various shapes are arranged to maintain openness and to take advantage of a wonderful patio.
- The granite-paved foyer is open to the large living room, which provides a terrific view of the covered patio.
- The octagonal dining room and den or study flank the foyer and also face the living room.
- The uniquely shaped family room, with a fireplace centered between a wall of

built-ins, has a dynamic view of the outdoors and is open to the kitchen.
- The spacious kitchen has an island range, a pantry and an octagonal nook.
- All of the living areas are enhanced by 11-ft.-high volume ceilings.
- Two nicely placed bedrooms allow for privacy. They have 9-ft., 4-in. ceilings and share a full bath, which is also accessible from the patio.
- The master suite is a wing in itself. The bedroom boasts a fireplace, walls of glass and a 9-ft., 8-in. ceiling. The posh bath includes a whirlpool tub, a corner shower and separate dressing areas.

Plan HDS-99-137

Bedrooms: 3	**Baths:** 2½

Living Area:

Main floor	2,656 sq. ft.
Total Living Area:	**2,656 sq. ft.**
Garage	503 sq. ft.

Exterior Wall Framing:
2x4 and 8-in. concrete block

Foundation Options:
Slab
(All plans can be built with your choice of foundation and framing. A generic conversion diagram is available. See order form.)

BLUEPRINT PRICE CODE: **D**

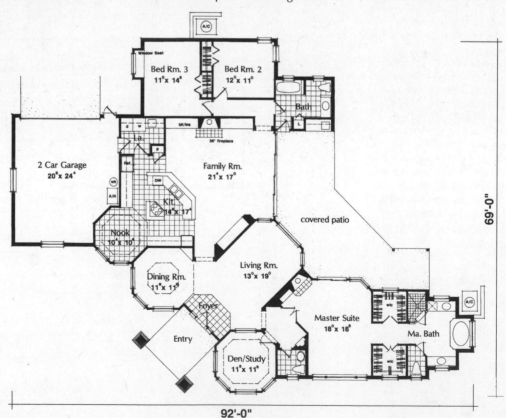

MAIN FLOOR

TO ORDER THIS BLUEPRINT, CALL TOLL-FREE 1-800-820-1283

Plan HDS-99-137

PRICES AND DETAILS ON PAGES 12-15

Fashionable Detailing

- A soaring entry portico and unusual window treatments make a bold, fashionable statement for this home.
- Inside, varied ceiling heights and special features lend a distinctive look and feel to each room.
- A 14-ft. stepped ceiling in the foyer gives way to the columned formal dining room and its 12-ft. stepped ceiling. Soffit planters outline the foyer and the living room.
- Decorative columns and a 12-ft. raised ceiling also highlight the living room, where sliding doors open to an expansive covered patio.
- A huge, angular counter with a floating soffit distinguishes the kitchen from the sunny breakfast nook. The adjoining family room has a 10-ft. ceiling and a fireplace accented with high, fixed glass and built-in shelves.
- The master suite has sliding glass doors to the patio and an arched opening to the lavish bath. The raised spa tub has louvered shutters to the sleeping area.
- Across from the den is a dual-access bath. The two bedrooms at the opposite side of the home enjoy private access to another full bath.

Plan HDS-99-161

Bedrooms: 3+	Baths: 3½
Living Area:	
Main floor	2,691 sq. ft.
Total Living Area:	**2,691 sq. ft.**
Garage	520 sq. ft.
Exterior Wall Framing:	2x4

Foundation Options:

Slab

(All plans can be built with your choice of foundation and framing. A generic conversion diagram is available. See order form.)

BLUEPRINT PRICE CODE: D

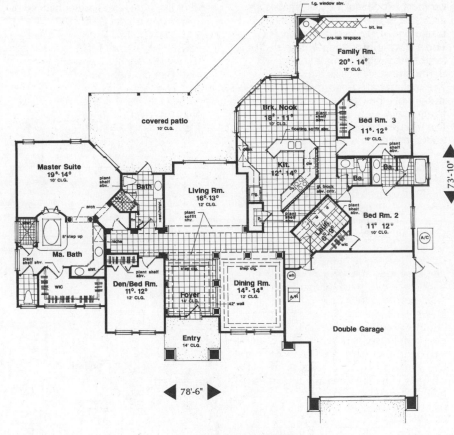

MAIN FLOOR

REAR VIEW

Stunning Estate for Scenic Sites

- A tiered roofline, expansive windows and a magnificent wraparound deck adorn this fantastic home, which is perfect for scenic building sites.

- The main floor is a masterpiece of open design, beginning with the sunny dining room that flows into the unique kitchen. The kitchen features an angled island cooktop/snack bar, a corner sink framed by windows and a nice pantry closet.

- The sunken living room is bordered by railings on two sides, keeping it visually open. A window-filled bay overlooks the deck, while a 12-ft. ceiling heightens the room's spaciousness. Other highlights include built-in bookshelves and a fireplace with a raised hearth and a built-in log bin.

- The luxurious master suite boasts a cozy window seat, a plush bath and a private sitting room with access to the deck.

- Downstairs, the recreation room offers another fireplace and double doors to a covered driveway or patio. One of the two bedrooms here offers a private bath and walk-in closet.

- Ceilings in most rooms are at least 9-ft. high for added spaciousness.

Plan NW-779	
Bedrooms: 3	**Baths:** 3½
Living Area:	
Main floor	1,450 sq. ft.
Daylight basement	1,242 sq. ft.
Total Living Area:	**2,692 sq. ft.**
Exterior Wall Framing:	2x6
Foundation Options:	

Daylight basement

(All plans can be built with your choice of foundation and framing. A generic conversion diagram is available. See order form.)

BLUEPRINT PRICE CODE: **D**

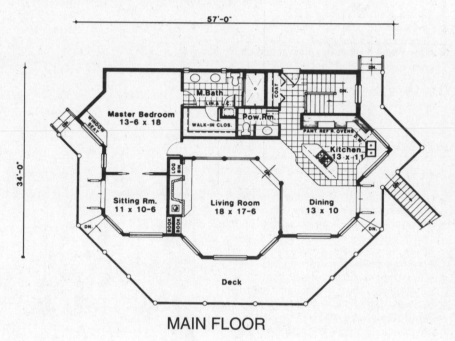

MAIN FLOOR

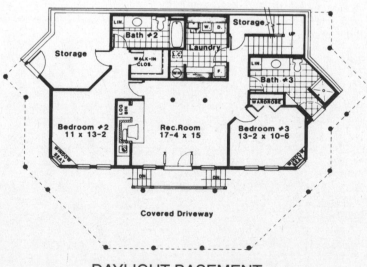

DAYLIGHT BASEMENT

TO ORDER THIS BLUEPRINT, CALL TOLL-FREE 1-800-820-1283

Plan NW-779

PRICES AND DETAILS ON PAGES 12-15

Made for You!

- After a long look at its solid facade and commodious living spaces, you may realize this striking two-story home was made for you!
- Greet your guests in the foyer, beneath its 17-ft.-high ceiling. Usher them into the formal dining or living room, or let them unwind in front of the family room's prominent fireplace. If the weather is nice, open the sliding glass doors to the backyard and enjoy a cool drink before dinner.
- A wide breakfast bay adjoins the island kitchen; a nearby desk keeps kids busy. Food can be kept warm in the butler's pantry near the dining room.
- Double doors introduce the upper-floor master bedroom, where another bayed window lets you drink in lofty views. The connecting room may serve as a calm retreat or a fourth bedroom. Young parents may dub it a nursery.
- At the end of the hall, the large bonus room would make a great game room! Its location allows rambunctious kids to let off a little steam on rainy weekends with minimal disruption for you.

Plan OH-234

Bedrooms: 3+	Baths: 2½
Living Area:	
Upper floor	1,151 sq. ft.
Main floor	1,285 sq. ft.
Bonus room	321 sq. ft.
Total Living Area:	**2,757 sq. ft.**
Standard basement	1,285 sq. ft.
Garage	660 sq. ft.
Exterior Wall Framing:	2x4

Foundation Options:

Standard basement

(All plans can be built with your choice of foundation and framing. A generic conversion diagram is available. See order form.)

BLUEPRINT PRICE CODE: D

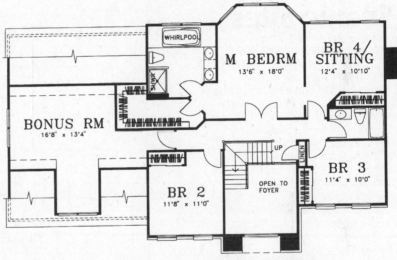

UPPER FLOOR

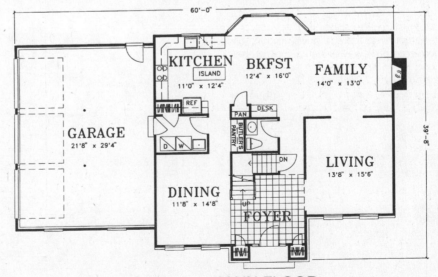

MAIN FLOOR

TO ORDER THIS BLUEPRINT,
CALL TOLL-FREE 1-800-820-1283

Plan OH-234

PRICES AND DETAILS
ON PAGES 12-15

185

Executive Excellence

- This executive home with a stucco exterior has a bright interior with flowing spaces and lots of windows.
- The two-story-high entry opens to the formal living and dining rooms, which are defined by decorative columns and enhanced by a shared 11-ft. ceiling.
- The island kitchen offers a corner windowed sink and a bayed morning room that merges with the family room.
- A fireplace warms the entire family area. Plenty of glass provides views of a large covered deck.
- A guest bedroom/study, a full bath and a utility room with a washer and dryer complete the main level.
- Upstairs, the master suite boasts an enormous walk-in closet and a lavish master bath with a boxed-out window, a spa tub and a separate shower.
- Two more bedrooms share another full bath. The third bedroom is expanded by an 11-ft. cathedral ceiling.
- Ceilings in all main-floor rooms are at least 9 ft. high for added spaciousness.

Plan DD-2725

Bedrooms: 3+	Baths: 3
Living Area:	
Upper floor	1,152 sq. ft.
Main floor	1,631 sq. ft.
Total Living Area:	**2,783 sq. ft.**
Standard basement	1,631 sq. ft.
Garage	600 sq. ft.
Storage	100 sq. ft.
Exterior Wall Framing:	2x4

Foundation Options:
Standard basement
Crawlspace
Slab

(All plans can be built with your choice of foundation and framing. A generic conversion diagram is available. See order form.)

BLUEPRINT PRICE CODE: D

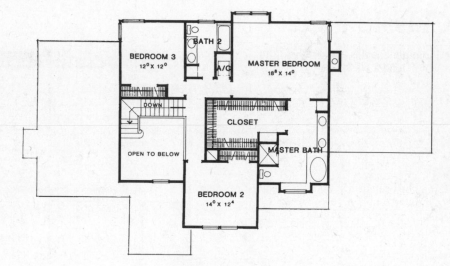

UPPER FLOOR

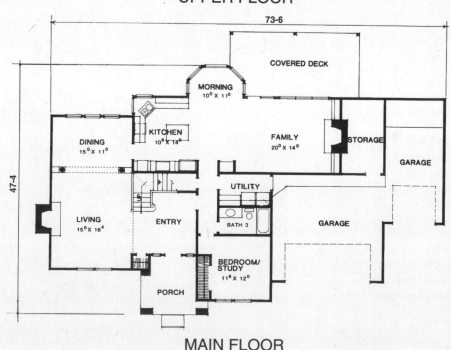

MAIN FLOOR

Plan DD-2725

TO ORDER THIS BLUEPRINT, CALL TOLL-FREE 1-800-820-1283

PRICES AND DETAILS ON PAGES 12-15

Classic Flair

- Prominent gables and a railed front porch lend a classic flair to this gorgeous country home.
- To either side of the sidelighted, two-story foyer, arched openings introduce the formal living and dining rooms.
- Straight ahead, the family room is warmed by a handsome fireplace and crowned by an impressive 18-ft. ceiling.
- A corner study with private bath access may be used as a bedroom.
- From the family room, a wide archway leads to the breakfast nook and the large island kitchen. A French door opens to the backyard.
- Upstairs, the master suite is topped by a 10-ft., 8-in. tray ceiling. The master bath enjoys a 13½-ft. vaulted ceiling above a delightful garden tub and a separate shower. A plant shelf above the closet adds a taste of the exotic.
- Along the balcony hall, arched openings give great views to the family room. Three more bedrooms offer private bath entrances; one bedroom boasts a walk-in closet.

Plan FB-5016-MARY

Bedrooms: 4+	Baths: 4
Living Area:	
Upper floor	1,408 sq. ft.
Main floor	1,426 sq. ft.
Total Living Area:	**2,834 sq. ft.**
Daylight basement	1,426 sq. ft.
Garage and storage	442 sq. ft.
Exterior Wall Framing:	2x4

Foundation Options:

Daylight basement

Crawlspace

(All plans can be built with your choice of foundation and framing. A generic conversion diagram is available. See order form.)

BLUEPRINT PRICE CODE:	D

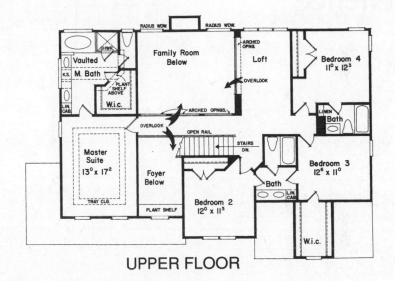

UPPER FLOOR

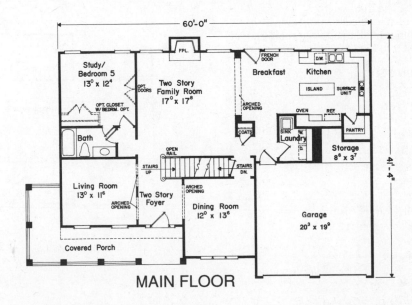

MAIN FLOOR

*TO ORDER THIS BLUEPRINT,
CALL TOLL-FREE 1-800-820-1283*

Plan FB-5016-MARY

*PRICES AND DETAILS
ON PAGES 12-15*

187

Symmetrical Bay Windows

- This home's ornate facade proudly displays a pair of symmetrical copper-topped bay windows.
- A bright, two-story-high foyer stretches to the vaulted Great Room, with its fireplace and backyard deck access.
- The island kitchen offers a snack bar and a breakfast nook that opens to the deck and the garage.
- The main-floor master suite features private deck access, dual walk-in closets and a personal bath with a corner garden tub. A laundry room and a bayed study are nearby.
- Upstairs, three secondary bedrooms and another full bath are located off the balcony bridge, which overlooks both the Great Room and the foyer.
- A second stairway off the breakfast nook climbs to a bonus room, which adjoins an optional full bath and closet.

Plan C-9010

Bedrooms: 4+	Baths: 2½-3½
Living Area:	
Upper floor	761 sq. ft.
Main floor	1,637 sq. ft.
Bonus room	347 sq. ft.
Optional bath and closet	106 sq. ft.
Total Living Area:	**2,851 sq. ft.**
Daylight basement	1,637 sq. ft.
Garage	572 sq. ft.
Exterior Wall Framing:	2x4

Foundation Options:

Daylight basement
Crawlspace
(All plans can be built with your choice of foundation and framing. A generic conversion diagram is available. See order form.)

BLUEPRINT PRICE CODE: D

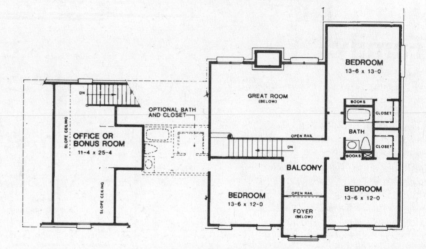

UPPER FLOOR

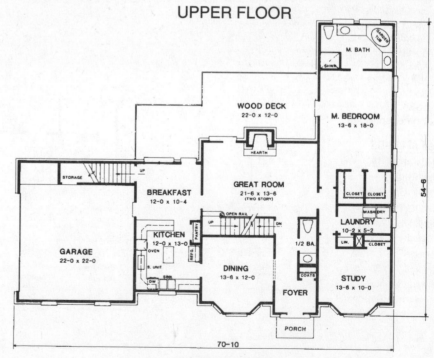

MAIN FLOOR

TO ORDER THIS BLUEPRINT, CALL TOLL-FREE 1-800-820-1283

Plan C-9010

PRICES AND DETAILS ON PAGES 12-15

A Family Tradition

- This traditional design has clean, sharp styling, with family-sized areas for formal and casual gatherings.
- The sidelighted foyer is graced with a beautiful open staircase and a wide coat closet. Flanking the foyer are the spacious formal living areas.
- The everyday living areas include an island kitchen, a bayed dinette and a large family room with a fireplace.
- Just off the entrance from the garage, double doors open to the quiet study, which boasts built-in bookshelves.
- A powder room and a deluxe laundry room with cabinets are convenient to the active areas of the home.
- Upstairs, the master suite features a roomy split bath and a large walk-in closet. Three more bedrooms share another split bath.

Plan A-118-DS

Bedrooms: 4+	Baths: 2½
Living Area:	
Upper floor	1,344 sq. ft.
Main floor	1,556 sq. ft.
Total Living Area:	**2,900 sq. ft.**
Standard basement	1,556 sq. ft.
Garage	576 sq. ft.
Exterior Wall Framing:	2x4

Foundation Options:

Standard basement

(All plans can be built with your choice of foundation and framing. A generic conversion diagram is available. See order form.)

BLUEPRINT PRICE CODE: D

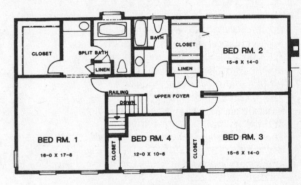

UPPER FLOOR

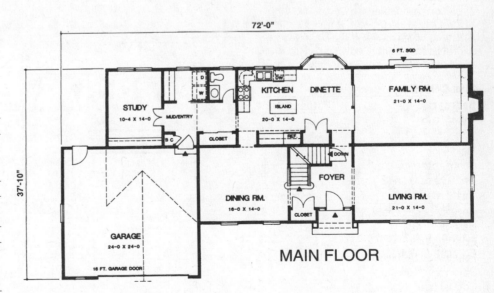

MAIN FLOOR

Sprawling French Country

- A hip roof and gable accents give this sprawling home a country, French look.
- To the left of the entry, the formal dining room is illuminated with a tall arched window arrangement.
- The spectacular living room stretches from the entry of the home to the rear. A vaulted ceiling in this expansive space rises to 19 ft., and windows at both ends offer light and a nice breeze.
- Angled walls add interest to the roomy informal areas, which overlook the covered lanai. The island kitchen opens to the adjoining morning room and the sunny family room.
- The spacious main-floor master suite is highlighted by a 13-ft. vaulted ceiling and a bayed sitting area. The master bath features dual walk-in closets, a large spa tub and a separate shower.
- Three extra bedrooms and two more baths share the upper level.

Plan DD-2889

Bedrooms: 4	Baths: 3½
Living Area:	
Upper floor	819 sq. ft.
Main floor	2,111 sq. ft.
Total Living Area:	**2,930 sq. ft.**
Standard basement	2,111 sq. ft.
Garage	622 sq. ft.
Exterior Wall Framing:	2x4

Foundation Options:
Standard basement
Crawlspace
Slab

(All plans can be built with your choice of foundation and framing. A generic conversion diagram is available. See order form.)

BLUEPRINT PRICE CODE: D

UPPER FLOOR

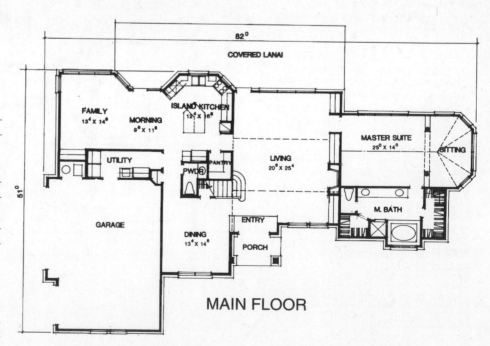

MAIN FLOOR

TO ORDER THIS BLUEPRINT,
CALL TOLL-FREE 1-800-820-1283

Plan DD-2889

PRICES AND DETAILS
ON PAGES 12-15

Super Features!

- Super indoor/outdoor living features are the main ingredients of this sprawling one-story home.
- Beyond the columned entry, the foyer features a 16-ft.-high ceiling and is brightened by a fantail transom. The dining room and the living room enjoy ceilings that vault to nearly 11 feet.
- The family room, with a 15-ft. vaulted ceiling, sits at the center of the floor plan and extends to the outdoor living spaces. A handsome fireplace flanked by built-in shelves adds excitement.
- The adjoining kitchen shares the family room's vaulted ceiling and offers a cooktop island, a large pantry and a breakfast nook that opens to the patio.
- The master suite is intended to offer the ultimate in comfort. A double-door entry, a 10-ft. tray ceiling and private patio access are featured in the bedroom. The master bath shares a see-through fireplace with the bedroom.
- Three secondary bedrooms share two full baths at the other end of the home.

Plan HDS-99-164

Bedrooms: 4	Baths: 3

Living Area:

Main floor	2,962 sq. ft.
Total Living Area:	**2,962 sq. ft.**
Garage	567 sq. ft.

Exterior Wall Framing:

2x4 and 8-in. concrete block

Foundation Options:

Slab

(All plans can be built with your choice of foundation and framing. A generic conversion diagram is available. See order form.)

BLUEPRINT PRICE CODE:	D

MAIN FLOOR

TO ORDER THIS BLUEPRINT,
CALL TOLL-FREE 1-800-820-1283

Plan HDS-99-164

PRICES AND DETAILS
ON PAGES 12-15

191

Exclusive Elegance

- A stunning array of elegant windows frames the columned, two-story-high entry of this exclusive home.
- Inside, bold columns define the foyer and the dining room, which is brightened by a wall of gracefully arched windows.
- The formal living room has a matching wall of windows, plus a two-way fireplace that is shared with the family room. Sliding doors in the family room

access a covered patio with a wet bar and an outdoor grill.
- The island kitchen gives way to a bright breakfast nook with patio access.
- The private master suite is absolutely superb, featuring a two-way fireplace that can be enjoyed from the sleeping area and from the lavish step-up spa tub. The sleeping area accesses the covered patio, while the bathing area is embraced by a sun-filled solarium.
- A bayed study, two bedrooms and two baths are on the left side of the home.
- The home features 16-ft. sloped ceilings throughout, with the exception of the two secondary bedrooms.

Plan HDS-90-801	
Bedrooms: 3+	**Baths:** 3
Living Area:	
Main floor	2,987 sq. ft.
Total Living Area:	**2,987 sq. ft.**
Garage	528 sq. ft.
Exterior Wall Framing:	2x4 and block
Foundation Options:	

Slab
(All plans can be built with your choice of foundation and framing. A generic conversion diagram is available. See order form.)

| **BLUEPRINT PRICE CODE:** | D |

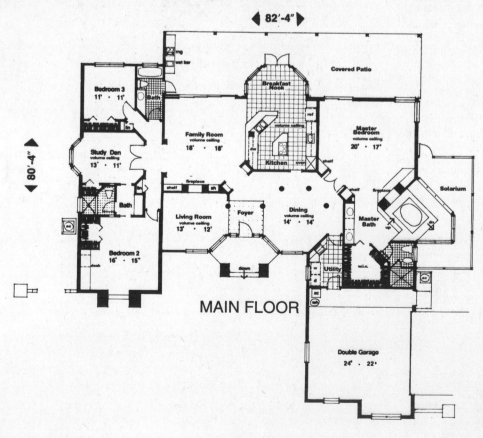

MAIN FLOOR

Plan HDS-90-801

Master Suite
Fit for a King

- This sprawling one-story features an extraordinary master suite that stretches from the front of the home to the back.
- Eye-catching windows and columns introduce the foyer, which flows back to the Grand Room. French doors open to the covered veranda, which offers a fabulous summer kitchen.
- The kitchen and bayed morning room are nestled between the Grand Room and a warm Gathering Room. A striking fireplace, an entertainment center and an ale bar are found here. This exciting core of living spaces also offers dramatic views of the outdoors.
- The isolated master suite features a stunning two-sided fireplace and an octagonal lounge area with veranda access. His-and-hers closets, separate dressing areas and a garden tub are other amenities. Across the home, three additional bedroom suites have private access to one of two more full baths.
- The private dining room at the front of the home has a 13-ft. coffered ceiling and a niche for a china cabinet.
- An oversized laundry room is located across from the kitchen and near the entrance to the three-car garage.

Plan EOF-60

Bedrooms: 4	Baths: 3
Living Area:	
Main floor	3,002 sq. ft.
Total Living Area:	**3,002 sq. ft.**
Garage	660 sq. ft.
Exterior Wall Framing:	2x6

Foundation Options:

Slab
(All plans can be built with your choice of foundation and framing. A generic conversion diagram is available. See order form.)

BLUEPRINT PRICE CODE: E

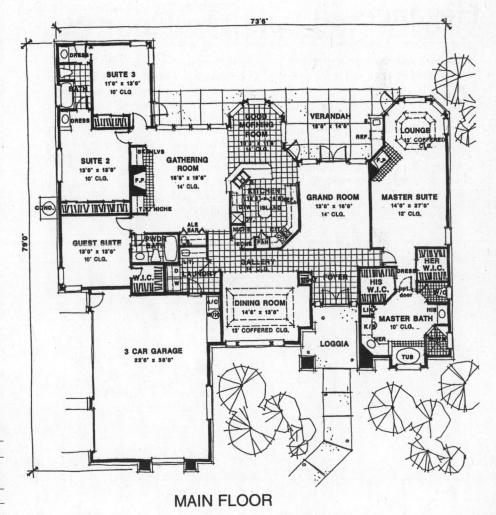

MAIN FLOOR

Plan EOF-60

PRICES AND DETAILS
ON PAGES 12-15

Angles Add Spark to Floor Plan

- Here's a one-story plan that provides plenty of space for active family living as well as business or personal entertaining.
- A majestic entry leads into a splendid sunken living room with fireplace, vaulted ceiling and built-in planter.
- A uniquely angled dining area is bathed in light from multiple windows and overlooks the living room.

- A stunning multi-sided kitchen includes a convenient island and adjoins a large pantry, breakfast nook and utility area.
- An incredible master suite boasts a magnificent bath, two huge walk-in closets and a striking bow window.
- A second bedroom also includes a large closet, and shares a walk-through bath with the parlor which could easily be a third bedroom, guest room or office.

Plan Q-3009-1A

Bedrooms: 2-3	Baths: 2½
Space:	
Total living area:	3,009 sq. ft.
Garage:	632 sq. ft.
Exterior Wall Framing:	2x4

Foundation options:
Slab only.
(Foundation & framing conversion diagram available — see order form.)

Blueprint Price Code: E

(floor plan diagram)

covered patio

bath 1

Mast. B. R.
21-4 X 19-10

lin.

clo.

lin.

clo.

clo.

Living
27-6 X 20-0
SUNKEN
CATHEDRAL CLG.

LINE OF 8' CLG.

PLANTER

Dining
12-0 X 15-6

dn.

GREENHOUSE

Kitchen
14-2 X 14-2
ISLAND

brkfst.
10-0 X 9-8

pantry

utility

dn.
Entry

bath

Bed Rm.
13-8 X 15-4

clo.

lin.

bath 2

Parlor
16-6 X 15-8

OPT. BED RM.

COVERED
ENTRY

PLANTER

Garage
31-4 X 20-2

91-0

47-0

TO ORDER THIS BLUEPRINT, CALL TOLL-FREE 1-800-820-1283

Plan Q-3009-1A

PRICES AND DETAILS ON PAGES 12-15

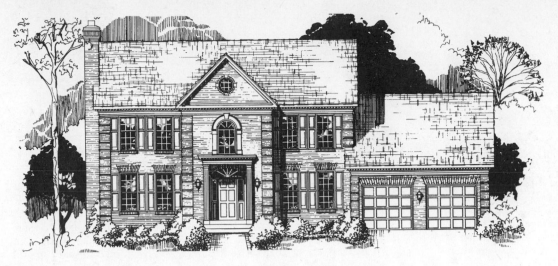

Stately and Roomy

- The exquisite exterior of this two-story home opens to a very roomy interior.
- The magnificent two-story-high foyer shows off a curved, open-railed stairway to the upper floor and opens to a study on the right and the formal living areas on the left.
- The spacious living room flows into a formal dining room that overlooks the outdoors through a lovely bay window.
- A large work island and snack counter sit at the center of the open kitchen and breakfast room. An oversized pantry closet, a powder room and a laundry room are all close at hand.
- Adjoining the breakfast room is the large sunken family room, featuring a 12-ft.-high vaulted ceiling, a cozy fireplace and outdoor access.
- The upper floor includes a stunning master bedroom with an 11-ft. vaulted ceiling and a luxurious private bath.
- Three additional bedrooms share a second full bath.

Plan CH-280-A

Bedrooms: 4+	**Baths:** 2½

Living Area:

Upper floor	1,262 sq. ft.
Main floor	1,797 sq. ft.
Total Living Area:	**3,059 sq. ft.**
Basement	1,797 sq. ft.
Garage	462 sq. ft.
Exterior Wall Framing:	2x4

Foundation Options:

Daylight basement

Standard basement

Crawlspace

(All plans can be built with your choice of foundation and framing. A generic conversion diagram is available. See order form.)

BLUEPRINT PRICE CODE:	**E**

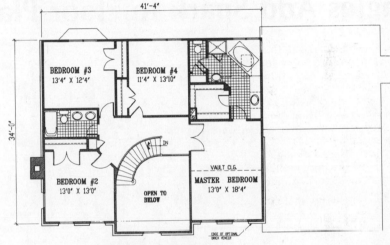

UPPER FLOOR

MAIN FLOOR

Grace and Space

- This plan is sure to be the talk of the town wherever it is built.
- A covered entry leads into a spacious foyer and straight ahead into a fantastic sunken family room with cathedral ceiling, fireplace, bar, sunroom/aviary and double-door egress to a covered patio.
- Formal living and dining rooms also are large, and traffic can flow easily from one to another when the need arises.
- The imaginative kitchen boasts a large work island, angled counter tops and plenty of space; also note the pantry and half-bath in the garage entryway.
- A large study off the foyer can serve beautifully for a home office or guest bedroom.
- The magnificent master suite features a cathedral ceiling, fireplace, double doors, and a skylighted bath with spa tub and shower, not to mention a large walk-in closet.
- Two secondary bedrooms share a second bath, and also contain large closets. The laundry area is convenient to all the bedrooms.

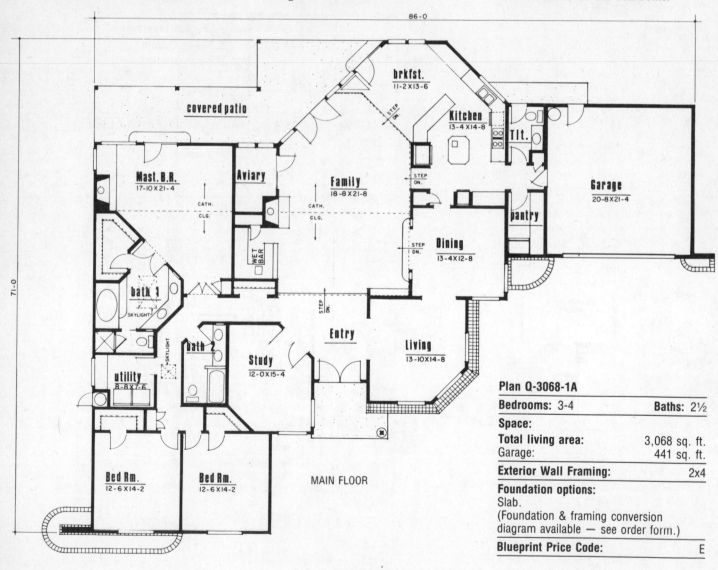

MAIN FLOOR

Plan Q-3068-1A	
Bedrooms: 3-4	**Baths:** 2½
Space:	
Total living area:	3,068 sq. ft.
Garage:	441 sq. ft.
Exterior Wall Framing:	2x4
Foundation options: Slab. (Foundation & framing conversion diagram available — see order form.)	
Blueprint Price Code:	E

TO ORDER THIS BLUEPRINT, CALL TOLL-FREE 1-800-820-1283

Plan Q-3068-1A

PRICES AND DETAILS ON PAGES 12-15

One-Floor Gracious Living

- An impressive roofscape, stately brick with soldier coursing and an impressive columned entry grace the exterior of this exciting single-story home.
- The entry opens to the the free-flowing interior, where the formal areas merge near the den, or guest room.
- The living room offers a window wall to a wide backyard deck, and the dining room is convenient to the kitchen.

- The octagonal island kitchen area offers a sunny breakfast nook with a large corner pantry.
- The spacious family room adjoins the kitchen and features a handsome fireplace and deck access. Laundry facilities and garage access are nearby.
- The lavish master suite with a fireplace and a state-of-the-art bath is privately situated in the left wing.
- Three secondary bedrooms have abundant closet space and share two baths on the right side of the home.
- The entire home features expansive 9-ft. ceilings.

Plan DD-3076	
Bedrooms: 4+	**Baths:** 3
Living Area:	
Main floor	3,076 sq. ft.
Total Living Area:	**3,076 sq. ft.**
Standard basement	3,076 sq. ft.
Garage	648 sq. ft.
Exterior Wall Framing:	2x4

Foundation Options:
Standard basement
Crawlspace
Slab
(All plans can be built with your choice of foundation and framing. A generic conversion diagram is available. See order form.)

BLUEPRINT PRICE CODE:	E

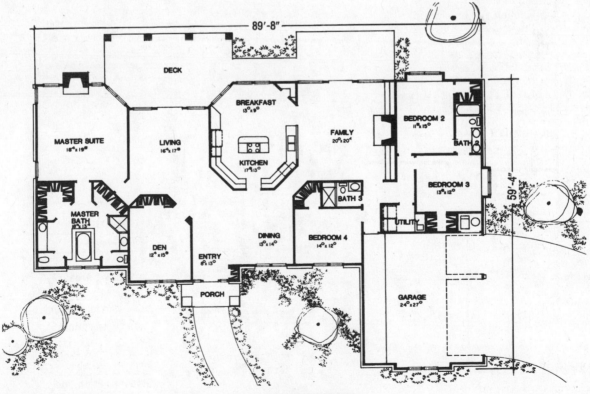

MAIN FLOOR

TO ORDER THIS BLUEPRINT,
CALL TOLL-FREE 1-800-820-1283

Plan DD-3076

PRICES AND DETAILS
ON PAGES 12-15

197

Spacious and Striking

- Alluring angles and an open, airy floor plan distinguish this impressive home, designed to take advantage of a sloping lot.
- A gorgeous covered deck and patio give guests a royal welcome.
- Designed for both entertaining and family gatherings, the home's main floor features a bright family room with an 11-ft.-high vaulted ceiling and fabulous windows. A two-way fireplace with a lovely semi-round planter is shared with the adjoining dining room.
- The combination kitchen and breakfast area features a 10-ft. vaulted ceiling, a center island and a high pot shelf.
- The roomy master suite boasts a 10-ft. vaulted ceiling and double doors to a private balcony. The sumptuous master bath includes a beautiful Jacuzzi, a separate shower and a walk-in closet.
- Three more bedrooms and three full baths are located on the lower floor.
- A second family room includes a wet bar and double doors to a large covered patio.

Plan Q-3080-1A

Bedrooms: 4	Baths: 4½
Living Area:	
Main floor	1,575 sq. ft.
Lower floor	1,505 sq. ft.
Total Living Area:	**3,080 sq. ft.**
Garage	702 sq. ft.
Exterior Wall Framing:	2x4

Foundation Options:

Slab

(All plans can be built with your choice of foundation and framing. A generic conversion diagram is available. See order form.)

BLUEPRINT PRICE CODE: **E**

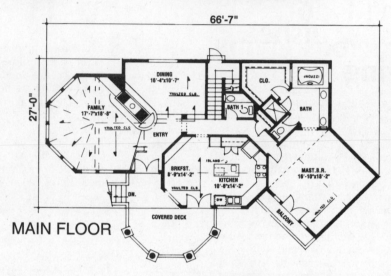

MAIN FLOOR

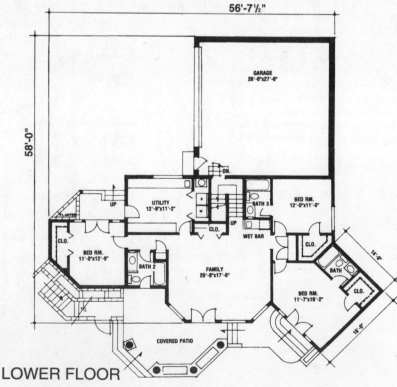

LOWER FLOOR

TO ORDER THIS BLUEPRINT, CALL TOLL-FREE 1-800-820-1283

Plan Q-3080-1A

PRICES AND DETAILS ON PAGES 12-15

Distinguished Living

- Beautiful arches, sweeping rooflines and a dramatic entry court distinguish this one-story from all the rest.
- Elegant columns outline the main foyer. To the right, the dining room has a 13-ft. coffered ceiling and an ale bar with a wine rack.
- The centrally located Grand Room can be viewed from the foyer and gallery. French doors and flanking windows allow a view of the veranda as well.
- A large island kitchen and sunny morning room merge with the casual Gathering Room. The combination offers a big fireplace, a TV niche, bookshelves and a handy snack bar.
- The extraordinary master suite flaunts a 12-ft. ceiling, an exciting three-sided fireplace and a TV niche shared with the private bayed lounge. A luxurious bath, a private library and access to the veranda are also featured.
- The two smaller bedroom suites have private baths and generous closets.

Plan EOF-62	
Bedrooms: 3	**Baths:** 3½
Living Area:	
Main floor	3,090 sq. ft.
Total Living Area:	**3,090 sq. ft.**
Garage	660 sq. ft.
Exterior Wall Framing:	2x6
Foundation Options:	

Slab

(All plans can be built with your choice of foundation and framing. A generic conversion diagram is available. See order form.)

BLUEPRINT PRICE CODE:　　　　　E

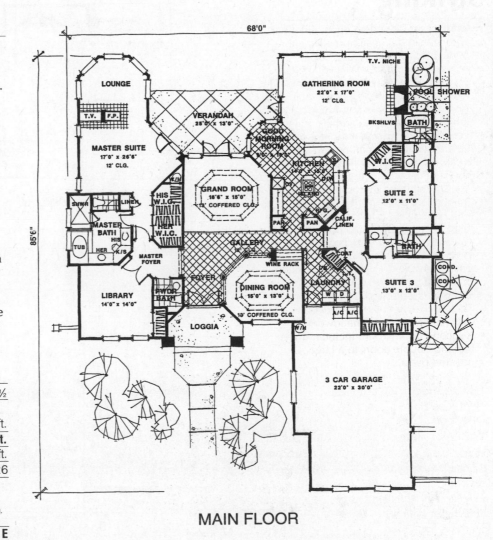

MAIN FLOOR

TO ORDER THIS BLUEPRINT,
CALL TOLL-FREE 1-800-820-1283

Plan EOF-62

PRICES AND DETAILS
ON PAGES 12-15

199

Tall Two-Story

- This gorgeous two-story is introduced by a barrel-vaulted entry and supporting columns. Inside, a spectacular curved staircase leads to a balcony overlook.
- Off the two-story-high foyer, a library with a 16-ft.-high vaulted ceiling is perfect for reading or study.
- A formal dining room opposite the library opens to the fabulous island kitchen. The kitchen offers an angled serving bar to the bayed breakfast area and adjoining living room.
- The spacious living room, with an 18-ft. vaulted ceiling, opens to a backyard patio. A fireplace flanked by built-in shelving warms the whole family area.
- The master bedroom boasts a 10-ft. gambrel ceiling, a sunny bay window and patio access. The spacious master bath offers his-and-hers walk-in closets, an oval tub and a separate shower.
- A second stairway near the utility room leads to the upper floor, where there are three more bedrooms, two baths and a bonus room above the garage. The bonus room could be finished as a game room, a media center or a hobby area.

Plan DD-3125

Bedrooms: 4+	Baths: 3½
Living Area:	
Upper floor	982 sq. ft.
Main floor	2,147 sq. ft.
Total Living Area:	**3,129 sq. ft.**
Unfinished Bonus	196 sq. ft.
Standard basement	1,996 sq. ft.
Garage	771 sq. ft.
Exterior Wall Framing:	2x4

Foundation Options:

Standard basement

Crawlspace

Slab

(All plans can be built with your choice of foundation and framing. A generic conversion diagram is available. See order form.)

BLUEPRINT PRICE CODE:	E

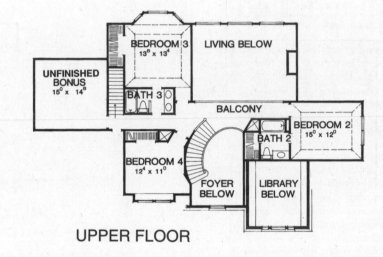

UPPER FLOOR

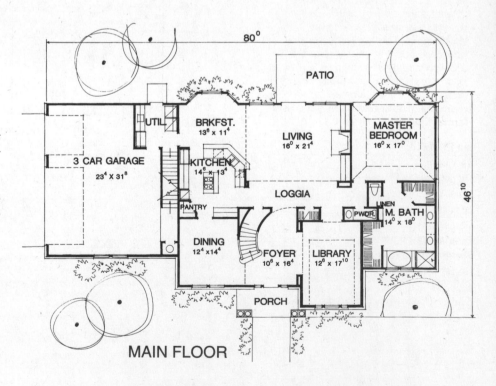

MAIN FLOOR

TO ORDER THIS BLUEPRINT, CALL TOLL-FREE 1-800-820-1283

Plan DD-3125

PRICES AND DETAILS ON PAGES 12-15

Natural State

- This home's nostalgic facade seems to blend with its natural surroundings, making it a prime choice for those who wish communion with the environment.
- There's plenty of room for interaction with nature. At the rear of the home, a covered patio flows into a fabulous deck, where a barbecue, a fun spa tub and built-in bench seats are arranged for the ultimate in excitement!
- The master bedroom cashes in on its location with a bayed window to view the festivities on the deck, and a private entrance in case the temptation to join in the frolicking becomes irresistible.
- A bay window also brightens the morning room, where your whole family may gather for waffles on those sleep-in Saturdays. In the fall months, you'll appreciate the kitchen's oversized island, which is big enough for four prize pumpkins!
- Your social obligations have not been overlooked, either. The large dining room practically guarantees successful formal dinners.

Plan DD-1914

Bedrooms: 3+	Baths: 2½
Living Area:	
Upper floor (bonus space)	1,216 sq. ft.
Main floor	1,917 sq. ft.
Total Living Area:	**3,133 sq. ft.**
Standard basement	1,820 sq. ft.
Garage and storage	467 sq. ft.
Exterior Wall Framing:	2x4

Foundation Options:

Standard basement
Crawlspace
Slab

(All plans can be built with your choice of foundation and framing. A generic conversion diagram is available. See order form.)

BLUEPRINT PRICE CODE:	E

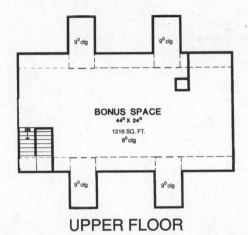

UPPER FLOOR

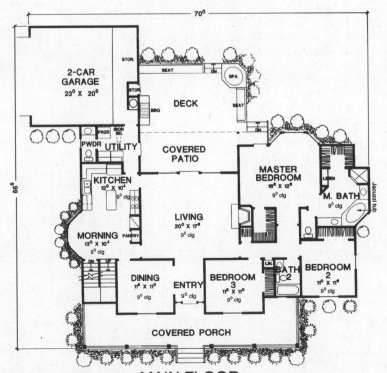

MAIN FLOOR

TO ORDER THIS BLUEPRINT,
CALL TOLL-FREE 1-800-820-1283

Plan DD-1914

PRICES AND DETAILS
ON PAGES 12-15

201

Stunning Country-Style

- A lovely front porch that encases bay windows provides a friendly welcome to this stunning country-style home.
- Inside, the main living areas revolve around the large country kitchen and dinette, complete with an island worktop, a roomy built-in desk and access to a backyard deck.
- A raised-hearth fireplace, French doors and a 12-ft., 4-in. cathedral ceiling highlight the casual family room.
- The formal dining room is open to the living room and features an inviting window seat and a tray ceiling. A French door in the bay-windowed living room opens to the relaxing porch.
- A quiet den and a large laundry area/mudroom complete the main floor.
- The upper floor showcases a super master suite with a bay window, an 11-ft., 8-in. tray ceiling, two walk-in closets and a private bath with a garden tub and its own dramatic ceiling.
- Three additional bedrooms share a full bath designed for multiple users.

Plan A-538-R

Bedrooms: 4+	Baths: 2½
Living Area:	
Upper floor	1,384 sq. ft.
Main floor	1,755 sq. ft.
Total Living Area:	**3,139 sq. ft.**
Standard basement	1,728 sq. ft.
Garage	576 sq. ft.
Exterior Wall Framing:	2x4

Foundation Options:

Standard basement

(All plans can be built with your choice of foundation and framing. A generic conversion diagram is available. See order form.)

BLUEPRINT PRICE CODE:	E

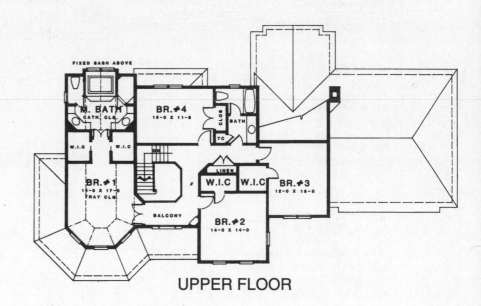

UPPER FLOOR

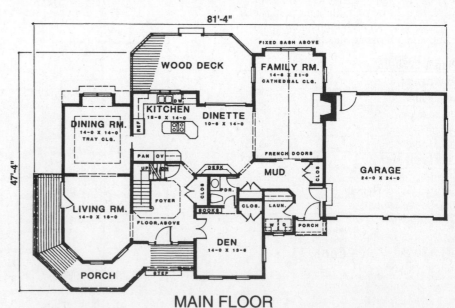

MAIN FLOOR

TO ORDER THIS BLUEPRINT, CALL TOLL-FREE 1-800-820-1283   Plan A-538-R   *PRICES AND DETAILS ON PAGES 12-15*

Traditional Elegance

- This home's stately traditional exterior is enhanced by a stunning two-story entry and brick with quoin corner details.
- The formal living and dining rooms flank the entry foyer.
- The informal living areas face the rear yard and include an island kitchen, a dinette bay and a sunken family room with a fireplace.
- The main floor also includes a handy mudroom that opens to the garage and flows back to a laundry room, a powder room and a sunny den or fifth bedroom.
- The upper floor houses four spacious bedrooms and two full baths, including a lavish master bath with a corner spa tub and a separate shower.

Plan A-2230-DS

Bedrooms: 4+	Baths: 2½
Living Area:	
Upper floor	1,455 sq. ft.
Main floor	1,692 sq. ft.
Total Living Area:	**3,147 sq. ft.**
Standard basement	1,692 sq. ft.
Garage	484 sq. ft.
Exterior Wall Framing:	2x6

Foundation Options:

Standard basement

(All plans can be built with your choice of foundation and framing. A generic conversion diagram is available. See order form.)

BLUEPRINT PRICE CODE:	E

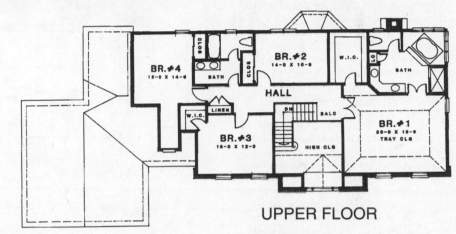

UPPER FLOOR

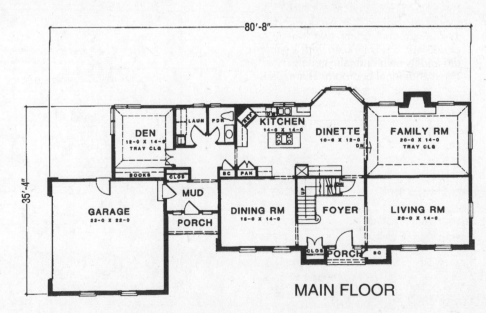

MAIN FLOOR

Creative Spaces

- This expansive home uses vaulted ceilings and multiple levels to create a functional, airy floor plan.
- The broad, vaulted entry foyer leads to the bayed living room, which is warmed by a striking fireplace. A few steps down, the dining room opens to a wide backyard deck.
- The island kitchen features a sunny sink area and a breakfast nook with deck access. A laundry room, a half-bath and a den or extra bedroom are also found on this level.
- Adjacent to the nook, the sunken family room boasts a wet bar, a second fireplace and a bright window wall with sliding glass doors to a lovely patio.
- Upstairs, the master suite includes a sunken bedroom with a private deck. The lavish master bath offers a sunken garden tub, a dual-sink vanity and a skylight near the private shower.
- Three large secondary bedrooms share another skylighted bath. Each bedroom has its own unique design feature.

Plans P-7664-4A & -4D

Bedrooms: 4+	Baths: 2½
Living Area:	
Upper floor	1,301 sq. ft.
Main floor	1,853 sq. ft.
Total Living Area:	**3,154 sq. ft.**
Daylight basement	1,486 sq. ft.
Garage	668 sq. ft.
Exterior Wall Framing:	2x4
Foundation Options:	**Plan #**
Daylight basement	P-7664-4D
Crawlspace	P-7664-4A

(All plans can be built with your choice of foundation and framing. A generic conversion diagram is available. See order form.)

BLUEPRINT PRICE CODE:	E

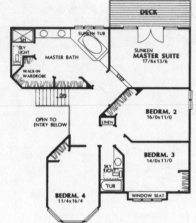

UPPER FLOOR

BASEMENT STAIRWAY LOCATION

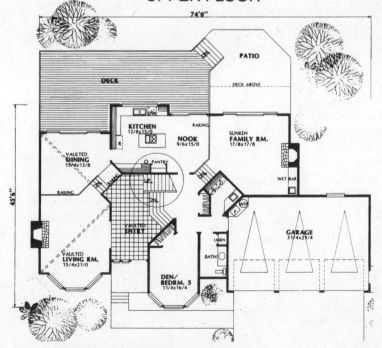

MAIN FLOOR

TO ORDER THIS BLUEPRINT,
CALL TOLL-FREE 1-800-820-1283

Plans P-7664-4A & -4D

PRICES AND DETAILS
ON PAGES 12-15

Mediterranean Masterpiece

- A captivating roofline, a stucco facade and a columned porte cochere create a stunning exterior for this home.
- A tiled foyer leads into the expansive sunken living room, which is served by a wet bar that can be accessed from the outdoor pool area.
- Pocket doors close off the kitchen and breakfast area from the dining room and living room. The kitchen offers a preparation island, a nearby laundry room and a serving bar to the adjoining family room. The breakfast area overlooks the screened patio and pool.
- The spectacular master suite boasts a bright sitting room and a fireplace set along a curved glass wall that overlooks the pool, spa and summer kitchen. The private, compartmentalized bath shows off a step-up tub, a separate shower and a huge walk-in closet.
- Two secondary bedrooms and a unique observation room occupy the upper floor. Each bedroom offers sliding glass doors to the large balcony.
- A guest room with a private bath is near the master suite on the main floor.

Plan HDS-99-138

Bedrooms: 4	Baths: 3½
Living Area:	
Upper floor	621 sq. ft.
Main floor	2,669 sq. ft.
Total Living Area:	**3,290 sq. ft.**
Garage	479 sq. ft.
Exterior Wall Framing:	2x6

Foundation Options:

Slab

(Typical foundation & framing conversion diagram available—see order form.)

BLUEPRINT PRICE CODE: E

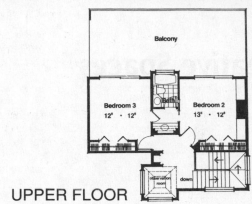

UPPER FLOOR

MAIN FLOOR

TO ORDER THIS BLUEPRINT,
CALL TOLL-FREE 1-800-820-1283

Plan HDS-99-138

PRICES AND DETAILS
ON PAGES 12-15

205

Lap of Luxury

- Entering this stunning, feature-filled one-story estate means entering a world of luxury and comfort.
- The open foyer is brightened by an arched transom window. Introduced by an archway, the adjacent formal dining room features a unique ale bar.
- The bright and airy parlor offers French doors to a covered backyard veranda. An outside stairway accesses the partial daylight basement.
- The island kitchen includes a menu desk, a pantry and a panoramic morning room.
- Inviting and spacious, the Gathering Room is enhanced by a media center

and a handsome fireplace with a built-in wood box.
- Double doors lead into the luxurious master suite, which features built-in bookshelves and cabinets. A sitting room provides private outdoor access. The master bath showcases a corner garden tub, a separate shower, dual vanities and roomy his-and-hers walk-in closets.
- A second bedroom, a guest suite, and a library or fourth bedroom complete the home's innovative floor plan.
- For added spaciousness, ceilings in the main living areas and in the master bedroom are 12 ft. high. Ceilings in the other bedrooms, the library and all three baths are 9 ft. high.

Plan EOF-63

Bedrooms: 3+	Baths: 3
Living Area:	
Main floor	3,316 sq. ft.
Total Living Area:	**3,316 sq. ft.**
Partial daylight basement	550 sq. ft.
Garage	496 sq. ft.
Exterior Wall Framing:	2x6

Foundation Options:

Partial daylight basement
(All plans can be built with your choice of foundation and framing. A generic conversion diagram is available. See order form.)

BLUEPRINT PRICE CODE:	E

MAIN FLOOR

*TO ORDER THIS BLUEPRINT,
CALL TOLL-FREE 1-800-820-1283*

Plan EOF-63

*PRICES AND DETAILS
ON PAGES 12-15*

European Look

- The beautiful stucco exterior of this European-style home features corner quoins and attractive arched windows.
- Inside, an 18-ft. tray ceiling and a plant ledge soar over the inviting foyer.
- A quiet study includes private access to a full bath, and would be an ideal guest room or extra bedroom.
- Columns neatly divide the combined living and dining rooms to the left. The bayed dining room opens to the deck.
- Double doors separate the formal areas from the island kitchen and the breakfast nook, where a menu desk, a walk-in pantry and a good-sized freezer room are much-appreciated features.
- An 18-ft. vaulted ceiling and a fireplace flanked by windows and bookcases highlight the family room. Elegant French doors provide deck access.
- Unless otherwise noted, every main-floor room includes a 9-ft. ceiling.
- Stairways in the foyer and the family room lead to the upper floor.
- A 14-ft. vaulted ceiling adds flair to the master suite, which boasts a private bath with a luxurious whirlpool tub.
- Two additional bedrooms and a vast bonus room are serviced by two full baths and a bright laundry room.

Plan APS-3302

Bedrooms: 3+	Baths: 4
Living Area:	
Upper floor	1,276 sq. ft.
Main floor	1,716 sq. ft.
Bonus room/4th bedroom	382 sq. ft.
Total Living Area:	**3,374 sq. ft.**
Standard basement	1,716 sq. ft.
Garage	693 sq. ft.
Exterior Wall Framing:	2x4

Foundation Options:

Standard basement
(All plans can be built with your choice of foundation and framing. A generic conversion diagram is available. See order form.)

BLUEPRINT PRICE CODE: E

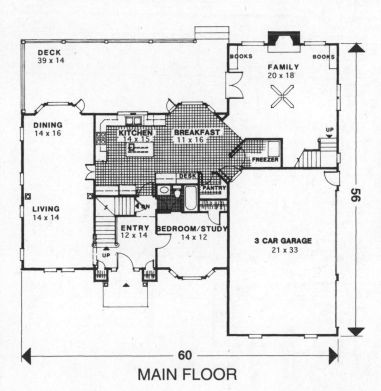

MAIN FLOOR

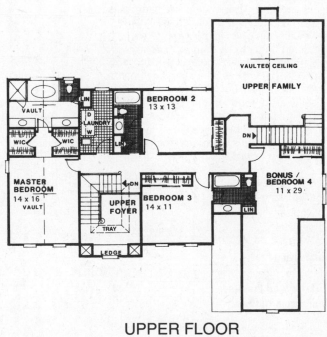

UPPER FLOOR

Nicely Adorned

- This nostalgic brick design is adorned with lovely columns, arches and half-round windows.
- Interior columns set off the main living areas from the foyer and gallery.
- A columned gallery directs traffic to a half-bath and the elegant dining room.
- The central family room offers a nice fireplace and a built-in media center.
- The focal point of the kitchen is its large island, which includes a handy bar sink.
- The fabulous morning room flaunts a 15-ft., 8-in. cathedral ceiling. Unless otherwise specified, 10-ft. ceilings are found throughout the main floor.
- The master suite boasts a dramatic corner fireplace, a sitting room and a private courtyard. The master bath hosts a Jacuzzi tub and a neat dressing table.
- Upstairs, an open game room offers French doors to an outdoor balcony.
- All three secondary bedrooms feature private bath access. A vaulted ceiling enhances the front bedroom, while 9-ft. ceilings are found in the rear bedrooms.
- The area above the stately porte cochere could be finished as a media room or a teen's bedroom. The ceiling slopes up from 5 ft. to 9 feet.

Plan GML-593

Bedrooms: 4+	Baths: 4½
Living Area:	
Upper floor	1,125 sq. ft.
Main floor	2,300 sq. ft.
Total Living Area:	**3,425 sq. ft.**
Media/teen room (unfinished)	303 sq. ft.
Exterior Wall Framing:	2x4

Foundation Options:

Slab

(All plans can be built with your choice of foundation and framing. A generic conversion diagram is available. See order form.)

BLUEPRINT PRICE CODE: E

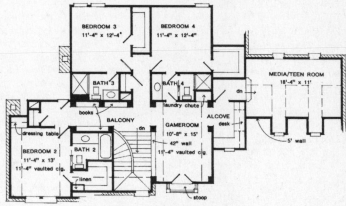

UPPER FLOOR

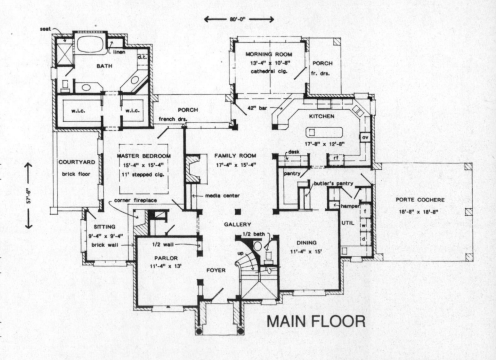

MAIN FLOOR

*TO ORDER THIS BLUEPRINT,
CALL TOLL-FREE 1-800-820-1283*

Plan GML-593

*PRICES AND DETAILS
ON PAGES 12-15*

Truly Nostalgic

- Designed after "Monteigne," an Italianate home near Natchez, Mississippi, this reproduction utilizes modern stucco finishes for the exterior.
- Columns and arched windows give way to a two-story-high foyer, which is accented by a striking, curved stairwell.
- The foyer connects the living room and the study, each boasting a 14-ft. ceiling and a cozy fireplace or woodstove.
- Adjacent to the formal dining room, the kitchen offers a snack bar and a bayed eating room. A unique entertainment center is centrally located to serve the main activity rooms of the home.
- A gorgeous sun room stretches across the rear of the main floor and overlooks a grand terrace.
- The plush master suite and bath boast his-and-hers vanities, large walk-in closets and a glassed-in garden tub.
- A main-floor guest bedroom features a walk-in closet and private access to another full main-floor bath.
- Two more bedrooms with private baths are located on the upper level. They share a sitting area and a veranda.

Plan E-3200

Bedrooms: 4	Baths: 4
Living Area:	
Upper floor	629 sq. ft.
Main floor	2,655 sq. ft.
Total Living Area:	**3,284 sq. ft.**
Standard basement	2,655 sq. ft.
Garage	667 sq. ft.
Exterior Wall Framing:	2x6

Foundation Options:

Standard basement

Crawlspace

Slab

(All plans can be built with your choice of foundation and framing. A generic conversion diagram is available. See order form.)

BLUEPRINT PRICE CODE: E

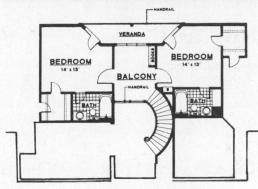

UPPER FLOOR

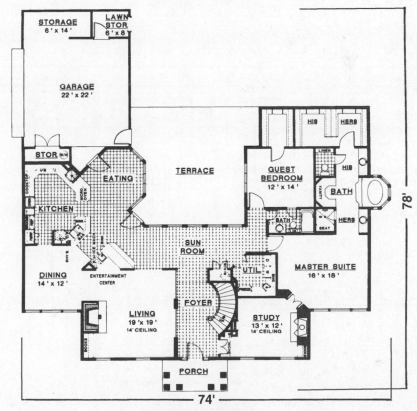

MAIN FLOOR

TO ORDER THIS BLUEPRINT,
CALL TOLL-FREE 1-800-820-1283

Plan E-3200

PRICES AND DETAILS
ON PAGES 12-15

209

Photo by Mark Englund/HomeStyles

Elegant Country

- This stately country home is filled with high elegance.
- Round-top windows brighten the living and dining rooms on either side of the long entry.
- Straight ahead, an 18-ft. ceiling crowns the family room, which is warmed by a handsome fireplace. Two sets of French doors flanking the fireplace lead to a huge deck.
- The secluded master suite boasts a stunning bath, with a step-up quarter-circle Jacuzzi tub under a columned

pergola, an arched window and a 12-ft. sloped ceiling!
- A peninsula cooktop/snack bar highlights the marvelously open kitchen. In one window-lined corner, a breakfast nook lies bathed in sunlight. A convenient porte cochere is nice for unloading groceries on rainy days.
- Unless otherwise specified, all main-floor rooms have 9-ft. ceilings.
- A game room at the top of the stairs may also be used as an extra bedroom.
- Along the balcony hall, two good-sized bedrooms enjoy private bath access. A third bedroom has a full bath nearby.

Plan E-3501	
Bedrooms: 4+	**Baths:** 3½
Living Area:	
Upper floor	1,238 sq. ft.
Main floor	2,330 sq. ft.
Total Living Area:	**3,568 sq. ft.**
Standard basement	2,348 sq. ft.
Garage and storage	848 sq. ft.
Exterior Wall Framing:	2x6

Foundation Options:

Standard basement
Crawlspace
Slab
(All plans can be built with your choice of foundation and framing. A generic conversion diagram is available. See order form.)

BLUEPRINT PRICE CODE: **F**

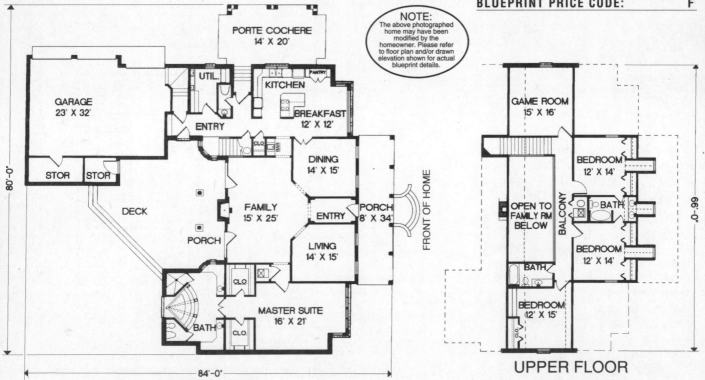

NOTE: The above photographed home may have been modified by the homeowner. Please refer to floor plan and/or drawn elevation shown for actual blueprint details.

MAIN FLOOR

UPPER FLOOR

Superb Views

- This superb multi-level home is designed to take full advantage of spectacular surrounding views.
- The two-story-high entry welcomes guests in from the covered front porch. An open-railed stairway and a 23-ft. domed ceiling are highlights here.
- The sunken living and dining rooms are defined by archways and face out to a large wraparound deck. The living room has a 13-ft. cathedral ceiling and a nice fireplace. The dining room offers a 9½-ft. domed ceiling and a wet bar.
- The octagonal island kitchen hosts a Jenn-Aire range, a sunny sink and a bayed breakfast nook. Nearby, the utility room reveals a walk-in pantry, laundry facilities and garage access.
- The quiet den boasts a second fireplace, a cozy window seat and deck access.
- The entire upper floor is occupied by the master bedroom suite, which has a spacious bayed sleeping room with a 12½-ft. cathedral ceiling. Other features include a huge walk-in closet, separate dressing areas and a private bath with a curved shower and a Jacuzzi tub.
- The exciting daylight basement has a recreation room, an exercise room and another bedroom, plus a sauna and a hot tub surrounded by windows!

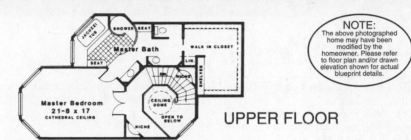

UPPER FLOOR

NOTE:
The above photographed home may have been modified by the homeowner. Please refer to floor plan and/or drawn elevation shown for actual blueprint details.

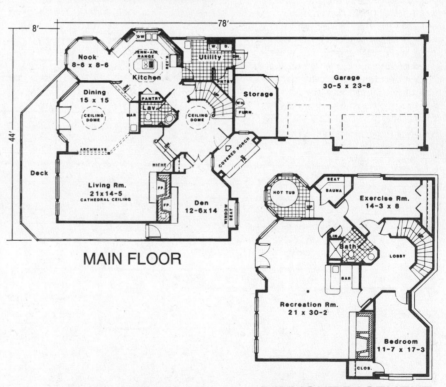

MAIN FLOOR

DAYLIGHT BASEMENT

Plan NW-229

Bedrooms: 2+	Baths: 2½
Living Area:	
Upper floor	815 sq. ft.
Main floor	1,446 sq. ft.
Daylight basement	1,330 sq. ft.
Total Living Area:	**3,591 sq. ft.**
Garage	720 sq. ft.
Exterior Wall Framing:	2x6

Foundation Options:

Daylight basement

(All plans can be built with your choice of foundation and framing. A generic conversion diagram is available. See order form.)

BLUEPRINT PRICE CODE: F

Photo by Mark Englund/HomeStyles

Stately Stone and Stucco

- A graceful combination of stone and stucco creates a warm and stately appearance for this charming home.
- The ornate, columned porch welcomes guests into the two-story-high foyer. Flowing to the right, the living room features a fireplace and a 15½-ft. vaulted ceiling. Decorative columns to the left set off the formal dining room.
- More columns introduce the two-story Great Room, which offers another fireplace and a handy back stairway.
- The open kitchen includes a work island and an angled serving bar to the bayed breakfast nook. French doors open to a covered backyard porch.
- The master bedroom boasts a three-sided fireplace and a 10½-ft. tray ceiling; while the peaceful sitting room and the luxurious garden bath each have a 16-ft. vaulted ceiling.
- Ceilings in all main-floor rooms are 9 ft. high unless otherwise specified.
- Upstairs, three bedrooms share two baths. The bonus room is a nice extra.

NOTE:
The above photographed home may have been modified by the homeowner. Please refer to floor plan and/or drawn elevation shown for actual blueprint details.

UPPER FLOOR

Plan FB-5345-JERN

Bedrooms: 4+	Baths: 3½
Living Area:	
Upper floor	928 sq. ft.
Main floor	2,467 sq. ft.
Bonus room	296 sq. ft.
Total Living Area:	**3,691 sq. ft.**
Daylight basement	2,467 sq. ft.
Garage	531 sq. ft.
Exterior Wall Framing:	**2x4**

Foundation Options:

Daylight basement

(All plans can be built with your choice of foundation and framing. A generic conversion diagram is available. See order form.)

BLUEPRINT PRICE CODE: **F**

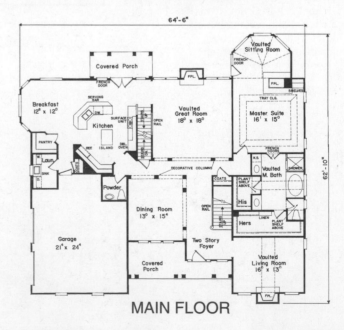

MAIN FLOOR

TO ORDER THIS BLUEPRINT, CALL TOLL-FREE 1-800-820-1283

Plan FB-5345-JERN

PRICES AND DETAILS ON PAGES 12-15

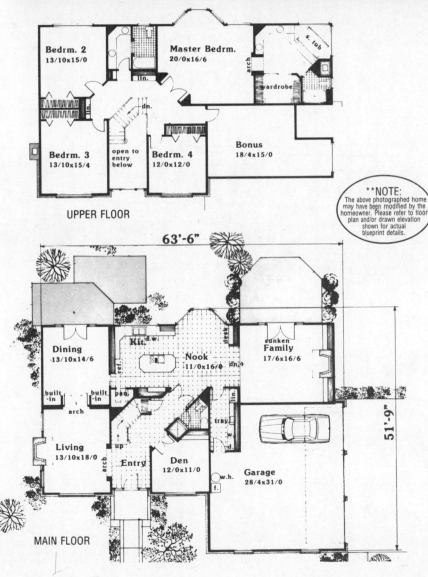

UPPER FLOOR

**NOTE:
The above photographed home may have been modified by the homeowner. Please refer to floor plan and/or drawn elevation shown for actual blueprint details.

MAIN FLOOR

European Charm

- Here's a home that not only exudes Old World charm, but also offers plenty of space for busy American families of today.
- French doors join the living and dining rooms, and the dining room offers easy access to an outside deck or patio.
- A huge kitchen/nook combination assures that those working in the kitchen will not feel isolated.
- The sunken family room beyond also features a fireplace and double doors to the rear.
- A front-facing den, with its adjoining bath, makes a great home office or a guest bedroom if needed.
- Upstairs, the master suite is spacious and includes an extravagant master bath and a big walk-in closet.

Plan R-2093

Bedrooms: 4-5	Baths: 3

Living Area:	
Upper floor	1,585 sq. ft.
Main floor	1,792 sq. ft.
Bonus room	351 sq. ft.

Total Living Area:	**3,728 sq. ft.**
Garage	878 sq. ft.

Exterior Wall Framing:	2x6

Foundation Options:
Crawlspace
(Typical foundation & framing conversion diagram available—see order form.)

BLUEPRINT PRICE CODE:	**F**

Exciting Angles and Amenities

- The interior of this elegant stucco design oozes in luxury, with an exciting assortment of angles and glass.
- Beyond the 14-ft.-high foyer and gallery is a huge parlour with an angled stand-behind ale bar and an adjoining patio accessed through two sets of glass doors.
- The diamond-shaped kitchen offers a sit-down island, a spacious walk-in pantry and a pass-through window to a summer kitchen.
- Opposite the kitchen is an octagonal morning room surrounded in glass and a spacious, angled gathering room with a fireplace and a TV niche.
- The luxurious master suite features a glassed lounge area and a spectacular two-sided fireplace, and is separated from the three secondary bedroom suites. The stunning master bath boasts a central linen island and an assortment of amenities designed for two.
- The library could serve as a fifth bedroom or guest room; the bath across the hall could serve as a pool bath.
- An alternate brick elevation is included

Plan EOF-59

Bedrooms: 4+	Baths: 4
Living Area:	
Main floor	4,021 sq. ft.
Total Living Area:	**4,021 sq. ft.**
Garage	737 sq. ft.
Exterior Wall Framing:	2x6

Foundation Options:

Slab

(All plans can be built with your choice of foundation and framing. A generic conversion diagram is available. See order form.)

BLUEPRINT PRICE CODE: **G**

MAIN FLOOR

Plan EOF-59

PRICES AND DETAILS ON PAGES 12-15

Spectacular Design

- The spectacular brick facade of this home conceals a stylish floor plan. Endless transoms crown the windows that wrap around the rear of the home, flooding the interior with natural light.
- The foyer opens to a huge Grand Room with a 14-ft. ceiling. French doors access a delightful covered porch.
- A three-sided fireplace warms the three casual rooms, which share a high 12-ft. ceiling. The Gathering Room is surrounded by tall windows; the Good Morning Room features porch access; and the island kitchen offers a double oven, a pantry and a snack bar.
- Guests will dine in style in the formal dining room, with its 13-ft. tray ceiling and trio of tall, arched windows.
- Curl up with a good book in the quiet library, which has an airy 10-ft. ceiling.
- A 12-ft. ceiling enhances the fantastic master suite, which is wrapped in windows. The superb master bath boasts a step-up garden tub, a separate shower, two vanities, a makeup table and a bidet.
- Two sleeping suites on the other side of the home have 10-ft. ceilings and share a unique bath with private vanities.

Plan EOF-8

Bedrooms: 3+	Baths: 3½
Living Area:	
Main floor	3,392 sq. ft.
Total Living Area:	**3,392 sq. ft.**
Garage	871 sq. ft.
Exterior Wall Framing:	2x6

Foundation Options:

Slab

(All plans can be built with your choice of foundation and framing. A generic conversion diagram is available. See order form.)

BLUEPRINT PRICE CODE:	E

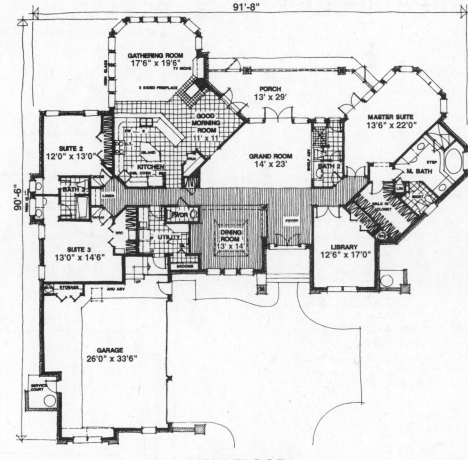

MAIN FLOOR

Photo by Mark Englund/HomeStyles

Ornate Design

- This exciting home is distinguished by an ornate facade with symmetrical windows and a columned entry.
- A beautiful arched window highlights the two-story-high foyer, with its open-railed stairway and high plant shelf. The foyer separates the two formal rooms and flows back to the family room.
- With an 18-ft. ceiling, the family room is brightened by corner windows and warmed by a central fireplace.
- Columns introduce the sunny breakfast area and the gourmet kitchen, which features an angled island/serving bar and a butler's pantry near the dining room. A laundry room and a second stairway to the upper floor are nearby.
- Ceilings in all main-floor rooms are 9 ft. high unless otherwise specified.
- Upstairs, a dramatic balcony overlooks the family room and the foyer.
- The master suite boasts a 10-ft. tray ceiling, a sitting room and an opulent garden bath with a 12-ft. vaulted ceiling. Three more bedrooms, each with a walk-in closet and private bath access, complete the upper floor.

Plan FB-5347-HAST

Bedrooms: 4+	Baths: 4
Living Area:	
Upper floor	1,554 sq. ft.
Main floor	1,665 sq. ft.
Total Living Area:	**3,219 sq. ft.**
Daylight basement	1,665 sq. ft.
Garage	462 sq. ft.
Exterior Wall Framing:	2x4

Foundation Options:

Daylight basement

(All plans can be built with your choice of foundation and framing. A generic conversion diagram is available. See order form.)

BLUEPRINT PRICE CODE:	E

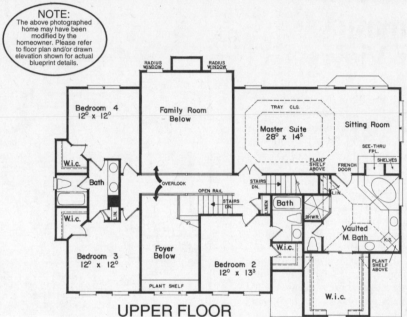

NOTE:
The above photographed home may have been modified by the homeowner. Please refer to floor plan and/or drawn elevation shown for actual blueprint details.

UPPER FLOOR

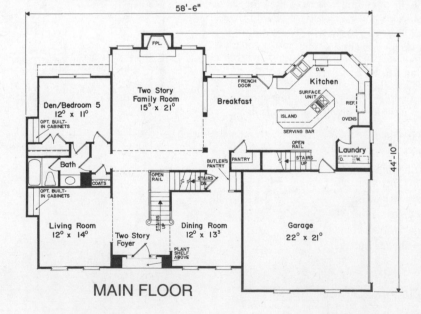

MAIN FLOOR

TO ORDER THIS BLUEPRINT, CALL TOLL-FREE 1-800-820-1283

Plan FB-5347-HAST

PRICES AND DETAILS ON PAGES 12-15

Dramatic Rear Views

- Columned front and rear porches offer country styling to this elegant two-story.
- The formal dining room and living room flank the two-story-high foyer.
- A dramatic array of windows stretches along the informal, rear-oriented living areas, where the central family room features a 17-ft.-high vaulted ceiling and a striking fireplace.
- The modern kitchen features an angled snack counter, a walk-in pantry and a work island, in addition to the bayed morning room.
- The exciting and secluded master suite has a sunny bayed sitting area with its own fireplace. Large walk-in closets lead to a luxurious private bath with angled dual vanities, a garden spa tub and a separate shower.
- The centrally located stairway leads to three extra bedrooms and two full baths on the upper floor.

Plan DD-2912

Bedrooms: 4	Baths: 3½
Living Area:	
Upper floor	916 sq. ft.
Main floor	2,046 sq. ft.
Total Living Area:	**2,962 sq. ft.**
Standard basement	1,811 sq. ft.
Garage	513 sq. ft.
Exterior Wall Framing:	2x4

Foundation Options:

Standard basement
Crawlspace
Slab

(All plans can be built with your choice of foundation and framing. A generic conversion diagram is available. See order form.)

BLUEPRINT PRICE CODE: D

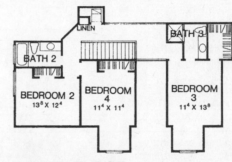

UPPER FLOOR

MAIN FLOOR

TO ORDER THIS BLUEPRINT,
CALL TOLL-FREE 1-800-820-1283

Plan DD-2912

PRICES AND DETAILS
ON PAGES 12-15

217

Photo by Mark Englund/HomeStyles

Angled Interior

- This plan gives new dimension to one-story living. The exterior has graceful arched windows and a sweeping roofline. The interior is marked by unusual angles and stately columns.
- The living areas are clustered around a large lanai, or covered porch. French doors provide lanai access from the family room, the living room and the master bedroom.
- The central living room also offers arched windows and shares a two-sided fireplace with the family room.
- The island kitchen and the bayed morning room are open to the family room, which features a wet bar next to the striking fireplace.
- The master bedroom features an irresistible bath with a spa tub, a separate shower, dual vanities and two walk-in closets. Two more good-sized bedrooms share another full bath.
- A 12-ft. cathedral ceiling enhances the third bedroom. Standard 8-ft. ceilings are found in the second bedroom and the hall bath. All other rooms boast terrific 10-ft. ceilings.

Plan DD-2802

Bedrooms: 3+	**Baths:** 2½
Living Area:	
Main floor	2,899 sq. ft.
Total Living Area:	**2,899 sq. ft.**
Standard basement	2,899 sq. ft.
Garage	568 sq. ft.
Exterior Wall Framing:	2x4
Foundation Options:	
Standard basement	
Crawlspace	
Slab	

(All plans can be built with your choice of foundation and framing. A generic conversion diagram is available. See order form.)

BLUEPRINT PRICE CODE: D

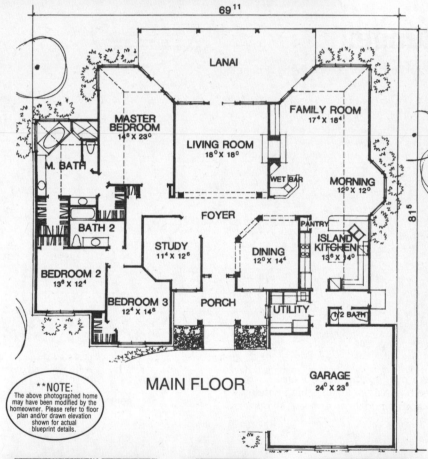

69⁻¹¹

LANAI

MASTER BEDROOM 14⁶ X 23⁰

LIVING ROOM 18⁰ X 18⁰

FAMILY ROOM 17⁴ X 18⁴

M. BATH

WET BAR

MORNING 12⁰ X 12⁰

BATH 2

FOYER

PANTRY

ISLAND KITCHEN 13⁶ X 14⁰

BEDROOM 2 13⁶ X 12⁴

STUDY 11⁴ X 12⁶

DINING 12⁰ X 14⁴

BEDROOM 3 12⁴ X 14⁸

PORCH

UTILITY

½ BATH

81⁵

NOTE:
The above photographed home may have been modified by the homeowner. Please refer to floor plan and/or drawn elevation shown for actual blueprint details.

MAIN FLOOR

GARAGE 24⁰ X 23⁸

REAR VIEW

TO ORDER THIS BLUEPRINT, CALL TOLL-FREE 1-800-820-1283

Plan DD-2802

PRICES AND DETAILS ON PAGES 12-15

Photo by Mark Englund/HomeStyles

Take the Plunge!

- From the elegant portico to the striking rooflines, this home's facade is magnificent. But the rear area is equally fine, with its spa, waterfall and pool.
- Double doors lead from the entry into a columned foyer where a 12-ft.-high ceiling extends into the central living room beyond. A sunken wet bar juts into the pool area, allowing guests to swim up to the bar for refreshments.
- The dining room boasts window walls and a tiered pedestal ceiling. The island kitchen easily services both the formal and the informal areas of the home.
- A large breakfast room flows into a warm family room with a fireplace and sliding glass doors to the patio and pool.
- The stunning master suite offers an opulent bath, patio access and views of the pool through a curved window wall.
- A railed staircase leads to the upper floor, where there are two bedrooms, a continental bath and a shared balcony deck overlooking the pool area.
- The observatory features high windows to accommodate an amateur stargazer's telescope. This room could also be used as an activity area for hobbies or games

NOTE: The above photographed home may have been modified by the homeowner. Please refer to floor plan and/or drawn elevation shown for actual blueprint details.

Plan HDS-99-154

Bedrooms: 3+	Baths: 3
Living Area:	
Upper floor	675 sq. ft.
Main floor	2,212 sq. ft.
Total Living Area:	**2,887 sq. ft.**
Garage	479 sq. ft.
Exterior Wall Framing:	2x4

Foundation Options:

Slab

(All plans can be built with your choice of foundation and framing. A generic conversion diagram is available. See order form.)

BLUEPRINT PRICE CODE: **D.**

UPPER FLOOR

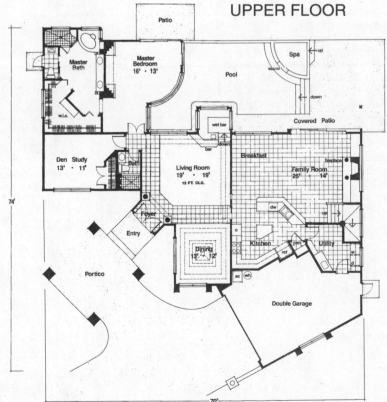

MAIN FLOOR

TO ORDER THIS BLUEPRINT,
CALL TOLL-FREE 1-800-820-1283

Plan HDS-99-154

PRICES AND DETAILS
ON PAGES 12-15

219

Home with Sparkle

- This dynamite design simply sparkles, with the main living areas geared toward a gorgeous greenhouse at the back of the home.
- At the front of the home, a sunken foyer introduces the formal dining room, which is framed by a curved half-wall. The sunken living room boasts a 17-ft. vaulted ceiling and a nice fireplace.
- The spacious kitchen features a bright, two-story skywell above the island. The family room's ceiling rises to 17 feet. These rooms culminate at a solar greenhouse with an indulgent hot tub and a 12-ft. vaulted ceiling. The neighboring bath has a raised spa tub.
- Upstairs, the impressive master suite includes its own deck and a stairway to the greenhouse. A vaulted library with a woodstove augments the suite. Ceilings soar to 16 ft. in both areas.

Plan S-8217

Bedrooms: 3+	Baths: 2
Living Area:	
Upper floor	789 sq. ft.
Main floor	1,709 sq. ft.
Bonus room	336 sq. ft.
Total Living Area:	**2,834 sq. ft.**
Partial basement	1,242 sq. ft.
Garage	441 sq. ft.
Exterior Wall Framing:	2x6

Foundation Options:

Partial basement
Crawlspace
Slab

(All plans can be built with your choice of foundation and framing. A generic conversion diagram is available. See order form.)

BLUEPRINT PRICE CODE: D

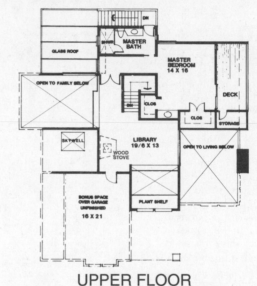

UPPER FLOOR

MAIN FLOOR

50' · 6"

62'

TO ORDER THIS BLUEPRINT, CALL TOLL-FREE 1-800-820-1283

Plan S-8217

PRICES AND DETAILS ON PAGES 12-15

Innovative Floor Plan

- The wide, covered front porch, arched windows and symmetrical lines of this traditional home conceal the modern, innovative floor plan found within.

- A two-story-high foyer guides guests to the front-oriented formal areas, which have views to the front porch.

- The hotspot of the home is the Great Room, with one of the home's three fireplaces and a media wall. Flanking doors open to a large backyard deck.

- The island kitchen and glassed-in eating nook overlook the deck and access a handy mudroom. High 9-ft. ceilings add to the aura of warmth and hospitality found on the main floor of this home.

- Another of the fireplaces is offered in the master suite. This private oasis also boasts a 13-ft.-high cathedral ceiling and a delicious bath with a garden tub.

- Upstairs, one bedroom has a sloped ceiling and a private bath. Three more bedrooms share another full bath.

Plan AHP-9360

Bedrooms: 5	Baths: 3½
Living Area:	
Upper floor	970 sq. ft.
Main floor	1,735 sq. ft.
Total Living Area:	**2,705 sq. ft.**
Standard basement	1,550 sq. ft.
Garage and utility area	443 sq. ft.
Exterior Wall Framing:	2x6

Foundation Options:

Standard basement
Crawlspace
Slab

(All plans can be built with your choice of foundation and framing. A generic conversion diagram is available. See order form.)

BLUEPRINT PRICE CODE: D

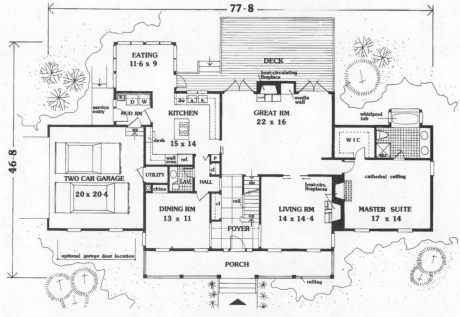

UPPER FLOOR

MAIN FLOOR

Luxurious Interior

- This luxurious home is introduced by an exciting tiled entry with a 17½-ft. vaulted ceiling and a skylight.
- The highlight of the home is the expansive Great Room and dining area, with its fireplace, planter, 17½-ft. vaulted ceiling and bay windows. The fabulous wraparound deck with a step-up hot tub is the perfect complement to this large entertainment space.
- The kitchen features lots of counter space, a large pantry and an adjoining bay-windowed breakfast nook.
- The exquisite master suite flaunts a sunken garden tub, a separate shower, a dual-sink vanity, a walk-in closet and private access to the deck area.
- The game room downstairs is perfect for casual entertaining, with its warm woodstove, oversized wet bar and patio access. Two bedrooms, a full bath and a large utility area are also included.

Plan P-6595-3D

Bedrooms: 3	Baths: 2½
Living Area:	
Main floor	1,530 sq. ft.
Daylight basement	1,145 sq. ft.
Total Living Area:	**2,675 sq. ft.**
Garage	462 sq. ft.
Exterior Wall Framing:	2x6

Foundation Options:

Daylight basement

(All plans can be built with your choice of foundation and framing. A generic conversion diagram is available. See order form.)

BLUEPRINT PRICE CODE: **D**

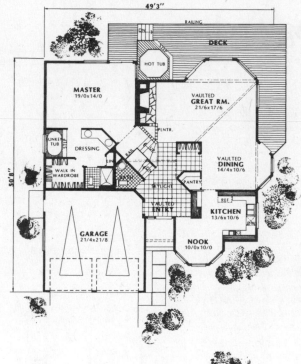

MAIN FLOOR

DAYLIGHT BASEMENT

Alluring Arches

- Massive columns, alluring arches and dazzling windows crowned by half-round transoms attract passersby to this gorgeous one-story showcase home.

- Inside, 12-ft. coffered ceilings are found in the foyer, dining room and living room. A bank of windows in the living room provides a sweeping view of the covered backyard patio, creating a bright, open effect that is carried throughout the home.

- The informal, family activity areas are oriented to the back of the home as well. Spectacular window walls in the breakfast room and family room offer tremendous views. The family room's inviting corner fireplace is positioned to be enjoyed from the breakfast area and the spacious island kitchen.

- Separated from the secondary bedrooms, the superb master suite is entered through double doors and features a sitting room and a garden bath. Another full bath is across the hall from the den, which would also make a great guest room or nursery.

Plan HDS-99-179

Bedrooms: 3+	**Baths:** 3

Living Area:

Main floor	2,660 sq. ft.
Total Living Area:	**2,660 sq. ft.**
Garage	527 sq. ft.
Exterior Wall Framing:	2x4

Foundation Options:

Slab

(All plans can be built with your choice of foundation and framing. A generic conversion diagram is available. See order form.)

BLUEPRINT PRICE CODE: D

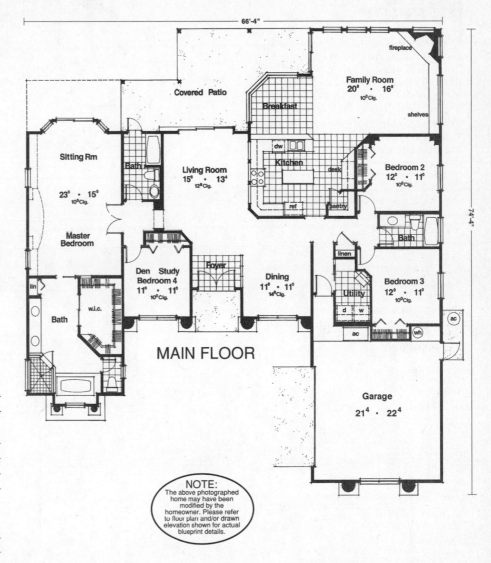

MAIN FLOOR

NOTE:
The above photographed home may have been modified by the homeowner. Please refer to floor plan and/or drawn elevation shown for actual blueprint details.

Privacy and Luxury

- This home's large roof planes and privacy fences enclose a thoroughly modern, open floor plan.
- A beautiful courtyard greets guests on their way to the secluded entrance. Inside, a two-story-high entry area leads directly into the living and dining rooms, which boast an 11-ft. vaulted ceiling, plus floor-to-ceiling windows and a fireplace with a stone hearth.
- The angular kitchen features a snack bar to the adjoining family room and a passive-solar sun room that offers natural brightness.
- A 14½-ft. vaulted ceiling presides over the family room. Sliding glass doors access a backyard patio with a sun deck and a hot tub.
- The luxurious master suite opens to both the front courtyard and the backyard hot tub area. The 11-ft.-high vaulted bath includes a dual-sink vanity, a raised garden tub, a separate shower and a corner walk-in closet.
- Two secondary bedrooms and another bath share the upper floor, which boasts commanding views of main-floor areas.

Plans P-7663-3A & -3D

Bedrooms: 3+	Baths: 3
Living Area:	
Upper floor	569 sq. ft.
Main floor	2,039 sq. ft.
Total Living Area:	**2,608 sq. ft.**
Daylight basement	2,039 sq. ft.
Garage	799 sq. ft.
Exterior Wall Framing:	2x4
Foundation Options:	**Plan #**
Daylight basement	P-7663-3D
Crawlspace	P-7663-3A

(All plans can be built with your choice of foundation and framing. A generic conversion diagram is available. See order form.)

BLUEPRINT PRICE CODE: **D**

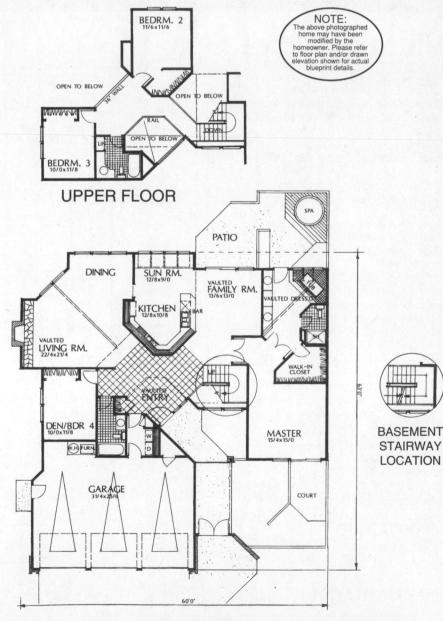

UPPER FLOOR

MAIN FLOOR

BASEMENT STAIRWAY LOCATION

NOTE:
The above photographed home may have been modified by the homeowner. Please refer to floor plan and/or drawn elevation shown for actual blueprint details.

TO ORDER THIS BLUEPRINT, CALL TOLL-FREE 1-800-820-1283 **Plans P-7663-3A & -3D** *PRICES AND DETAILS ON PAGES 12-15*